Now choose life

Titles in this series:

NEW STUDIES IN BIBLICAL THEOLOGY

Series editor: D. A. Carson

Now choose life

THEOLOGY AND ETHICS IN DEUTERONOMY

J. Gary Millar

APOLLOS

APOLLOS (an imprint of Inter-Varsity Press),
38 De Montfort Street, Leicester LE1 7GP, England
Email: ivp@uccf.org.uk
Website: www.ivpbooks.com

INTERVARSITY PRESS
PO Box 1400, Downers Grove, Illinois 60515, USA
Email: mail@ivpress.com
Website: www.ivpress.com

First published 1998
Reprinted 2002

British Library Cataloguing in Publication Data
A catalogue record for this book is available from the British Library.

UK ISBN 0–85111–515–2

Library of Congress Cataloging-in-Publication Data
This data has been requested.

USA ISBN 0–8308–2606–8

Set in Times New Roman
Printed and bound in Great Britain by Creative Print and Design (Wales), Ebbw Vale

For Fiona

who follows the Lord wholeheartedly

(Deuteronomy 1:36)

Contents

Series preface

New Studies in Biblical Theology is a series of monographs that address key issues in the discipline of biblical theology. Contributions to the series focus on one or more of three areas: 1. The nature and status of biblical theology, including its relations with other disciplines (*e.g.* historical theology, exegesis, systematic theology, historical criticism, narrative theology); 2. the articulation and exposition of the structure of thought of a particular biblical writer or corpus; and 3. the delineation of a biblical theme across all or part of the biblical corpora.

Above all, these monographs are creative attempts to help thinking Christians understand their Bibles better. The series aims simultaneously to instruct and to edify, to interact with the current literature, and to point the way ahead. In God's universe, mind and heart should not be divorced: in this series we will try not to separate what God has joined together. While the notes interact with the best of the scholarly literature, the text is uncluttered with untransliterated Greek and Hebrew, and tries to avoid too much technical jargon. The volumes are written within the framework of confessional evangelicalism, but there is always an attempt at thoughtful engagement with the sweep of the relevant literature.

Dr Millar's volume nicely nestles into the second category described above. This study helps make sense of the book of Deuteronomy – not only of Deuteronomy as a whole, but of many difficult passages within it precisely because Dr Millar keeps his eye on the flow of thought and the literary and theological shape of the entire book. Here and there he also includes tantalizing hints about the ways in which the theology of Deuteronomy should be integrated into the entire canon.

This sixth volume of the series will benefit not only serious students of Scripture, but preachers who want to work their way through Deuteronomy in the course of their regular ministry.

D. A. Carson
Trinity Evangelical Divinity School, Deerfield, Illinois

Author's preface

This book has been born of the conviction that not only does the message of Deuteronomy take us to the very heart of biblical theology, but that it is unmatched in its relevance for the affluent western church of today. Moses' preaching aims to equip God's people for life in a prosperous, pluralistic context – to enable them to keep moving forward even when they have settled down. It is my conviction of the relevance of Deuteronomy for the church that has brought me back to it again and again, and while I hope that this book makes some small contribution to the critical study of Deuteronomy, my greater burden is that it might enable some pastors and teachers to bring its vibrant message to bear on churches and communities in a new and more relevant way. My study of Deuteronomy has repeatedly made me stop and gasp at God's unfolding grace, and I pray that *Now Choose Life* may help others to do the same.

My interest in Deuteronomy began during my studies in Aberdeen, where my teachers in both Old and New Testament, notably William Johnstone, Howard Marshall, Max Turner and Ken Aitken, encouraged me to dig deeper. Thanks to a grant from the Department of Education in Northern Ireland, I was able to pursue doctoral studies at The Queen's College, Oxford. This book is, in fact, a substantially revised version of my DPhil thesis *The Ethics of Deuteronomy*. I owe a substantial debt to my supervisor, Prof. John Barton, for his gracious and thoughtful guidance, and not least for asking Dr Gordon McConville, then of Wycliffe Hall, to act as an informal second supervisor. Gordon's friendship, stimulation, constructive criticism and generous invitation to co-author a monograph (*Time and Place in Deuteronomy*, JSOTS 179, Sheffield: JSOT Press, 1994), did more to shape my thinking than anything else. He also read and commented on part of this manuscript. At various stages along the way I have benefited from the advice of Gordon Wenham, Chris Wright, Paul Barker and Bruce Winter of Tyndale House, Cambridge; and, as this book began to take shape, from the wisdom of D. A. Carson and of Mark Smith of Inter-Varsity Press. Thanks are also due to Ruth Moore for her help in preparing the manuscript.

I have long believed that theology is best done within the context of the church, and the support and prayers of the congregations of Elmwood Presbyterian Church in Lisburn, Co. Antrim, Gilcomston South Church of Scotland, Aberdeen, St Andrew's Church, Oxford and latterly Hamilton Road Presbyterian Church, Bangor, Co. Down, have been vital to me throughout my years of study. Without them, and others who have listened to me teach and preach Deuteronomy, there would have been little point in pursuing this work.

From the beginning, my parents, John and Lorna Millar, were unstinting in supporting me in every way, and both they and my wife's parents, Warner and Sheena Hardie, have consistently been a real encouragement and example in godliness. It is my wife, Fiona, however, to whom I owe the most. As well as being a loving soulmate, she constantly encouraged me both to keep my work grounded in reality and to live out the message which I have sought to pass on. It is with gratitude and joy that I dedicate this book, such as it is, to her, with the prayer that it may encourage some to preach more relevantly and live more faithfully for the Lord Jesus Christ.

Bangor, December 1997   *J. Gary Millar*

Abbreviations

AB	Anchor Bible
AnBib	Analecta Biblica
ANE	Ancient Near East(ern)
ANET	*Ancient Near Eastern Texts Relating to the Old Testament*, Pritchard, J. B. (ed.) (Princeton: Princeton University Press, 1950)
AOS	American Oriental Society
AT	Altes Testament
AUSS	*Andrews University Seminary Studies*
AZTANT	Abhandlungen zur Theologie des Alten und Neuen Testaments
BASOR	*Bulletin of the American Schools of Oriental Research*
BBB	Bonner biblische Beiträge
BDB	Brown, F., Driver, S. R., & Briggs, C. A., *Hebrew and English Lexicon of the Old Testament* (Oxford: Oxford University Press, 1906)
BEThL	Bibliotheca ephemeridum theologicarum lovaniensium
BK	Biblischer Kommentar, Altes Testament
BN	*Biblische Notizen*
BVSAW	Berichte über die Verhandlungen der Sächsischen Akademie der Wissenschaften zu Leipzig
BWANT	Beiträge zur Wissenschaft vom Alten und Neuen Testament
BZ	*Biblische Zeitschrift*
BZAW	Beiheft zur Zeitschrift für die Alttestamentliche Wissenschaft
CBQ	*Catholic Biblical Quarterly*
EQ	*Evangelical Quarterly*
EJT	*European Journal of Theology*
ET	English translation
EThL	*Ephemerides Theologicae Lovanienses*
EvTh	*Evangelische Theologie*
ExpT	*Expository Times*

FRLANT	Forschungen zur Religion und Literatur des Alten und Neuen Testaments
GKC	*Gesenius' Hebrew Grammar*, Kautsch, E. (ed.), tr. Cowley, A. E. (Oxford: Oxford University Press, 1910)
HKAT	Handkommentar zum Alten Testament
HTR	*Harvard Theological Review*
HUCA	*Hebrew Union College Annual*
ICC	International Critical Commentary
IDB	*Interpreter's Dictionary of the Bible*
IEJ	*Israel Exploration Journal*
Int	*Interpretation*
JAOS	*Journal of the American Oriental Society*
JBL	*Journal of Biblical Literature*
JETS	*Journal of the Evangelical Theological Society*
JJS	*Journal of Jewish Studies*
JNES	*Journal of Near Eastern Studies*
JPOS	*Journal of the Palestine Oriental Society*
JSOT	*Journal for the Study of the Old Testament*
JSOTS	Journal for the Study of the Old Testament Supplement Series
JSS	*Journal of Semitic Studies*
JTS	*Journal of Theological Studies*
KJV	King James Version
NCB	New Century Bible Commentary
NEchB	Die Neue Echter Bibel
NF	Neue Folge
NIBC	New International Biblical Commentary
NICOT	New International Commentary on the Old Testament
NIV	New International Version
NS	New Series
OBO	Orbis Biblicus et Orientalis
OBT	Overtures to Biblical Theology
OT	Old Testament
OTL	Old Testament Library
OTS	*Oudtestamentische Studiën*
PEQ	*Palestine Exploration Quarterly*
REB	Revised English Bible
RB	*Revue Biblique*
RSV	Revised Standard Version
SBAB	Stuttgarter Biblische Aufsatzbände, Altes Testament
SBLDS	Society of Biblical Literature Dissertation Series
SBS	Stuttgarter Bibelstudien

SBT	Studies in Biblical Theology
SJT	*Scottish Journal of Theology*
SVT	Supplements to Vetus Testamentum
ThBl	*Theologische Blätter*
THAT	*Theologisches Handwörterbuch zum Alten Testament*, Jenni, E., & Westermann, C. (eds) (Munich: Chr. Kaiser Verlag, 1971, 1976)
ThQ	*Theologische Quartalschrift*
ThZ	*Theologische Zeitschrift*
TOTC	Tyndale Old Testament Commentary
TRev	*Theologische Revue*
TSFB	*Theological Students' Fellowship Bulletin*
TWAT	*Theologisches Wörterbuch zum Alten Testament*, Botterweck, G. J., Ringren, H., & Fabry, H.-J. (eds) (8 vols, Stuttgart: Kohlhammer, 1970–95)
TynB	*Tyndale Bulletin*
VT	*Vetus Testamentum*
WBC	Word Biblical Commentary
WMANT	Wissenschaftliche Monographien zum Alten und Neuen Testament
ZAW	*Zeitschrift für die Alttestamentliche Wissenschaft*
ZkTh	*Zeitschrift für katholische Theologie*

Introduction

Old Testament ethics and Deuteronomy

When it comes to making ethical decisions, what do we do with the Old Testament? This is one of the most important and hotly debated issues in the church today. Are we simply to jettison the Hebrew Bible as irrelevant to (post)modern society? Is it legitimate to adopt a 'pick and mix' approach to the moral teachings of the Bible? Does the Bible as a whole, or even the Old Testament, speak with one voice on matters of morality? Such questions take us into the realm of Old Testament ethics. This book aims to make a small contribution to the ongoing discussion by exploring the book of Deuteronomy.[1]

What are we trying to do?

It is important at the outset to define what we mean by 'Old Testament ethics'. The very idea of separating the 'ethical' material from the rest in the Bible is a little questionable. As Brevard Childs has said:

> The initial and fundamental point to make is that the Old Testament's portrayal of ethical behaviour is inseparable from its total message respecting Israel, that is to say from its theological content. There is no such thing as an autonomous ethic of the Old Testament, nor can Old Testament ethics be restricted to so-called 'ethical' passages of the Bible (1992: 676).

Yet this crucial aspect of biblical studies must not be neglected, if we are to provide answers to the questions which the church and, at times, the whole of society are throwing our way.

The discipline of Old Testament ethics has often been shrouded in a cloud of vague terminology: even in the academic world, 'Old Testament ethics' is used to mean different things by different people. In this book, 'Old Testament ethics' is used to describe the branch of Old

---

[1] Readers who are simply interested in the exegesis and interpretation of Deuteronomy for its own sake may wish to begin reading at chapter 1.

Testament study which is concerned with the moral teaching, whether implicit or explicit, of the Hebrew Scriptures. 'The ethics of the Old Testament' is used in a general way to denote the huge variety of moral action (and justification for such action) described or commended in the text of the Old Testament.[2] Where other writers depart from this convention, it will be pointed out.

Unfortunately, there is no definitive volume on 'the ethics of the Old Testament' which we can use as a benchmark as we begin our study. In fact, there is not even agreement on how one might go about producing such a work.[3] The hiatus in significant progress in this area has, in recent years, been pointed out repeatedly; but, as we shall see, we have now entered a much more creative phase in the study of the ethics of the Old Testament.

I believe that 'Old Testament ethics' can usefully be resolved into three closely related components. This will help us to clarify the task which lies before us, and to evaluate earlier work in this area.

The analysis of the ethics of the Old Testament

Anyone studying Old Testament ethics must begin by analysing or describing the ethical stance or stances of the biblical text. The aim, at this stage, should be to understand the ethical material *on its own terms*. The foundation of Old Testament ethics, then, must always be exegesis. Careful reading will inevitably highlight contrasts and similarities between various texts. This, in turn, may suggest ways of organizing ethical material around specific themes or ideas, which leads on to the second component of Old Testament ethics.

The synthesis of the ethics of the Old Testament

Whether one is working with the Old Testament as a whole, with a particular book, or even with part of a book, there comes a time when it is important to investigate if or how the pieces of the jigsaw fit together. This step can be called 'synthesis'.

Some writers have tried to provide a comprehensive account of the ethics of the Old Testament in its entirety. Most have either sought to relate all ethical texts to a key concept such as covenant, or attempted to synthesize a hypothetical 'Israelite mindset', which might underlie the moral teaching of the Bible. Others have focused on trying to construct the 'ethics' of a single book or writer.

---

[2] The use of this term does not in itself presuppose a single ethical perspective undergirding the canonical text.

[3] Rudolf Smend writes that the problem of producing an 'ethics of the Old Testament' is even thornier than writing an Old Testament theology (1982: 423).

Clearly, analysis and synthesis are closely linked: there can, of course, be no attempt to put together the ethics of Deuteronomy, for example, until the initial exegetical work has been done. Then attempts to systematize may shed further light on the exegesis of the text. It is extremely important, however, to differentiate between these related tasks.

The application of the ethics of the Old Testament

Analysis and synthesis, then, form the bedrock of the study of Old Testament ethics. There are, however, many people who want to take things a step further: to apply this material to life in the modern world in some way. This task of applying Old Testament ethics today, while being, in my view, tremendously interesting and important, is not the goal of this book. I shall concentrate on analysis and synthesis, while hoping along the way to open up stimulating possibilities for application to be followed up elsewhere. It is worth noting, however, that any attempt to apply Old Testament ethics in a Christian context instantly raises the question of the relationship between the Old and New Testaments. Any serious treatment of how these texts speak to the contemporary world would, of necessity, begin here.

Conclusion

My simple breakdown of Old Testament ethics into exegesis/analysis, synthesis and application provides the rationale for my study of the ethics of Deuteronomy. Most energy will be devoted to analysing and describing the ethical teaching of the text of Deuteronomy in context. From this exegetical base, I shall move on to examine the possibility of a synthesis of the ethics of the book. This is probably the most important part of this study and has far-reaching implications. If it is impossible to speak of 'the ethics of Deuteronomy' in a coherent and meaningful way, then it is unlikely that a more ambitious attempt to outline the ethics of the Old Testament could succeed. On the other hand, if this is successful, then it must be of help in charting a course towards the synthesis of the ethics of the Old Testament as a whole. This synthesis, in turn, may open up new ways of applying its ethical teaching to the church and the society of which we are a part.

This division of Old Testament ethics into three closely related tasks is also extremely useful in evaluating the work that has been done on Old Testament ethics in recent years. It is to this that we now turn.

What has gone before

This is an exciting time for those interested in Old Testament ethics.

The most stimulating and potentially most important work of the twentieth century was produced in its last few years. To understand (and appreciate) today's creativity, we must, of course, begin much earlier. As there are many recent, helpful surveys of work done in Old Testament ethics,[4] this need not detain us unduly, but it is extremely valuable to spend some time developing specific insights from earlier writers which are relevant to the study of the ethics of Deuteronomy in the context of the ethics of the Old Testament as a whole.

In the twentieth century, the study of the ethics of the Old Testament fell into three relatively distinct phases. First came several substantial attempts to produce 'the ethics of the Old Testament'. In the wake of the failure to do this came a time of questioning the validity of such an approach and some suggestions for a new methodology. In recent years, the mood has swung again, and a new interest in synthesis is returning. We shall glean what we can from each of these in turn.

Early attempts at synthesis

Any discussion of the study of the ethics of the Old Testament this century is almost bound to start with Johannes Hempel's book, *Das Ethos des Alten Testaments* (1964).[5] This long and complex work tries to determine the distinctive features of an 'Israelite ethical mindset' by what amounts to a sociological analysis (Hempel 1962: 153–157).[6] Hempel's central conclusion is that the ethics of the Old Testament are based on the concept of obedience to the will of Yahweh: the moral material in the biblical text is not so much worked out as 'given'. Hence, there is something irrational and arbitrary about the 'ethos of the Old Testament' (1964: 87, 90). This is reflected in the rather obvious fact that the 'Israelite ethic' (all these designations are Hempel's own) is religious rather than, say, political.

Having made this pivotal observation, Hempel goes on to argue that the two chief characteristics of this 'obedience ethic' are 'decision' (*Entscheidung*) and 'separation' (*Abgrenzung*) (1964: 29). He discusses these in turn, and both parts of his explanation prove interesting in the context of our study.

Hempel argues that the concept of 'decision' initially emerged from

---

[4] An exhaustive bibliography can be found in Otto 1991. Also see C. J. H. Wright 1992a; 1993; Rodd 1994.

[5] The first edition (1938) was supplemented rather than fully revised.

[6] His analysis traces the development of three strata of primitive Israelite society – semi-nomadic cattle-breeders, agricultural peasants and Canaanite city dwellers – and the ethical phenomena corresponding to the socio-historical changes. Later sociological approaches, *e.g.* Smend 1982, built on this.

the competition for the affections of Israel between the redeemer god, Yahweh, and the gods of the Canaanites. It was then adapted by subsequent 'movements' to suit their own agenda. The prophets, for example, called for a decision which touched on every area of life, but focused on social justice in particular (1964: 106–109). In every case, however, the religious decision is to be understood in this context of obedience; throughout the history of Israel, salvation (whether military intervention or return from exile and the revival of true religion) was always dependent on obedience.

This reveals the three primary characteristics of the 'decision' for Hempel: it was the inevitable consequence of living among the nations; it showed the concrete, practical nature of Israelite ethics; and it was perpetual, for the ethos of Israel demands a continuing life of obedient decision. As we shall see, this could almost be a summary of the rationale for the ethical teaching of Deuteronomy.

Then Hempel turns his attention to his other proposed expression of obedience: the concept of separation (*Abgrenzung*), principally from other nations. This idea, he insists, has its origins in ancient taboo laws, which have been overlaid with the language of obedience to the covenant God, primarily in the biblical laws. Unfortunately, Hempel is more interested in the origins of this idea than in exegesis of the text, yet he has clearly uncovered one of the striking features not only of biblical laws in general, but of Deuteronomy 12 – 26 in particular.

One of the obvious strengths of Hempel's work is his determination to do justice to the diversity of the ethical material contained in the Old Testament, which he attributes to the chequered political and economic history of Israel and the rapid movement of ideas from the surrounding cultures (1964: 5). Along the way he makes some crucial observations: for instance, he points out that it is possible for two 'ethics' to share the same prescriptions and prohibitions while arising from fundamentally different conceptions of moral action (1964: 29).

Overall, his scheme has much to commend it. Separation and decision are crucial categories, not only in Deuteronomy, as we shall see, but also throughout much of the Hebrew Scriptures. The important role played by of the will of Yahweh in the ethics of the Old Testament can hardly be doubted. Yet Hempel's work is deeply flawed.[7]

For a start, Hempel simply *assumes* that there is an Old Testament ethic, common to every Israelite in every generation, which comes through all the individual authors. As a result, he fails to capture the diversity (whether sociological, theological or ethical) of Israel's

[7] This has been clinically exposed by Barton 1978: 44–51.

national life at any given moment, and across the centuries. Hempel struggles to differentiate between what Israelites may have believed *en bloc*, what sections of the community may have adhered to, and what a given writer was trying to communicate.

I would suggest that he also overplays the 'irrationality' of the Old Testament concept of obedience. The biblical writers (as Hempel himself admits) do not simply pass on 'primitive' ideas; for instance, a pragmatic motive clause is often attached to laws. The obedience demanded can hardly then be called 'irrational'. So overall, his approach tends to flatten the biblical picture.[8]

While there is much to be valued in Hempel's work, his method is far from satisfactory. Neither his analytic nor his synthetic work is entirely adequate. Unfortunately, the lengthy section on ethics in Walther Eichrodt's *Theology of the Old Testament* (the other major attempt to write the ethics of the Old Testament in the first half of the twentieth century) shows similar weaknesses.[9]

As one would expect in the context of an attempt to write a theology of the Old Testament, Eichrodt's work on ethics is unashamedly synthetic. From the beginning, he seeks to quantify how Israel acted, what they were aiming for and why they lived as they did, under the rubric of 'The Norms of Moral Conduct', 'The Goods of Moral Conduct' and 'The Motives of Moral Conduct'. In each case, his conclusion is essentially the same: Israel's moral behaviour is shaped by God's command, aims to please him through obedience and is motivated by respect for (and even fear of) the one who lays down ethical absolutes.

The prophetic movement plays a crucial part in Eichrodt's reconstruction. It was the prophets who took Israel beyond an *ad hoc* 'popular morality'.[10] As Yahwism began to make an impact, a new Israelite moral conscience was born. Rules for living suddenly began to 'acquire a share in the timeless and unconditioned quality of the holy' (1967: 319). A coherent 'system' of ethics began to emerge which was expressed in terms of obeying the will of Yahweh. At the cutting edge of this moral shift were the prophets (1967: 317).

---

[8] Levenson shows the variety of motivation in law and ethics, and in particular that 'not all ethos was thought to issue from mythos' (1980: 53).

[9] 'The Effect of Piety on Conduct (Old Testament Morality)' (Eichrodt 1967: 316–379). See also the rather disappointing work of van Oyen (1967).

[10] Eichrodt cites evidence from 'early Israel' (stretching from the patriarchs to the monarchy) in such a haphazard way that one is left with the feeling that this morality dropped out of the sky. For instance: 'Her moral consciousness was rooted in the basic facts of human life as given in Nature' (1967: 319). Rogerson (1982: 28–29) speaks of 'natural morality' in a similar way.

The prophets expressed conformity to the will of God 'as a whole personal attitude to the will of God as revealed in its moral majesty', and attempted to unify all existing ethical norms under this concept (1967: 327). The primitive idea of the fear of God, for example, was rehabilitated as motivation for doing good in the context of covenant (1967: 371–372). Such changes, in turn, redefined the *aims* of moral conduct: people no longer sought 'goods' or benefits for their own sake, but the divine approval of which the goods were evidence (1967: 350).[11] So the prophetic movement not only succeeded in establishing God's right to define obedience, but affirmed that his pleasure was the ultimate aim of obedience. This gave a new degree of coherence to the ethics of Israel, and goes some way to explaining the impact of the prophetic preaching.[12]

It is hardly surprising that Eichrodt also turns to his prophetic preoccupation with the will of Yahweh to find the most cogent expression of the motives for living a moral life. Some 'natural social instinct' may have provided a framework for early life in the family or kin-group, but it took the introduction of this 'absolute Ought' of the divine will, to overcome man's innate selfishness to provide a coherent motivational framework (1967: 367).[13]

Eichrodt measures the ethical contributions of other 'movements' in Israel's history against this prophetic ideal. He suggests, for instance, that later generations developed new rules to eradicate moral deficiencies of 'early Israel' (1967: 337–338). This, however, led to a narrow, particularist mentality, which focused exclusively on obedience to the *law*, losing touch with the prophetic elements of the tradition, especially the emphasis on fellowship with the divine. Others rejected legalism and sought asceticism, which also departed from the prophetic legacy.

The priestly tradition modified prophetic teaching in another way: they affirmed that a relationship with God was the supreme blessing, yet tried to maintain the ancient stress on enjoying the blessings which life brings.[14] They also exchanged the goal of conformity to the will of God

---

[11] Eichrodt argued that a 'primitive eudaemonism' had been transformed by Yahwism, but then returned under the influence of Canaanite religion, which promoted personal gain and power. The prophetic movement provided a critique of such a view.

[12] 'Where the goods for which men are striving and the norms governing their conduct are heterogeneous, the norms are always in danger of serving only as means to an end, and thereby losing their character of absolute obligation. Only where the goal of action is homogeneous with the norm is there any guarantee of the coherence and strength of ethics'(Eichrodt 1967: 349).

[13] He sees this emerging first at Sinai, and then developed in the prophetic movement.

[14] The priestly position is 'characterized by an organic synthesis of earthly blessing and the supreme gift of salvation' (Eichrodt 1967: 363).

to conformity to the image of God: the highest motive for moral action becomes the desire to be 'modelled on the pattern of the divine' (1967: 373). In the chaos of the exile, however, the coherence and power of the prophetic model were never matched, and it is this which Eichrodt sees as constituting the true Israelite ethos:

> As little as any other major civilized religion does that of Israel know of morality apart from religion. On the contrary, we would expect from our knowledge of the Israelite view of God that here above all the derivation of moral conduct from the all-ruling will of God would be pursued with especial vigour; and as we turn the pages of the Old Testament, this expectation is completely confirmed. From the earliest to the latest period it is God's demand, which comes vested with absolute authority, which is the strongest and dominating motive of human conduct. The power of good rests entirely on the recognition of God as the One who is good. Of moral behaviour for the sake of an abstract good there is none (1967: 316).

He then concludes his discussion with the following succinct summary of his position:

> It is the loftiness of the obligation, the spirituality of the central good, the unconditional character of the Ought, and the perfect unity of these three aspects of moral conduct in the divine Thou as known in the gift of his favour, which give the ethics of the Old Testament their unique inner greatness (1967: 379).

Eichrodt's attempt to construct the ethics of the Old Testament is extremely thought-provoking, but also has several methodological weaknesses. First, like Hempel, he is prone to oversimplify the ethical diversity of a socially complex nation over a vast period of time. A more serious deficiency, however, is his failure to admit the diversity of Israelite society *at any given time*. A third problem arises from his attempts to synthesize an Old Testament ethic from the concept of the will of Yahweh alone. As a result, he does not give sufficient emphasis to the diverse biblical material even, for example, within the prophetic tradition itself. In general, his descriptive and analytical work proves to be less useful than one would have hoped, because it is so coloured by his desire to synthesize 'the ethics of the Old Testament' in terms of his 'unconditional Ought'. Overall, his conclusions seem a little one-dimensional and he falls into the trap of distorting material in an effort to squeeze it into his rather narrow system (see Childs 1985: 205–207).

The main post-war influences in the study of Old Testament ethics have, then, been Hempel and Eichrodt. Other contributions appeared sporadically but had little impact on the wider debate (see *e.g.* Davidson 1959; Fletcher 1971). The tragedy is that, despite all the good things they have to offer, both Eichrodt and Hempel struggle to avoid two damning errors. In reducing the ethos of the Hebrew Bible to a concept of the will of Yahweh and investing it with an irrational arbitrariness, they fail to do justice to the careful complexity of Israelite moral thought reflected in the texts themselves. They also end up blurring the vigorous detail of the various aspects of ethics in the Old Testament in their attempts to synthesize a coherent ethic. As a result, the integrity of their analyses is impaired. These are obviously mistakes which we must be careful not to repeat.

The failure of their attempts to describe the ethics of the Old Testament on a grand scale and to provide a satisfactory synthesis of the 'ethos' initially did little to encourage anyone to build on this work. A general scepticism regarding the viability of making any statement which applied to the Old Testament as a whole (resulting largely from the work of James Barr and the demise of the 'biblical theology movement') contributed to the malaise (Barr 1961; Childs 1970). Eventually, however, re-examination of their work led to the emergence of new possibilities in Old Testament ethics.

Reflections on methodology

In the wake of the 'failure' of the grand schemes of those who sought to write the definitive 'Old Testament Theology' or 'Old Testament Ethics', it is hardly surprising that it was a case of 'back to the drawing-board' for those trying to say something meaningful about the sweep of the Old Testament. Of necessity, the rebuilding of a satisfactory rationale and method for studying Old Testament ethics has been a painstaking process. There has been no *magnum opus* to plot a path for subsequent study. Instead we have seen a host of small but significant contributions from a wide variety of sources.[15] Several of these demand careful consideration.

The work of John Barton marked a sea-change in the field of Old Testament ethics. The real strength of Barton's work lies in his clear definition of what we are trying to do when we study Old Testament

---

[15] Crenshaw & Willis (1974) typically contains useful material but fails to deal with methodological issues.

ethics.[16] In particular, he has dispelled confusion by distinguishing between the (socio-historical) ethics of the Israelites and the ethics of the Old Testament.[17] The historical and sociological study of the nature and development of morality in ancient Israel is valid and fascinating, but it is not Old Testament ethics, which is concerned solely with the study of the lifestyle presented as normative by the text of the Old Testament itself.

This basic premise leads him to speak in rather general terms of the 'the common flavour or atmosphere, a certain style of approach to moral questions' which characterizes the Old Testament (1983: 115). This 'atmosphere' can best be captured by adopting a loose 'pseudo-framework' when describing the ethics of the Old Testament. Barton's framework consists of three basic ethical categories: (1) obedience to God's command; (2) conformity to natural law; (3) imitation of God.[18] It is fair to say that Barton wants to say something about the 'big picture' without actually getting involved in synthesis proper.

In a similar way, while Barton's primary interest is not in applying the Old Testament to life today, he does make several comments about how this might be done. Unfortunately, it is here that his work is at its weakest. He helpfully points out some of the pitfalls; for instance:

> The problem that we immediately face when we try to discover what actual moral principles or norms can be extracted from the OT text is that the OT text does not seem designed as a mine from which these things are meant to be extracted (1983: 123).

But he becomes a little vague when suggesting how such obstacles might be overcome, arguing, for example, that we should 'allow what it [the text] is saying *on its own terms* to work on our minds, as we face

---

[16] Barton's methodological studies are the most important: see Barton 1978; 1983; 1996. He has also done some analytical work: see Barton 1974; 1979; 1981.

[17] 'The ethics of the Old Testament and the ethics of ancient Israelite society do not necessarily coincide, and the latter may not be represented altogether accurately by the former. Old Testament ethics is a theological construction, a set of rules, ideals and principles theologically motivated throughout and in a large part religiously sanctioned. Were the principles by which real Israelites actually lived quite so closely determined by religious faith? It may be that they were, but we cannot without further ado assume so' (McKeating 1979: 70).

[18] Rogerson 1982; Schmid 1963. Compare also Fletcher's four 'models': (1) responding to the divine deeds; (2) reflecting the divine nature; (3) living as a people under the divine ruler; (4) obeying the divine command (1971). His 'canonical' method, however, limits the usefulness of his study. See also Otto 1991; C. H. J. Wright 1992a.

the issues on which we ourselves must make our own ethical decisions' (1983: 124).

Overall, however, Barton's contribution has been immense. He laid some methodologically sound ground rules for all who follow, and began to rehabilitate the synthetic task, albeit in a relatively weak sense. In addition, his tripartite ethical model provides a useful way to compare and contrast ethical perspectives across the biblical corpus.

Once Barton had clarified what we are doing when we 'do' Old Testament ethics, it allowed others to grapple with some of the other methodological questions which he had not addressed so effectively.

Perhaps the most intriguing question which Barton had raised was that of how the Old Testament can have an impact on decision-making in the faith community in any meaningful way. John Goldingay touched on this in his *Approaches to Old Testament Interpretation* (1981).[19] He set this out in terms of the way in which Scripture commands us (its prescriptivity), provides us with exemplary material (albeit somewhat incidentally as it engages in its primary task of relating God's salvation history), declares values, defines the appropriate response to creation and shapes our character. There are obvious points of contact with Barton's work here, not least in the realm of how the text is supposed to shape our character, as we allow it to work on our minds. While he takes us a little further than Barton, ultimately Goldingay's work founders on the same rock. It may be true that the ethical material in the Old Testament will shape our character, but that is largely irrelevant to describing, synthesizing and even applying the moral implications of the text! Oliver O'Donovan writes:

> If these are ways of saying we must not consult the Bible in the same way we consult a railway timetable, but that our decisions must arise out of a long reflection on the biblical ethic understood in the light of biblical theology, then they are surely right, but equally surely irrelevant. How the biblical ethic may be appropriated, internalized, accepted into our thought-patterns once we have discovered it is not the question that we set out to answer. The sudden appearance of these psychological observations in the last scene of the drama suggests that the tragedian has killed so many characters in the course of the action that he has had to borrow a *deus ex machina* from another play (1973: 23).

---

[19] He discusses 'the ways in which Scripture shapes our life' (Goldingay 1981: 38–43).

In a more recent work on Old Testament theology, Goldingay hints at a more specific method of using the Old Testament in decision-making (1987: 36). This involves plotting the 'trajectories' of themes through the canon and extrapolating to modern situations. This seems an intriguing idea, but it is an aside which is not developed at any length. Following his oft-quoted comment on the lack of interest in Old Testament ethics in *A Century of Old Testament Study*, R. E. Clements has sought to do his bit to redress the balance.[20] He denies that the Old Testament deliberately seeks to promulgate abstract, timeless moral norms, but, in terms reminiscent of Barton, he allows that 'overall the Old Testament literature appears to be feeling its way towards the formulation of universal principles of morality' (1984: 17).[21] Clements points to a continuous process of applying, refining and reapplying the basic insights of Yahwism to the plethora of social and political situations in which Israel found herself. In his view this eventually produced broad and durable ethical expressions, which are of some use to the church. It seems to me that the manner in which Israel refined and reapplied the tenets of Yahwism might repay careful study, but Clements focuses more on the well-worn norms which emerge.

During this time of methodological reflection, other short papers appeared which covered essentially the same ground. Each discussed how the ethics of the Old Testament might be properly described, and expressed some doubts about how appropriate and/or viable it might be to attempt some kind of synthesis of the ethics of the Old Testament. Some writers also betrayed a desire to recover the Old Testament for the life of the church. No clear consensus emerged, but this period of discussion seemed to stimulate new attempts to tackle the synthetic task in a serious and responsible way.

The re-emergence of synthesis

The publication of *Toward Old Testament Ethics* by Walter Kaiser Jr (1983), after an absence of such a volume in English for over half a century, promised much, not least in its modest, yet hopeful, title. Kaiser made the first serious attempt since Eichrodt to express the

---

[20] 'The subject of OT Ethics has proved to be a most difficult one to deal with, and has, in fact, generally been treated as a subsidiary part of the wider study of OT Theology. The literature devoted to it has been surprisingly sparse, and the complex interaction of historical, sociological and religious factors has made it a subject in which it has been difficult to avoid the merely superficial' (Clements 1976: 107). His own contributions to the debate are Clements 1984; 1992.

[21] R. R. Wilson (1988) investigates how Israel made its decisions by examining the ethical use of Deuteronomy in the Deuteronomistic history. This also shows methodological similarities to Barton.

ethical content of the Old Testament as a coherent whole. Unfortunately, despite providing an up-to-date account of the study of Old Testament ethics on both sides of the Atlantic and a competent evaluation of methods used in describing and applying the ethics of the Old Testament, Kaiser mystifyingly sets all this aside to revert to the essentially pre-critical approach of W. S. Bruce, seeking to developing a framework from the 'ethical high-points' of the Decalogue, Holiness Code and Deuteronomic law and so on. Some helpful exegetical points result, but he makes no effort to tackle the problems of unity and diversity on the social and temporal planes, nor to suggest how the material might relate to current problems. The main significance of this work lies in its restoration of the synthetic aspect of Old Testament ethics to the scholarly agenda.

It is hardly surprising that the pioneer of 'canonical criticism', Brevard Childs, has made a telling contribution to the reinstatement of synthesis as a valid exercise. He has done so directly in *Old Testament Theology in a Canonical Context* (1985) and more recently in his magisterial *Biblical Theology of the Old and New Testaments* (1992), as well as indirectly through the work of his students.

Childs sets out his own canonical position as follows:

> Rather than to suggest that the route of Old Testament ethics is to pursue far more radically the application of sociology in reconstructing small areas of Israelite culture, I would argue that the task of Old Testament ethics is to acknowledge this canonical corpus as a theological construct which is only indirectly related to an historical and empirical Israel, and to pursue rigorously the theological witness of this biblical witness as the privileged sacred writings of Israel, the people of God (1992: 676).[22]

He argues that his canonical method frees the ethical witness of the Old Testament for the church today, without having to resort to such a-biblical concepts as 'middle axioms' or general principles. Childs consistently attempts to address the diversity of individual strands of the text (*e.g.* the narrative witness, prophetic witness, *etc.*) while maintaining an emphasis on their continuity.[23]

---

[22] Childs's canonical theology will be familiar from his other writings. The degree to which one is convinced by his view of ethics will depend on one's view of his wider work.

[23] His later work builds on the ideas developed in his earlier discussion, as the shared title, 'The shape of the obedient life' might suggest; see Childs 1985: 204–221.

The central feature of Childs's work is the belief that ethical action must always be defined in terms of response to God's action. The contrast between morally flawed human actions (*e.g.* of the patriarchs) and divine action highlights this fundamental point (1985: 220). This is an important observation, but, as with much of his work on ethics, it needs to be developed further. As it stands, Childs's work is too brief to have a significant impact on the current discussion.

One of his former students, Bruce Birch, has sought to apply just such a canonical approach in a more thoroughgoing way.[24] In particular, Birch is interested in making Old Testament narrative more available as a moral resource, yet he handles a variety of genres in a refreshing and illuminating way. His insight that the multiplicity of genres in the Old Testament is a major obstacle in producing a coherent account of biblical ethics is very helpful, as is his accessible description of the ethics displayed across the range of genres. The problems start when Birch seeks to move beyond description.

Ultimately, his canonical assumptions lead him inexorably to view the text as a unified narrative crystallizing at one historical moment, and the emphasis on the diversity of the Old Testament witness is somehow lost. His desire to apply his insights is laudable: however, in language not far removed from that of Barton or Goldingay, he simply appeals to the power of the biblical story (apparently flowing from some canonizing moment in the dim and distant past) to mould and transform the character (1991: 34).

The most interesting (and probably the most methodologically sound) work on Old Testament ethics yet seen has emerged relatively recently from Christopher Wright and Waldemar Janzen. Confusingly, they both take a 'paradigmatic approach', although, as we shall see, their work differs in several important respects.

Christopher Wright's *Living as the People of God* (UK) / *An Eye for an Eye* (US) (1983; aptly subtitled 'The Relevance of Old Testament Ethics') is an accessible attempt to develop a responsible way of handling the diverse ethical material in the Old Testament.[25] Wright's method is neither purely descriptive nor synthetic; rather, he suggests a loose framework which embraces a variety of ethical perspectives, and shows how such a model has potential for comparing and

---

[24] Birch & Rasmussen 1976; Birch 1988; 1991.

[25] A collection of Wright's work on Old Testament ethics was published in 1995, and this covers a wide range of subjects in the field and repays careful study, but does not advance his basic approach beyond that set out in his seminal work.

contrasting ethical material, as well as applying Old Testament ethics to contemporary problems.

In developing his 'ethical triangle', comprising three 'angles' which he terms 'theological' (God), 'social' (Israel) and 'economic' (the land), Wright provides us with a powerful analytical tool.[26] He argues that this ethical triangle allows any 'ethical' passage of the Old Testament to be understood in its proper theological context:

> Whenever we seek to interpret any passage ethically, by locating it within this framework, seeing where it 'fits' and how it functions, we shall be seeing it in the light of the main 'beams' of Israel's spiritual constitution – namely the great themes of election, redemption, law and land (1983: 63).

Wright examines each of these 'angles' in turn, and then sets off on a brief voyage through ethical themes, such as 'economics', 'politics' and 'society', to show how his proposed framework functions in interpreting and applying Old Testament ethical material. There is so much of value in this section of the book that one is left longing for a more rigorous treatment from Wright at a later date.

There is no doubt that Wright cogently presents a basic conceptual unity undergirding the ethics of the Old Testament. His framework accounts admirably for the pre-exilic situation. It does, of course, have its weaknesses: in the exilic period the 'triangle' inevitably becomes a little distorted, and it is difficult to see how the wisdom tradition fits in. But my major criticism of Wright's work is a familiar one. The material is fitted so neatly and skilfully into the framework that the variety of Old Testament literature is not allowed sufficient room to breathe. The 'ethical triangle' inevitably has the effect of smoothing developments and discontinuities. Despite these drawbacks, Wright has pointed the way towards a description of the 'atmosphere' of the Old Testament ethical witness, and a synthesis which can accommodate a range of Old Testament themes.

The usefulness of Wright's approach, however, does not stop there. It also points the way to new possibilities of applying the text in a responsible and appropriate way. The key to this lies in considering Israel as God's paradigm:

> A paradigm is something used as a model or example for other cases where a basic principle remains unchanged, though details

---

[26] This idea was first mooted by von Waldow 1974.

differ. It commonly refers, for example, to patterns in grammatical inflection – a verb, say, taken to exemplify the way endings or prefixes will go for other verbs of a similar type. A paradigm is not so much imitated as applied. It is assumed that cases will differ but, when necessary adjustments have been made, they will conform to the observable pattern of the paradigm (1983: 43).

For Wright, the Old Testament provides 'case studies' involving God's paradigm, Israel. These case studies are then 'to be applied to the infinite complexities' of the rest of human experience. He argues that Israel, the people of God, was not merely a medium for the message of God to the world, but a part of the message itself. It is not so much a matter of isolating principles from the narrative as seeing the (ethical) message enmeshed in the complex narrative of national and individual life. Wright claims that God spoke *incarnationally* through Israel in the Old Testament, in much the same way as he did through Christ in the New. So Israel's 'very existence and character as a society were to be a witness to God, a model or paradigm of his holiness expressed in the social life of a redeemed community' (1983: 43). Wright's work has much in common with that of Michael Schluter, Roy Clements and others at the Jubilee Centre in Cambridge.[27] They have adapted and extended this 'paradigmatic' method to enable the application of the Old Testament to the twentieth century to inform social and political action, with some success.[28]

Wright has written widely in the area of Old Testament ethics: both the publication of a revised version of his doctoral thesis (1990), where he traces the material concerning family, land and property in a vigorous and insightful way, and *Walking in the Ways of the Lord* (1995), a valuable collection of his articles and booklets, have been most welcome. Yet there is still vast potential for his seminal work to be followed up.

At one level, the work of Waldemar Janzen, *Old Testment Ethics: A Paradigmatic Approach*, has sought to do just that. He perceives three weaknesses in Wright's work, arguing that (1) Wright does not take sufficient account of the variety of ethical perspectives in the Old Testament; (2) he distinguishes too sharply between individual and

---

[27] Schluter & Clements 1989; 1990; Schluter 1984. There was much cross-fertilization of ideas during time spent in Cambridge by all concerned.

[28] This model provided the theological basis for the 'Keep Sunday Special Campaign', which, under Michael Schluter, engineered the only major parliamentary defeat of Margaret Thatcher during her premiership.

social ethics; (3) he occasionally falls back on appealing to 'principles' (1994: 75). Janzen presents a sound case, and develops an interesting alternative approach. He defines a 'paradigm' as follows:

> A personally and holistically conceived image of a model that imprints itself immediately and non-conceptually on the characters and actions of those who hold it (1994: 27–28).

Despite the wordiness of his definition, the idea behind it is relatively simple. Janzen argues that, as they were told stories, the people of Israel instinctively picked up what it meant to live in a godly way. They were not presented with principles, but with narratives about real people. He suggests, with some force, that this way of looking at the Old Testament is in keeping with the personal modes of thought we find there, in a way that a typically western attempt to extract 'principles' does not.

Janzen suggests that five such 'paradigms' can be found in the Old Testament: a familial paradigm, a priestly paradigm, a wisdom paradigm, a royal paradigm and a prophetic paradigm. The task of studying Old Testament ethics can then be summed up very simply: it should be our aim to discover 'Israel's inner image of a loyal family member, of a dedicated worshipper, of a wise manager of daily life, of a just ruler and of an obedient proclaimer of the prophetic word' (1994: 20).[29] Of these, the familial paradigm enjoys an ultimate primacy, and to a degree subsumes the other four. He sees the three features of life, land and hospitality lying at the heart of this paradigm.

There are several very clear strengths in this approach. For one thing, Janzen does justice to the narrative context of much of the ethical material in the Hebrew Bible. He makes the valuable point that stories are not told in the Old Testament simply to illustrate self-interpreting, abstract principles. The details of the text do not become superfluous once we have identified the 'moral' (1994: 57–58). Janzen also highlights the fact that even the legal codes in the Old Testament are now embedded in a narrative context which must shape their impact. He argues that the function of law in Israel is the shaping of character and community among God's redeemed people (1994: 62). What separates Israel from her neighbours is not always the content of her laws, but the fact that they find their meaning within their national story.

Janzen argues that this paradigmatic approach has three other distinct advantages. It asserts that, in the Old Testament, ethical behaviour is modelled primarily in a specific and concrete way, which fits well with

---

[29] He compares such concepts to our idea of a 'good driver' (1994: 28).

what we know of Hebrew thought. It also suggests a plausible mechanism by which laws, prophetic preaching, and so on, may have been generated to promote or buttress ethical teaching. But, perhaps most significant for our study, it has enormous potential for synthesizing the ethics of the Old Testament and applying them to life today. On the one hand, if one can reconstruct these paradigms, then one is well on the way to producing a coherent version of Old Testament ethical teaching; on the other, 'It holds promise for laying hold of the Old Testament canon's ethical substance in a sufficiently comprehensive yet concrete form to be manageable and useful in Christian ethical discourse' (1994: 79).[30]

This potential becomes clear as Janzen begins to develop each of his five paradigms. One of his most interesting conclusions concerns the Decalogue (and, by extension, other collections of law). In contrast to many writers, he argues that the Decalogue is *not* a summary of ethical teaching: it is intended to be 'sampling in scope' rather than comprehensive, yet, in its narrative context, it maintains a comprehensive function, calling Israel to remember all their covenantal obligations (1994: 89–91).

Overall, Janzen has gone a long way to establishing his central contentions:

> I believe that this paradigmatic structure embraces the canonical Old Testament's message in a comprehensive way. In its several paradigms it gathers up ethical content expressed in a great variety of literary genres. It provides a focus in the familial paradigm that is more proper and adequate than a single principle, such as love, justice or shalom, can offer. Instead of making individual texts, such as the Decalogue or the social justice oracles of the prophets, central through reductionist selection, it provides a framework within which these, too, can function more adequately as they are integrated into the Old Testament's total ethical thrust (1994: 178).

For all its power, however, Janzen's work has some questionable aspects. These surround his view of the 'familial paradigm'. I have some reservations about his characterization of the familial paradigm in terms of life, land and hospitality. While there is no doubt that each of these ideas is fundamental to the ethics of the Old

---

[30] Janzen also provides a delicately nuanced treatment of the use of the Old Testament in the light of the New Testament in his final chapter.

Testament, at times Janzen appears to use these categories so broadly (particularly when speaking of hospitality) as to remove them far from what one might imagine to be the subconscious ideal which every Israelite carried around in his or her head. In this, I believe, Janzen leaves himself open to the very criticism which he levels so effectively at Wright: his familial paradigm, like Wright's ethical triangle, becomes too general to do justice to the many ethical facets of the text.

Perhaps a more serious weakness is Janzen's failure to demonstrate convincingly that the familial paradigm is, in fact, pre-eminent.[31] Particularly in the case of the royal and prophetic paradigms, it seems that any attempt to see these models as in any sense derived from the familial is contrived. In a footnote at one point, Janzen admits that his list of four 'supportive' paradigms may not be complete (as there is no place, for example, for apocalyptic) (1994: 80 n. 70). This is an important point, for I believe that if we eliminate the primacy of the familial paradigm, and are prepared to admit new categories as we come across them, we may have a power-ful, appropriate method for the synthesis of the ethics of the Old Testament, and a helpful starting-point for our studies in Deu-teronomy.

Conclusions

This short survey of trends in Old Testament ethics has shown that there are still gaps in the picture. The analytical, synthetic and applicatory tasks have not yet been dealt with in a satis-factory way, either in theory or in practice. The resolution of the tension arising from the unity and diversity of the Old Testament is particularly problematic, and will have a key role in develop-ing an appropriate methodology for the study of the ethics of Deu-teronomy.

Studying the ethics of Deuteronomy

Why study the ethics of Deuteronomy?

This book has been written for two basic reasons. First, we simply do not have detailed studies of the ethics of the different strata of the biblical text (whether construed as books, genres or sources). Without such studies, we cannot hope to begin to determine the 'common

---

[31] This is reflected in some of Janzen's own comments. For instance, he seems to admit that the priestly paradigm adds something distinct from the familial (1994: 118).

atmosphere' of the Old Testament, let alone produce the definitive word on ethics. Deuteronomy is a good place to start.[32]

In addition, Deuteronomy provides us with a fascinating opportunity to tackle an issue with much wider ramifications: that of unity and diversity in the Old Testament. Perhaps more than any other book, Deuteronomy can claim to be pivotal in the study of the Old Testament. This may be true for historical reasons, but it can also be argued on theological and literary grounds. More energy has probably been devoted to the source analysis of Deuteronomy than to that of any other book. It has been subjected to a wider range of interpretations than has any other book. It is beyond question, for example, that, while exhibiting some contact with the preceding pentateuchal material, it has affinities in certain aspects with both the prophetic and wisdom traditions. And yet the rhetoric of Deuteronomy obviously sets parts of it, at least, in a league of its own as far as theological preaching is concerned. Therefore, Deuteronomy presents a unique challenge and testing-ground for an investigation of the methods and viability of both the analytical and the synthetic task set out above. The variation of genre and content will surely stretch any descriptive method. In turn, this, along with the accumulated weight of source and redactional theories, presents a stern test for any attempt at synthesis. If efforts to produce a synthesis of the ethics of Deuteronomy fail, then there can be no hope of moving beyond this to the ethics of the Old Testament.

One feature of Deuteronomy makes it particularly suitable as a case study for the viability of synthesis. That is its character as a book of transition. One of the prominent concerns of the book as it presents itself is to redefine the wilderness ethics of Israel for life in the land. Childs states:

> A predominant function of the book of Deuteronomy in relation to the preceding books of the Torah, was toward redirecting the original vertical model of the divine commands to later generations of those who had not experienced the thunder of Horeb (1992: 678).

Thus, alongside the value in studying Deuteronomy for its own sake, here is a potential key for unlocking the inner dynamic of the ethics of the Old Testament. Deuteronomy is avowedly a recasting of old ethical material for a new situation: in some ways a new revelation, yet one

---

[32] Maarsingh's examination of ethical themes in the laws is the only major study of the book's ethics (1961).

which is perceived to be continuous with the old. This is evidently of great significance for both synthesis and application.

The earlier works failed, above all, to do justice to either the unity or the diversity of the text. In a sense, this is the key issue in attempting to study any dimension of the theology of the Old Testament.

The problem of unity and diversity

Biblical scholars have long been asking whether the ethical material in the Old Testament is merely an accumulation of disparate units, or whether it may, in fact, be possible to detect some kind of undergirding pattern or atmosphere; that is, unity in the diversity. The tendency in the modern period has been to emphasize diversity at the expense of unity. This has dominated to the extent that the affirmation of overwhelming diversity has become part of the presuppositional framework of Old Testament study.

It is very easy to resolve the dialectic of unity and diversity by simply ignoring one of the poles. It is very difficult to preserve it in a thoroughgoing way.[33] To emphasize either the uniformity or the diversity of the Old Testament at the expense of the other, however, is an error. O'Donovan is helpful here:

In fact the search for diversity is as much the result of a prior methodological decision as the search for harmony, and cannot be defended on purely empirical grounds. Empirical investigation reveals points of diversity and points of harmony too (1973: 19).

Barton also highlights this:

Our sense that the moral stance of the OT is simply chaotic derives largely from the fact that it is so much a part of our common western heritage that we cannot stand far enough away to recognize the family likeness among its writings, and thus to see how markedly they differ, as a whole, from those of other major religious and ethical systems. And, if we are biblical critics, our very detailed study of the OT will make us acutely aware of differences within it, which, seen from the outside, are actually comparatively minor. It is important to keep a sense of proportion (1983: 126–127).

---

[33] See Spriggs's (1974) comparison of the OT theologies of Eichrodt and von Rad: Eichrodt stresses unity at the expense of diversity, while von Rad makes the equal and opposite error.

The question of unity and diversity in the Old Testament has been discussed at great length in other contexts.[34] The issue here is how to build methodological safeguards into this work which will prevent either differences or similarities from being obscured. What I am seeking is an 'analytic' technique which facilitates a synthesis *if the text itself demands it*, without glossing over diversity.

General methodological issues in the study of Deuteronomy

In studying any portion of the Old Testament one is faced with the problem of how the processes of composition of the text bear upon its interpretation. This problem is particularly acute in Deuteronomy, which has spawned a huge range of literary-critical studies; so even to speak of the ethics (or theology) of Deuteronomy is a perilous and complex exercise.

Traditionally, biblical scholars have started with the assumption that Deuteronomy reflects a variety of different theological perspectives. The first step is then to identify these strata of the text, and the next to try to place them on the historical timeline. Then, it is argued, it is possible to shed light on the theology (or theologies) of the book by comparing and contrasting these different literary and theological layers. By nature, such an approach is bound to emphasize diversity and discontinuities, and ultimately tends to produce a literary (or at best theological) history rather than 'theology'.[35]

Today, however, this method of studying the text does not hold sway in the way it once did. Partly as a result of recent developments in literary criticism, and partly due to a desire to recover the biblical text for the church, there has been a growing emphasis on reading the text *holistically*. 'Canonical' criticism and the so-called 'new literary' criticism have both sought to provide a theoretical justification for reading the final text as a literary unit. While neither of these 'schools' denies that the book is the product of a complex redactional history, the findings of historical criticism are sidestepped as an irrelevance to the 'meaning' for the modern 'reader' of the text.

In practice, these contrasting approaches to the text can actually appear very similar. In the case of Deuteronomy, if one sees the final form of the book as a careful reworking of older material in the interests of Josiah's reform, or as a later thoroughgoing attempt to enlist the Josiah tradition by 'Deuteronomistic' theologians in the exile, or even

---

[34] Goldingay (1984; 1987) critiques attempts to handle this tension and proposes some novel approaches. See also Reventlow 1979; Hasel 1982; McConville 1987.

[35] See *e.g.* Merendino 1969 or Mittmann 1975.

as a post-exilic creation, then the result will still come close to reading the text holistically. This shows that reading texts in this way does not always imply that historical questions have been set aside.

My interest in Deuteronomy grew out of a suspicion that a preoccupation with source criticism and redaction criticism in recent years has blinded many people to the extent of the literary and theological coherence of the book. This study, is, in some ways, an attempt to test the validity of this suggestion. Beginning with a holistic reading of the book, and aiming to produce a coherent, thoroughgoing account of the ethics of Deuteronomy, should, in principle, allow the conviction that this book does display a high degree of unity to be assessed.

Pragmatic considerations also make such an approach appropriate. If one wants to get round to saying anything meaningful about the ethics of the book (without getting bogged down in literary-critical issues), there are only two choices: one must either build on someone else's literary-critical work or begin with the final form of the text. For the reasons set out above, I have adopted the latter, and shall, for the moment, assume that a holistic reading of Deuteronomy is possible.

I make no assumptions at the outset about a particular setting. This, it could be argued, means that any discussion of the text will lack historical 'rootedness'. I am not, however, arguing that historical questions should be ignored: on the contrary, I shall attempt to take the historical implications of my study seriously. I am not suggesting that my integrated reading of the book is radically different from more conventional traditio-historical approaches.

Of course, it could be argued that it will be no surprise if, by assuming that it is possible, I manage to make a good case for a synchronic reading. It is true that the point at which one 'jumps' into the hermeneutical circle (or spiral) may have a profound influence on what one finds, but there really is little that can be done to avoid such a problem. Ultimately my approach can be vindicated or rebutted only on the basis of the detail of the pages which follow.

Conclusion

I have argued that the discipline of Old Testament ethics has not succeeded, despite many helpful individual works, in describing, synthesizing or applying the moral teaching of the text in any satisfactory way. In recent years the debate has centred upon exposing the inadequacies of previous work and hesitantly pointing the way forward.

The Old Testament cannot be treated as a parcel of ethics dropped from heaven (or crystallizing at some canonizing moment) or as a history of ethics in Israel. Yahweh did not present Israel with a beginner's set of norms and principles on Sinai and continue filling in gaps until every possible situation had been covered at the end of Chronicles! The biblical text reflects an ongoing struggle to address basic questions fundamental to the existence of individual and community in relationship with Yahweh. There is unity because these questions were essentially the same for each generation and because they asked the questions of the same revealing God. There is diversity because new situations and times of national upheaval inevitably mark vigorous activity in seeking ethics for the new order.

This book aims to study the ethics of Deuteronomy in their theological context in a way which allows for the possibility of inherent unity without ignoring diversity of genre and perspective. This may be one small step toward rediscovering the ethical content of the Old Testament as a whole.

Chapter One

Ethics and covenant

To say that covenantal ideas play a central role in Deuteronomy is hardly to make a startling claim, for they are prominent on almost every page of the text. This chapter examines how the Deuteronomic view of covenant shapes the ethical teaching of the book.[1]

The origins and development of covenant thought and language in Deuteronomy have been discussed at great length. In the first part of this chapter, I shall attempt to chart a course through the claims that the structure of Deuteronomy as a whole can be accounted for by comparison with ancient near-eastern (ANE) treaty forms, and suggest a slightly modified approach along the way. Then I shall move on to examine some of the exhortation in the book and discuss its ethical implications. Finally, I shall examine the role of the covenant metaphor in the Deuteronomic presentation of national history, and make a few suggestions on how we might read the book in the light of my findings.

Ethics and the covenant form

Determining the relationship between the *form* of a text and its *content* is never easy, but it is a vital part of interpretation. This explains why a vast amount of energy has been expended in trying to prove that Deuteronomy borrows its form from certain ancient treaty documents. This is clearly an important question for us: if the whole book has been carefully arranged to resemble a particular kind of international 'covenant', then we would expect the nature of this covenant to shape the ethical teaching of the text. So we must begin by looking at the arguments over the structure of Deuteronomy.

---

[1] Of course, I am very aware of the complex debate which has raged in recent years over the origins of covenant thought and language in Israel. In this chapter, I use 'covenant' in a broad sense to denote Yahweh's relationship with Israel, rather than limiting it to a specific word-group.

Deuteronomy in its ANE context

Since Bickerman's original recognition of parallels between Deuteronomy and ANE treaty forms (1950–51) was picked up and developed by George Mendenhall in 1954, the 'treaty question' has dominated the form-critical study of Deuteronomy. The basic contention was that Deuteronomy, like these treaties, followed a simple pattern:

1. Introduction
2. Historical prologue
3. Details of the agreement
4. Ratification ceremony
5. Conclusion (including threats of punishment and incentives to obedience).

The precise details have been covered exhaustively many times.[2] To summarize the debate, it seems fair to say that attempts to establish a distinct ANE treaty genre into which Deuteronomy fits neatly have not succeeded. Neither the efforts of Mendenhall (1954), Kitchen (1965) and Kline (1963) to demonstrate formal dependence on Hittite vassal treaties of the second millennium, nor the competing endeavours of McCarthy (1978) and others to forge a link with Assyrian treaties of the first, have gained a consensus.[3]

Ernest Nicholson has highlighted the problems which must be overcome by anyone suggesting that Deuteronomy was directly modelled on an ancient 'diplomatic' accord (1986: 68). For a start, Deuteronomy is not *presented* as either a treaty or any kind of legal document, and its scope ranges far beyond the confines of a suzerain–vassal relationship. Nicholson also makes the simple but important observation that the term 'king' is not used of Yahweh in the book (with the possible exception of 33:5). This obviously weakens any claim that Deuteronomy is consciously emulating the treaty form.[4] The case against dependence is strengthened by the difficulty of explaining the role of chapters 1 – 3, 4, 5 and 28 in such a scheme. Attempts to

---

[2] For a sympathetic view of the treaty analogy see *e.g.* McCarthy 1978; Baltzer 1960. For a later summary see Nicholson 1986: 56–82.

[3] See also Frankena 1965. Weinfeld tries to combine both views (1991: 9).

[4] While his explanation of this is weak (that any comparison of Yahweh to an Assyrian overlord would be utterly inappropriate), failing to take proper account of the metaphorical nature of 'covenant' on any reading of the book, this does not undermine his case.

produce a neat correlation have tended to undermine the distinctive elements of the text itself.[5]

On balance, I am convinced that it is best to abandon attempts to identify Deuteronomy with particular international treaty documents, and to focus instead on how the Deuteronomist has reshaped common ideas to serve his own theological and ethical agenda, drawing on diplomatic language and concepts and, *mutatis mutandis*, using them to characterize Israel's relationship with her God.[6]

Similar scepticism towards overzealous efforts to tie down the origins of covenant language in Deuteronomy is found in Kalluveettil's study (1982). He shows that covenantal ideas were not restricted to the national level, but pervaded every type of relationship in the ANE. So we must be careful, even where there are similarities with treaty material, to ensure that the authors of the treaties and of the biblical text are not simply drawing on the same common stock of ideas.

Having sounded these warnings, there are some theologically significant parallels between Deuteronomy and extant treaties. In the same way as treaties legislate for a situation which has arisen primarily through the action of the suzerain, Israel's covenant relationship with Yahweh has its foundation in divine action. But even here, there are important differences. God has not conquered Israel, but freed her from oppression (the only military action in view is Yahweh's defeat of Israel's enemies, whether in Egypt or the Transjordan; see *e.g.* 2:24–25). Israel stands in the position of vassal and yet her people are conquerors rather than the conquered! Throughout the narrative of the opening chapters Yahweh is presented as the one who disposes territory and determines the outcome of battles. Israel's part is merely obedient response to the divine command. This is the central insight of the treaty model.

Although Yahweh is not explicitly named as the king of Israel (in contrast to the theology of Yahweh's kingship in some of the Psalms), it is clear that Israel is subject to him, both in the light of his power and his particular interest in the life of the nation. There is no hint of negotiation in the drafting of this treaty – it is divine pronouncement in

---

[5] A classic example of the danger so perceptively pinpointed by Muilenburg (1969: 1–18) of becoming too preoccupied with form at the expense of content.

[6] 'The Near Eastern covenant idea provided Israel with a significant metaphor for the exposition of the relationship which existed between Yahweh and herself' (Thompson 1964: 23). Both Wenham's suggestion that Deuteronomy conforms to a distinct Old Testament covenant genre (1970: 152–181) and Craigie's proposal that the book should be read against the background of Ex. 1 – 15 (1978a: 78–83) share this basic recognition.

the wake of divine action. This pronouncement has been couched in the language of international treaty and transformed to address the unique situation of the covenant relationship between Yahweh and Israel. It is in this atmosphere that the ethical preaching of Deuteronomy exists.

The parallels with ANE treaties show that the Deuteronomist has used covenant as a metaphor for Israel's relationship to Yahweh. This metaphor must now be unpacked. I shall attempt to begin this task by re-examining the shape of the book as a whole.

The shape of Deuteronomy and the concept of decision

Opinion is split over the best way to divide up the text of Deuteronomy. Many have suggested that the editorial phrase 'and Moses said to Israel ...' marks off 1:6 – 4:40 and 5:1 – 28:68 as the two main parts of the book. Others, often influenced by treaty parallels, have proposed more complex divisions. But I think that several important features of the book have been largely overlooked.

One major problem for those who take 5:1 – 28:68 as a discrete unit is that there is clearly a significant break in the text at the end of chapter 11, where exhortation gives way to the collection of laws. While this transition can be exaggerated (it is true that chapters 11 and 12 are carefully integrated), there is a marked rhetorical shift as we move from the preaching of chapter 11 to the legal imperatives of chapter 12. This makes it difficult to see how 5:1 – 28:68 can be taken as the central panel of the book.[7] I would suggest that it is much better, for reasons which I shall explain, to see the collection of laws stretching from 12:1 to 26:19 as the core of the book.

Matters are more complicated when we come to the remaining parts of the text, loosely referred to as the 'framework'.[8] Chapters 1 – 11 fall fairly naturally into four parts: the historical prologue of chapters 1 – 3, chapter 4 (which seems to stand alone), the rehearsal of the Decalogue in chapter 5 and the 'sermonic' material in chapters 6 – 11. Although each section of the text has its own character, they combine to create a theological and rhetorical progression, calling Israel to do what God has commanded. These chapters are united by the concept of *decision*.

At every stage, the Deuteronomist is interested in depicting the choices confronting Israel in the past, present and future. The first three chapters deal with decisions made by Israel in the past and the new

---

[7] In fact, the phrase 'and Moses spoke ...' (5:1; 29:1) has more to do with a deliberate identification of Moab with Horeb than with the literary structure of the book as a whole, as I will show in the next chapter.

[8] This is useful shorthand for chapters 1 – 11, 27 – 34, but does not imply any particular view of the relationship of the parts of the book.

opportunity to obey in the present. Chapter 4 sharpens the focus on the present, while also anticipating choices to be made in the near and distant future. The preaching of chapters 6 – 11 returns to the imminent decisions facing Israel at Moab and within the land, continuing to draw on examples of the nation's appalling record of past disobedience. So whatever one thinks about the literary history of these chapters, they display a careful and coherent development in their present form.

This view has not found many proponents in recent times, but support comes from Andrew Mayes, commenting on the closing verses of chapter 11:

> These verses are intended as a conclusion to the whole of chs. 1-11, in that after all the history and the exhortation, they bring Israel to the point of decision. The verses are also a prelude to what follows, since the decision which is now set before Israel concerns obedience or disobedience to the law which is about to be proclaimed (1981: 217).

Despite his source-critical focus, Mayes recognizes the clear evidence for an overarching purpose in the selection, expression and arrangement of chapters 1 – 11. The organizing principle which binds these words together is the decision demanded by the covenant relationship.

The content of this decision is expounded in various ways. In chapters 1 – 3, Israel must choose to press on to Canaan, putting past failures behind them. Chapter 4 issues a clear challenge to live in conformity to the divine revelation, whether at Horeb or Moab. The recapitulation of the Decalogue in chapter 5 then paves the way for the Deuteronomist's explicit appeal for a total personal response, in chapter 6, which is developed in chapters 7 – 11.[9]

It is extremely interesting, however, that for the most part, the choices facing Israel (or the obedience which is demanded) are construed in abstract terms. The nation is repeatedly called to serve God, obey, or listen, but with the exception of purging the land of Canaanites and establishing a pattern of family instruction in the covenant relationship, the all-embracing obedience commanded by Yahweh remains ill-defined. This, I believe, gives us an important pointer to the function of these chapters.

I would suggest that this feature of the text reveals that the primary role of chapters 1 – 11 is to set the collection of laws in chapters 12 –

---

[9] This is presented in covenantal language, in the light of Yahweh's unique historical intervention in the life of Israel (Hempel 1964: 105–152; Kuyper 1952: 338).

26 in the context of a crucial decision faced by the nation, brought about by Yahweh's insistence that they must respond to him at Moab. Above all, the nation must choose to love God, and to demonstrate this love by obedience. This proposal will be developed in the next chapter, but for the moment it is enough to notice that the 'laws and statutes', which have remained tantalizingly hidden throughout chapters 1 – 11 (although they are clearly related in some way to the Decalogue – see 5:1), are made explicit in 12:1 onwards. Chapters 1 – 26, it seems, are bound together in a uniform concern to encourage Israel to choose covenantal obedience.

Much too often, chapters 27 – 34 have been treated as some kind of composite appendix to Deuteronomy, loosely related to its general concerns, but peripheral to the central thrust of the book. The many difficulties in interpreting individual pericopes have discouraged attempts to discover how these chapters may contribute to the message of the book as a whole.

I would argue, however, that there are grounds for reading this part of the book as the climax of a carefully conceived work, with a particular interest in ethical behaviour among God's people. It is my contention that this disparate material is also held together by a common interest in the decisions to be faced throughout Israel's existence. Here the stress is placed explicitly on the *outcome* of the decision faced by the nation. The enunciation of blessing and curse in chapters 27 – 28 graphically presents Israel with a choice, as does the covenant-renewal ceremony of chapter 29, however the details are interpreted. Chapter 30 explores the ramifications of this and future decisions.

It is quite obvious that in chapters 31 – 34 there is a change in mood, as the preaching of Moses becomes the reflections of the dying leader. But even here, the interest in decision persists. Both in the Song of Moses and in the account of the great leader's death, the implications of making the wrong decision lurk in the background.

This general overview of the text furnishes us with the following simple structure:

1 – 11	Israel at the place of decision
12 – 26	The decision spelled out
27 – 34	The outcome of decision

Such a division is, of course, quite crude, but it does serve to illustrate that the preaching of the book as we now have it construes some kind of 'decision' as the primary obligation arising from covenant relationship with Yahweh (see also Lenchak's more detailed rhetorical analysis,

1993: 1–37). Like ancient treaties, at a general level, Deuteronomy consists of an account of the recent past (how the relationship between the parties has arisen), a statement of the behaviour required in view of this new relationship, and concluding matters such as the consequences of disobedience. Within this simple and logical pattern, Israel is presented with a real choice within the covenant arrangement.

Deuteronomy clearly arose in the covenantal atmosphere of the ANE. The innovation of the Deuteronomist is derived from the nature of the God of Deuteronomy, who is primarily a God of grace. This God has brought Israel to a point of decision, and through this book defines the decision which he demands, and which will benefit his people. This is made even more apparent by the proliferation of the language of choice and decision in Deuteronomy.

Ethics and covenant language

The language of Deuteronomy and the concept of decision

The whole book of Deuteronomy is packed with appeals to make the proper response to Yahweh's initiatives in the life of the nation. In fact, this preoccupation with exhortation is the most striking feature of the book's language (Amsler 1977: 11–22). I would suggest that this adds further weight to the suggestion made in the last section, that Deuteronomy is a book which is fundamentally concerned with *decision*.

A high degree of creativity is evident, as the writer draws on metaphors from everyday life, as well as on ancient treaties, in expounding his own view of Israel's relationship with Yahweh and pressing a decision upon Israel. There are at least fifteen ways of referring to the action to be taken in response to the divine 'command' (*miṣwâ*). These will be considered in turn, roughly in order of prominence, and a few comments offered on each.

The least interesting of the Deuteronomist's ways of enjoining Israel to follow God is the use of *'śh*, 'hear' (*e.g.* 6:1–2; 11:22; 26:16; 30:8) and this needs no further comment. The use of *šm'*, however, is more intriguing. While the word is used to mean 'hear' or 'listen' in a straightforward 'physical' sense in many places in Deuteronomy, it is clear that in others the verb carries a more developed nuance.[10] We find *šm'* meaning to preside over a lawsuit (1:16, 17; 17:12), to answer prayer (9:19; 10:10; 26:7) and to understand foreign languages (28:49),

---

[10] The subjects are Yahweh (1:34, 45; 3:26; 5:28; 23:6; 33:7); Israel (1:43; 9:2; 13:12; 17:4; 29:3); the nations (2:25); the gods (4:28); the heavens (32:1). See also 4:32; 29:18. The passages 13:9; 17:13; 19:20; 21:21 deal with deterrents.

but normally the verb carries the connotation of hearing *and acting*, rather than simply recognizing sounds. In 4:1, for example, Israel is commanded to 'listen to' the statutes and ordinances in such a way that they carry them out. Similar injunctions to 'hear the law' are found throughout the text.[11] Closely related to this is the often repeated command to 'listen to the voice of Yahweh'.[12] The two ideas are used in such close proximity that it is very difficult to see any distinction between obeying the law and listening to God's voice. This is hardly surprising when we examine the other major idea connected with the use of *šm'* in Deuteronomy.

There is a deliberate association of *šm'* with the theophany at Sinai/Horeb. Eight times in chapters 4 and 5 the verb occurs in the context of divine revelation, and at the end of chapter 5 in particular there is a marked emphasis on *šm'*.[13] The verb appears in five consecutive verses and links hearing the divine voice at Horeb, receiving the Mosaic law and the obedience (*i.e. šm'*) required of Israel in response (*e.g.* 4:27). Thus we see that the writer has carefully drawn together the ideas of actually hearing the voice at Horeb, the content of the revelation (whether expressed in terms of the 'voice of Yahweh' or the commandment, statutes, *etc.*) and the response required of Israel in his use of this single verb. It is interesting to note in passing that the 'Shema' in chapter 6 comes as the climax of this development of this theme of divine revelation, and is therefore thoroughly grounded in the response required of Israel by this God who reveals himself.

There is a strong possibility that the Deuteronomist found inspiration for his use of the verb *šmr* in the world of treaties. The verb is common, occurring in the contexts of general injunctions to be careful, of Yahweh keeping his oath and also of abstaining from certain behaviour (2:4; 7:8; 23:10). In addition, *šmr* is the basis of the stereotyped warning 'Be careful lest you …',[14] as well as the expression 'take care and guard yourselves' (4:9, 23; 12:28). The vast majority of occurrences of the verb, however, comes where Israel is enjoined either to 'keep the commands' (where the 'commands' or equivalent are the direct object of *šmr*)[15] or to 'be careful to carry out the commands',

[11] 4:1, 6, 10; 5:1; 6:3, 4; 7:12; 11:13, 27, 28; 12:28; 13:4; 27:9; 28:13; 30:17; 31:12, 13.

[12] 4:30; 5:27; 8:20; 9:23; 13:15, 19; 15:5; 26:14, 17; 27:10; 28:1, 2, 15, 45, 62; 30:2, 8, 10, 12, 13, 20.

[13] 4:12, 33, 36; 5:23, 24, 25, 26, 27; also 18:16.

[14] 4:23 and 11:16 (plural) ; 6:12; 8:11; 12:13, 19, 30; 15:9 (singular).

[15] 4:2, 40; 5:10, 29; 6:2, 17; 7:11, 12; 8:2, 6; 10:13; 11:1, 8, 22; 13:5, 19; 17:19; 26:17, 18; 27:1; 28:9, 45; 29:8; 30:10, 16; 33:9.

where *šmr* and *'šh* are collocated.[16] As 26:17–18 and 29:8 show, there is little difference between these ways of expressing the response demanded of Israel.

The presence of the word pair *zkr*[17] / *škh*[18] (remember / not forget) contributes to the atmosphere of decision – at this significant point in history and in the future, Moses calls the people to remember Yahweh. In 4:23, 31, Israel is warned against the dire consequences of forgetting the covenant of Yahweh. Elsewhere it is Yahweh himself whom they are in danger of forgetting (6:12; 8:11, 14, 19; 32:18), or, on occasion, his words or their past experiences (4:9; 25:19; 26:13). Where Israel is told to remember, the history of the nation (and particularly the exodus) is stressed,[19] although not to the exclusion of Yahweh (8:18; 25:18).

The choice facing Israel is also cast in terms of whom they will serve (*'bd*). The writer periodically calls the nation to serve Yahweh (6:13; 10:12, 20; 11:13; 13:5), but by far the most common use of the verb is in drawing attention to Israel's past (and future) proclivity for rejecting Yahweh in favour of other gods.[20] This may well be further evidence of the influence of suzerain–vassal treaties on the metaphors which the Deuteronomist chooses to adapt.

As the book unfolds we can see a persistent thread dealing with fear (*yr'*) in the life of the nation. Israel is repeatedly assured that there is no need to be afraid of her enemies,[21] and reminded that it is really the nations around who should be afraid of her (2:4, 25; 28:10). There is, however, a definite place for 'fear' in Israel's relationship with Yahweh; this becomes apparent both in direct injunctions and in descriptions of the appropriate attitude within such a relationship.[22] Alongside the fear of Yahweh himself, fear of the judicial consequences of departing from the will of Yahweh is presented as a powerful deterrent in national life (13:12; 17:13; 19:20; 21:21). The language of 'fearing Yahweh' seems to take us beyond any contemporary model, although it may borrow from the area of international conflict. The Deuteronomist has reshaped the concept, insisting that it is within Israel's power to choose whom she shall fear.

---

[16] 4:6; 5:1, 32; 6:3, 25; 8:1; 11:32; 12:1; 13:1; 15:5; 16:12; 17:10; 19:19; 23:24; 24:8; 26:16; 28:1, 13, 15, 58; 29:8; 31:12; 32:46.

[17] 5:15; 7:18; 8:2, 18; 9:7; 15:15; 16:3, 12; 24:18, 22; 25:17; 32:7; and nominal form in 25:9.

[18] 4:9, 23, 31; 6:12; 8:11, 14, 19; 9:7; 25:19; 26:13; 32:18.

[19] 5:15; 7:18; 15:15; 16:3, 12; 24:18, 22.

[20] See 4:19, 28; 5:9; 7:4, 16; 8:19; 11:16; 12:30; 13:3, 7, 14; 17:3; 28:36, 64; 29:17, 25; 30:17; 31:20.

[21] *E.g.* 1:21, 29; 3:2, 22; 7:18, 19; 20:1, 3, 8; 31:6, 8.

[22] See 4:10; 5:29; 6:2, 13, 24; 8:6; 10:12, 20; 13:5; 14:23; 17:19; 25:18; 31:12, 13.

In apparent contrast to the fear of Yahweh, we have the celebrated Deuteronomic injunctions to love (*'hb*). The book opens with an exposition of the love which Yahweh has shown to Israel (in marked contrast to any extant treaty). It is only in the light of God's love that Israel is commanded to respond in kind (4:37; 7:8, 9, 13; 10:15, 18). The first prescription of a loving *response* comes in the Shema, but after the watershed of 10:12 we encounter the necessity of Israel loving Yahweh repeatedly.[23] 'Love' here amounts to a total response which encompasses every aspect of the life of the nation and of the individual to the initiatives of her God.

The precise nuance of the command to 'cleave' to Yahweh (*dbq*) is difficult to tie down (4:4; 10:20; 11:22; 13:5; 30:20). There are only forty occurrences of the verb in biblical Hebrew, spread throughout the canon (Andersen & Forbes 1989: 302). Only the Psalms have more instances (seven) than Deuteronomy. In places, including the celebrated command of Genesis 2:24, it clearly implies personal intimacy, while in others, nothing more than actual, physical 'sticking' is in view (*e.g.* Jb. 29:10). We can say with confidence, however, that the writer is talking about a decisive, irreversible commitment.

Several other expressions are used further to elucidate the response of Israel. Caleb is spoken of as fulfilling Yahweh's will (*ml'*; 1:36). Elsewhere an all-embracing response to God is described in terms reminiscent of the wisdom literature (6:7–8; 11:18–20), and the nation is called not to turn (*swr*) to the left or right.[24] Throughout it is clear that Yahweh appeals to the people on the basis of his 'record' of covenant faithfulness, and asks that they make their decision on this rational basis (4:39; 7:9; 8:5; 9:3, 6; also 31:13).

One final feature which deserves comment is the way in which, at some points in the book, the Deuteronomist piles up several of his favourite expressions for the response demanded of Israel, to emphasize his urgent appeal for decision.[25] This technique is used at certain key points in the text (*e.g.* the end of chapter 11), but also occurs almost at random throughout the book in a variety of forms. 10:12–13 is one example. Israel is called to 'fear' Yahweh, 'walk in his ways', 'love and serve' him and to 'guard his commands and statutes'. Even in the legal

[23] 10:15, 18; 11:1, 13, 22; 13:4; 19:9; 30:6, 16, 20.
[24] 5:32; 17:11, 20; 28:14; with 2:27 as a possible historical paradigm for this behaviour.
[25] 6:1–2; 8:6; 10:12, 20; 11:1, 13, 22; 13:4, 18; 14:1–3; 19:9; 26:12–15; 27:10; 28:1, 9, 13–14; 30:1–10, 16, 20. Toombs argues that these present the 'wider and narrower meanings of obedience' (1965: 407).

section of the book, the Deuteronomist is at pains to remind his readers that he is presenting a coherent theological and ethical agenda. This may also be why the noun *miṣwâ* occurs regularly as the lone singular in the phrase 'the commandment, the statutes and the ordinances' (rather like the more familiar uses of *tôrâ* and *derek*).[26] Along with the variety of verbal forms used, the 'commandment' and other nominal forms combine in Deuteronomy to represent an overall response which Yahweh deserves and demands.

It is plain, then, that Deuteronomy is overflowing with exhortation. The unmatched concentration of parenetic vocabulary confirms that the prevailing atmosphere of the book is the ethical decision facing Israel. Useful work has been done in tracing some of this language to the diplomatic milieu.[27] One must not, however, underestimate the distinctiveness of Israelite thought, even when it has borrowed extensively from its neighbours. Ultimately such a background is only a *starting-point* for determining the intentions of the Deuteronomist. Even when we have discovered the source of his ideas, we are still some way short of discerning his message.

Deuteronomy is not a treaty document. It has, however, emerged from a world where vassal treaties were relatively common, and something of the language and thought of response to an arrangement imposed 'from above' has found its way into the book. Talk of 'treaty' or covenant was in the air, and was seized upon by the Deuteronomist to convey facets of the relationship of Israel with Yahweh, and primarily to emphasize the need to make an instant, thoroughgoing response.[28]

The singular–plural variation in Deuteronomy

There is one outstanding linguistic feature which requires some comment. This is the well-known shift from use of the second person

---

[26] 5:31 (28); 6:1, 25; 7:11; 8:1; 11:8, 22; 15:5; 17:20; 19:9; 26:13; 27:1, 10^k; 30:11; 31:5. See also the singular pronoun in 30:12, 13 referring to what has gone before. Amsler speaks of writers who 'sont animés d'un authentique souci de cohérence éthique' ('are driven by an authentic concern for ethical coherence') (1977: 18).

[27] *yd'* (usually 'to know') has been linked to Akkadian and Ugaritic treaty parallels ('recognizing treaty stipulations as binding') (Huffmon 1966; Huffmon & Parker 1966); *'hb* (to love) given an emotionless background (Moran 1963: 75–80; McCarthy 1965); *sᵉgullâ* (treasured possession), *yšr* (upright), *'bd* (serve), *brk* (bless), *'rr* (curse) and phrases such as 'going after other gods' and 'with all your heart' traced to this milieu (Moran 1963: 85–87).

[28] This was not the only metaphor he used; see the discussion of familial ideas in the next section, and Kalluveettil 1982: 90–91. The fact that the term *ḥeseḏ* (lovingkindness) is an integral part of 'covenant' thought throughout the Old Testament, yet is without parallel in treaty contexts, provides a timely warning (Clark 1992: 256–267).

singular form to the corresponding second person plural and *vice versa* (see *e.g.* 4:19–20).

This phenomenon was systematically applied as a criterion of source analysis by Staerk (1894) and Steuernagel (1894), and in more recent times was developed by Minette de Tillesse (1962).[29] Building on the work of Martin Noth, Minette de Tillesse argued that the singular and plural passages reflect different theological positions. Many literary-critical studies rely heavily on this understanding.[30] It is not, however, without its problems.

Lohfink has shown that 'number-mixing' in chapters 5 – 11 is unreliable for source analysis and should rather be seen as a stylistic and rhetorical device for attracting attention.[31] This has been accepted by Weinfeld, Braulik and Seitz, among others.[32] Parallels in treaty material and biblical texts have also been pointed out.[33] In the light of what we have seen of Deuteronomy's preoccupation with decision, it may be that the alternation is used to underline the demands made upon both individual and community by the covenant relationship.

This phenomenon of number-mixing has not been examined exhaustively, nor has a thoroughgoing solution been provided. We have seen, however, that its reliability as a systematic tool for redactional analysis is questionable. Its presence does not necessarily exclude the holistic reading I have been proposing and may, in fact, strengthen the case for seeing ethical implications in the covenant relationship set out in this chapter.

Ethics and 'covenant history'

The simple outline of the text and brief discussion of vocabulary presented above strongly suggest that 'decision' is an important category in Deuteronomic theology. This is borne out when we examine

[29] Staerk 1894: 78–93; Steuernagel 1894 (throughout); Minette de Tillesse 1962. It was argued that the plural passages share the Deuteronomistic historian's concern to denounce idolatry and expound a conditional view of the covenant. See also Begg 1994.

[30] *E.g.* Mittmann 1975; Rose 1975; Preuss 1982.

[31] Lohfink 1963: 237ff. Mayes uses the division to support his 'double redaction' theory, but admits that '4:19 cannot be taken from its context despite the change of address' and that in 10:12 – 11:32 'attempts to carry through a division on the basis of the change from singular to plural do not appear to be successful' (Mayes 1981: 154, 207).

[32] Weinfeld 1991: 15; Braulik 1978a: 146–150; Seitz 1971: 309; McConville 1993: 36–38.

[33] For treaty parallels see Mayes 1981: 35–37; Baltzer 1960: 33, 71; Fitzmyer 1967: 107. Also Ex. 22:19–23; Jos. 7:12ff.; 8:2b; 11:10ff.

the way in which the book regards the recent history of this infant nation, for Deuteronomy presents the history of Israel in its entirety as leading up to the critical moment of decision at Moab. Much of this material will be considered in detail in the rest of this book, but it is worth pausing here to note the proliferation of historical references, and the way in which they are chosen to serve the ethical preaching of the Deuteronomist as he calls Israel to decision.

Chapters 1 – 3

After 1:1–2 sets the entire book in the context of the history of Yahweh's dealings with Israel, there is an immediate reference to the defeat of the kings of the Transjordan (verse 4). Sihon and Og play an important role in the historical prologue (and beyond) as a paradigm of successful conquest under Yahweh in the life of the nation.[34]

The next incident to be picked out is that of the delegation of Moses' authority (and presumably responsibility for subsequent actions), which leads into a pointed rehearsal of the spy narrative and initial refusal (and subsequent failure) to enter the land at Kadesh Barnea. The theologically weighted account of the second tortuous journey to Moab, including the details of the encounters with Sihon and Og, brings the nation to Beth-Peor (see Nu. 25:1–5).

Chapters 4 – 11

On leaving the 'historical prologue', the prominence of past events in the Deuteronomic scheme does not noticeably decrease. Chapter 4 not only makes explicit reference to and use of the events of Baal-Peor (verses 3–4, 46), but moves into a lengthy 'meditation' on the events of Horeb (verses 10–40).

The Horeb theme is picked up again immediately in chapter 5, where it is the subject of further theological and ethical reflection. The second half of chapter 6 draws on the events of the exodus and the rebellion at Massah, whereas chapter 7 considers the exodus in the light of the patriarchal promises.

From this point to the beginning of the laws, the nation's recent experience comes even more to the fore. Chapter 8 is essentially an affirmation of the Lord's care for Israel in the wilderness and the resultant ease with which the potential danger was negotiated. This implies that the starkly contrasting abundance of the land can only be enjoyed on the same basis, that is, in dependence upon Yahweh. After a

[34] See 3:21, and also 1:4; 2:24, 30, 31, 32; 3:1, 2, 3, 4, 6, 10, 11, 13; 4:46, 47; 29:6; 31:4.

short allusion to the fear of giants which kept Israel from the land, chapters 9 - 10 return to Horeb to recall the apostasy of the golden calf incident. In the course of this we read the catalogue of Israelite rebellion (9:22–23), the parenthesis dealing with the death of Aaron and the designation of the Levites to carry the ark (10:6–9). The climax of the rhetoric of these chapters is also prefaced by a welter of historical references – to the blessing of Israel through progeny (10:22), the plagues (11:3), the drowning of the Egyptian army (11:4) and the deaths of Dathan and Abiram (11:6). All these references, either implicitly or explicitly, serve to sharpen the decision facing Israel at Moab.

Chapters 12 – 26

One would not normally expect to find a wealth of historical content in a new collection of laws. But as well as the use of shorthand allusions to the uniqueness of Israel (*e.g.* 14:1–2), the fulfilment of promise (*e.g.* 12:20) or the exodus (17:17–18), we find other, longer references to history. In the list of regulations for admission to the assembly, the basis for prohibiting Moabites is traced to the poor treatment of Israel on the way to Canaan and the Balaam incident (23:4–6). In contrast, Egypt's 'entertainment' of Israel (verse 7) leads to a relaxed provision for them! In the case of virulent skin diseases (24:9), the presumptuous actions of Miriam and her resultant punishment are recalled to provide an encouragement to conform. Strangely, the Amalekites are also cited at the end of chapter 25 (verses 17–19). A final historical allusion comes in the conclusion to the laws in chapter 26. Whatever the origins of the 'credo' (verses 5–10), it has the effect of setting the archetypal response to the laws firmly in the context of the history of the covenant between Yahweh and Israel.

Chapters 27 – 34

As in the collection of laws, the nature of the material in the closing section of the book does not lend itself to extended historical allusion, but even here we find the Deuteronomist using the past to inform the future.

Much of the long list of curses in chapter 28 is cast in terms of the experiences of Egypt. It turns out that chapters 29 and 30 use the past in the same way as chapters 1 – 11. For example, 28:69 recalls the events at Horeb in the context of the covenant, and the journey from Egypt to Transjordan is revisited in 29:1–8. The painful realities of life in Egypt (29:16ff.), and the sobering destruction of Sodom and Gomorrah (verses 23–28) continue the emphasis on historical events. Sihon and Og reappear in 31:4, and a final (extended) appeal to the experience of

Israel in relationship with Yahweh comes in the poetry of the Song of Moses, particularly in 32:7–22.

This brief overview of the use of historical material simply shows that the way in which the nation is reminded of past experiences in order to call her to a decision in the present is one of the most prominent features of Deuteronomy. This, in turn, adds further weight to the suggestion that the Deuteronomic theology of 'covenant' is best understood in an ethical context, calling to people to respond to the grace of God. A final aspect of the covenantal material in the book makes this even clearer.

Ethics and the fulfilment of covenant promises

The final aspect of covenant thought in Deuteronomy, which is related to this whole area of ethical/theological choice, concerns the fulfilment of promise which Yahweh made to the 'fathers' (or to Abraham, Isaac and Jacob).

In Deuteronomy, to speak of the fulfilment of promise is, in essence, to speak of the land.[35] Of course, in some places in the book, this fulfilment is spoken of in general terms (e.g. 4:31; 9:27). In others, notably 7:12–15, the promise extends beyond the land, to prosperity and population growth (see also 1:8–11; 6:3; 10:22; 13:18) and even international pre-eminence. In the vast majority of cases, however, the expectation focuses on the *land* itself (Diepold 1972: 76). The proliferation of direct references to the occupation of the land as promise-fulfilment makes this all too clear.[36]

For the author, Israel is entering a good land given by God. The fact that the land is given to fulfil the promise goes some way towards explaining the enthusiastic language in which it is described. Whether a strip of semi-fertile real estate on the edge of the Mediterranean warrants such extravagant praise or not, it is repeatedly pronounced 'good' (*ṭôḇ*).[37] The description of 8:7–10 is typical. When this is augmented by the designation 'flowing with milk and honey', it begins to look as if the land which the Israelites are about to enter is being described as a new paradise.[38] The expansive contrast in 11:10–12

---

[35] For an exhaustive study of the references to the promise in Deuteronomy see Skweres 1979: 87–191.

[36] See 1:20–21, 25, 35; 3:18, 20; 4:1, 40; 6:1, 10, 18; 7:1, 8, 12; 8:1, 18; 9:5; 10:11; 11:9, 21; 12:1; 19:8; 26:3, 15; 27:3; 30:20; 31:7, 21, 23; 34:4.

[37] See 1:25, 35; 3:25; 4:21f.; 6:18; 8:7, 10; 9:6; 11:17.

[38] See 6:3; 11:9; 26:9, 15; 27:3; 31:20; cf. Ex. 3:8, 17; 13:5; 33:3; Lv. 20:24; Nu. 13:27; 14:8; 16:13, 14. For parallels in Ugaritic, see *ANET* 140; Gordon 1965: 168. On

between the 'barrenness' of the alluvial floodplains of the Nile and Canaan supports this.

We must not miss the fact that this is making a theological rather than an agricultural point. Israel's land is so good because it is the long-awaited gift of God in fulfilment of his promise:

> ... the land of Israel becomes almost a kind of paradise. It did not bother the Israelites that the reality fell considerably short of that. Canaan appeared to them as a paradise not because of its character as a land but because it was a gift of Yahweh (von Waldow 1974: 497).

But that is not all; the land is also the locus of Israel's relationship with Yahweh. 'Drinking the rain of heaven' is then seen to be an affirmation of the land as the place of relationship, and not a puzzling comment on the relative merits of irrigation and rainfall. While physical abundance in the land does not lie outside his concerns, the primary matter is Israel's relationship with God as signified by the land. In the wilderness, the survival or physical comfort of the nation was not the ultimate purpose of Yahweh's intervention (see *e.g.* 8:3). In Yahweh's land, material blessing should sharpen the focus on the potential intimacy occupation of this land provides. The ultimate indicative is not the land which Yahweh gives, but the relationship which that land affords.[39]

The land then, is clearly a good gift, but the emphasis on the land is always matched by the insistence that the land has been given by Yahweh. Plöger has provided a very helpful analysis of the 'gift' language in the book (1967: 121–129). Of the 174 occurrences of *ntn*, a significant proportion relate to the land in one of the following combinations: *ntn* + *'ereṣ* (give + land); *ntn* + *'ereṣ* + *yrš* (give + land + possess); *ntn* + *'ereṣ* + *naḥᵃlâ* (give + land + inheritance); *ntn* + *'ereṣ* + *nāḥᵃlâ* + *yrš* (give + land + inheritance + possess); *ntn* + *ᵃdāmâ* (give + ground). Yahweh is also portrayed as giving the derivative benefits of occupying Canaan: cities (6:10–12; 13:13; 20:6); towns (16:14, 18; 17:2); subjects (17:6; 19:1); rest (12:9); herds and flocks (12:21) and so

---

paradisal language see Miller 1969: 457; Plöger 1967: 78 (speaking of 'eschatological good'); Bächli 1962: 156; Waterhouse 1963.

[39] Including the ideal of rest – 3:30; 12:10; 25:19. This is supported by von Rad, despite his opposition to the idea of Yahweh's ownership of the land: 'The life of the chosen people in the 'pleasant land', at rest from all enemies round about, the people owning their love for God and God blessing his people – this is the epitome of the redeemed nation as Deuteronomy sees it' (von Rad 1966b: 95).

on, but there is no doubt that the land is the gift *par excellence* from which all other blessings flow.[40]

The fulfilment of the promise, from the Deuteronomist's point of view, however, demands a response from Israel. Plöger shows that while the land is often presented as an unconditional gift of Yahweh (which Israel must simply accept), occupation also seems to be conditional upon the obedience of Israel (*e.g.* in 11:8–9).[41] I believe that this tension is the basis for much of the ethical material in Deuteronomy.

It must be admitted that this is not how the paradox between the unconditional and conditional elements has often been understood. Many writers have seen this tension as evidence of two contradictory perspectives. Von Rad, for example, distinguished between a 'historical' conception of the land (which was unconditional, drawing on the promises made to the patriarchs), and a later 'cultic' conception (which focused on Yahweh's ownership of the land and the conditions which he laid down for a successful tenancy). This led to his celebrated claim that Deuteronomy marks a 'declension from grace into law' (1966b: 85).

A more influential, literary-critical solution was proposed by Noth and Perlitt, among others, in von Rad's wake.[42] For them, the contradiction between an unconditional view ('grace', or the land as a gift) and a conditional position ('law', or the land as a reward for obedience) arose as early (unconditional) Deuteronomic material was reinterpreted by the Deuteronomistic circle, who superimposed a legalistic understanding of Yahweh's relationship with Israel upon it.[43]

Each of these views, however, rests on an arbitrary assumption that an emphasis on promise and gift necessarily excludes the view that the

---

[40] The variation in recipients of the gift stresses continuity: 'The land is given "to them" or "to you" or "to us". Deuteronomy can say that Yahweh swore to give it to our fathers or Yahweh swore to our fathers to give it to *us*. There is no real distinction. The promise to the fathers was a promise to us. The gift to the fathers was a gift to us. The recipients coalesce' (Miller 1969: 454).

[41] McConville shows that the giving of Yahweh is imitated by Israel in 15:7ff.; 16:5ff.; 18:14 (1984: 12–13).

[42] The attractiveness of this to German Lutherans may arise, in part, from a view of law as inferior to gospel.

[43] Noth states of his Deuteronomistic historian: 'It seems that, following tradition, he liked to describe the relationship between God and people as a "covenant"; here he did not have in mind the act of making a covenant in its original sense but rather the permanent regulation, as defined in the law of the relationship between God and people' (1981: 135). Perlitt reaches the same conclusion, tracing a change from the Deuteronomic grace of Dt. 7 to the exilic Deuteronomistic conditionality of Dt. 5 (1969: 46).

land ultimately belongs to Yahweh.[44] This is unwarranted, as Plöger has shown that these ideas are inextricably linked: Yahweh is the one with the right to dispose of the land in the way that he sees fit, because he is ultimately the one to whom the land belongs.[45] The two ideas cannot be separated.[46] Whatever the theological and literary problems raised by attempting to hold the distinct concepts of promise/gift and divine ownership together, they cannot be solved by any such historical or literary reconstruction. Such approaches are also built on the presupposition that the presence of conditionality necessarily undermines any unconditional element. This is wooden and assumes that all tension has its origins in the literary history of the text, thus effectively denying any one author all claims to subtlety, or the ability to produce a multi-layered text. This will not do.

I believe that a creative tension between land as gift and land to be possessed is inherent in not only the Deuteronomic theology of land, but the entire message of the book. There is some precedent for departing from the view of von Rad and others. A wide range of scholars, including Mayes, Polzin, Wright and Diepold, have already argued that both conditionality and unconditionality are a fundamental part of the rhetoric of Deuteronomy.

Mayes, despite his views of the redaction of the text, is loath to ascribe the tension between the covenantal elements to mere contradiction. He observes that the introduction of the possibility of repentance and forgiveness in the final chapters goes some way toward resolving 'the tension between the idea that Israel's status as the people of Yahweh precedes and is independent of the covenant, and the idea that disobedience to the covenant demands bring punishment and destruction'. He expands his position in a most helpful way:

In this connection the land plays a significant role as the very

---

[44] See *e.g.* Hyatt 1970: 152–170; Nicholson 1973: 27; C. J. H. Wright 1990: 5–23.

[45] Wright points out that the land is referred to as Yahweh's long before the conquest; Ex. 15:13–17 is a pre–Deuteronomic example of a link between promise and ownership (C. J. H. Wright 1990: 11–13). Also Clements 1965b: 51–53.

[46] Von Rad's arguments are weakened further by the special pleading he is forced to indulge in when the very 'traditions' he is striving to separate occur together in his 'little Credo' (26:1–2). A cultic conception, embracing the agrarian celebration of tithes, firstfruits and so on, comes in the same breath as the recognition that the land is Yahweh's gift to Israel. An earlier comment reveals the inconsistency of his own thought on the subject: 'It is surely inherent in the inner logic of early Israelite belief that thanksgiving for the harvest should stand side by side with, and indeed be contained within, thanksgiving for deliverance from bondage and for the gift of the promised land' (von Rad 1966b: 4). See also Miller 1969: 457.

place at which the tension is most taut. On the one hand the land is the place where the law is to be obeyed; but on the other, it also appears as the place which Israel cannot possess unless she obeys the law. *These views are not simply to be assigned to different authors or editors in Deuteronomy; rather they result from the adoption and modification of the covenant or treaty form in which Deuteronomy is presently expressed* (1981: 78–79, italics mine).

Mayes argues that the tension is grounded in the covenantal atmosphere of the book, which highlights both the grace of Yahweh and the responsibilities of Israel. The covenantal realities of today and the promises made to the fathers in the past produce a paradox which lies at the heart of the book.[47]

Robert Polzin uses a very different method, drawing heavily on modern literary theory, to reach similar conclusions. Polzin hears two opposing voices in Deuteronomy, which interact to create the overall message of the text.[48] This theological dialogue produces an involved ideological and temporal construction, which cannot be resolved into contradictory sources:

One of the immediate results of this exceedingly complex network of utterances within utterances is the deliberate representation in Deuteronomy of a vast number of intersecting statements, sometimes in agreement with one another, sometimes interfering with one another. *This enables the book to be the repository of a plurality of viewpoints, all working together to achieve an effect on the reader that is multidimensional* (1980: 26, italics mine).

For Polzin, the 'ultimate semantic authority' of the book is not to be found merely by determining which redactional layer is the most recent, but by 'engaging' with the creativity of the Deuteronomist as a literary artist (1980: 68). Polzin's work is most stimulating, although the radically different philosophical basis of his work hinders any detailed interaction with those working with a historical-critical paradigm.

Wright's approach is much simpler, but no less powerful for that. He tackles the issue theologically, arguing that the theme of *sonship* allows

---

[47] I am indebted to D. A. Carson for pointing out that this tension can be traced back to the much broader and more comprehensive tension that is bound up with all genuine theism: God is both sovereign/transcendent and personal, and never less than both.

[48] Different 'voices' exalt Moses and undermine his authority (Polzin 1980: 39).

the conditional and the unconditional to co-exist perfectly naturally:

> What kind of relationship can it have been to produce this duality in which the indicative of God's grace is explicitly unconditioned yet requires Israel's obedience and response? The answer, it seems, is to be found in the relationship of Israel's 'sonship of Yahweh' which is expressed in many parts of the Old Testament. As a living, personal relationship, Israel's 'sonship' involved this organic tension or duality by its inherent nature (C. J. H. Wright 1990: 15).[49]

There is, then, plenty of support for the notion that the various material on land belongs together. The important question that remains, however, concerns how this land theology functions in the book as a whole. This is where the category of decision comes into its own. I believe that the 'indicatives' and 'imperatives' concerning the land, to use Diepold's designation, dovetail in a way which gives a graphic exposition of the decision which Israel faces (1972: 76–104).

Diepold's excellent study of the land in Deuteronomy comes closest to setting out such an understanding. He characterizes distinct ways in which the land is related to the ethical injunctions facing Israel: (1) the land is the context of Israel's obedience; (2) obedience is the condition of entering the land; (3) obedience is the condition of continued occupation of the land (1972: 91). Alternatively, one could say that the land is the context of the covenantal decision, the motivation for decision, the reward for decision and even the yardstick of decision.

The land as context for decision

First and foremost, the land is the place where Israel has the opportunity to enact God's commands (1972: 94). This is made abundantly clear at almost every significant point in the book (*e.g.* 6:1; 12:1; 26:1; 27:1). The land, given by God, is the place in which Israel must make her ethical choices and live in obedience. Thus it plays a fundamental part in the covenantal relationship itself.

Brueggemann articulates this intimate relationship between land and covenant relationship in these terms:

> Israel's involvement is always with the land and with Yahweh, never only with Yahweh as though to live only in intense

---

[49] Also, 'Deuteronomy sees nothing incongruous about basing a law safeguarding the essential relationship to Yahweh on an appeal to the father–son relationship' (McCarthy 1965: 145–146).

obedience, never only with land as though simply to possess and manage (1978: 52).

He even goes as far as to say that 'only in the land is Israel primarily a people of Torah' (1978: 60). This is because Yahweh has given Israel this land as a place in which to enjoy relationship with him expressed in obedience; this land is the divinely appointed context for decision.

The land as motivation for decision

It is this 'givenness', however, which also provides the rationale for ethical action in the land. God had acted; now Israel must respond. God has given a land; now Israel must give her wholehearted obedience.[50] Miller articulates the link between God's action and Israel's in a helpful way, highlighting Israel's responsibilities in occupying the land:

> The two notions of Yahweh's giving and Israel's taking are brought together in the expression 'the land which Yahweh gives you to possess' (3:19; 5:31; 12:1; 15:4; 19:2, 14; 25:19; cf. 1:39; 4:1; 17:14; 26:1). In a similar way 7:1f. juxtaposes *Yahweh's bringing* Israel into the land and *Israel's coming* into the land, *Yahweh's giving over* of the enemy of Israel and *Israel's smiting* of the enemy. The ideas of divine gift and human participation are not incompatible but rather a part of the whole (1969: 455–456).

It is too simple, then, to say that the fulfilment of the promise is the aim of the occupation. In Deuteronomy, partial fulfilment has already taken place. Yahweh has assured Israel that the land is theirs. In his grace, he has already handed over the deeds to them. This should act as an encouragement to them to go in and possess it.

The land as reward for obedience

From the opening chapters onwards, it is clear that only if Israel obeys will she actually be able to enjoy the fulfilment of the promise to the patriarchs. Only by reversing the failures of the past and faithfully negotiating the challenges of the future will the infant nation enjoy this divine reward (*e.g.* 4:1; 8:1; 11:8; *etc.*). But the relationship between the fulfilment of promise and obedience does not, of course, end here.

---

[50] Diepold 1972: 88, 101; Kuyper 1952: 333–34. We have also seen the reciprocal use of *ntn* (give), but Yahweh and Israel are respectively the subjects of the following verbs: *hdp* (drive out) (9:4/6:19); *yrš* (inherit) (9:4; 11:23; 18:12/ 7:17; 9:1, 3, 23; 10:11; 11:23; 18:14); *šmd* (destroy) (9:3/7:24); *'bd* (8:20/7:24; 9:3).

Even the successful subjugation of Canaan is only a first step to fulfilment of the promise.

Enjoyment of life with Yahweh in the land (as fulfilment of the covenant promise) is an open-ended and dynamic reality. For this to be realized, Israel must continue to obey: this is the only way to enjoy long life with Yahweh in the land promised to the fathers.[51] This idea of a promised land, waiting first to be occupied and then enjoyed by an obedient people, is the most powerful incentive to make the right decisions before God. Deuteronomy has taken the land itself and turned it into the most powerful rhetorical device, which presses home the urgency and import of the decision facing the nation on the plains of Moab (Diepold 1972: 98).

The land as measure of decision

The successful conquest and occupation of the land serve to provide the most obvious index, or measure, of the obedience of God's people. The primary consequence of disobedience will be loss of land. This is made clear not only in chapters 4 and 30, but also in the series of curses, and is at least implied in, for instance, chapters 8 and 11. Throughout Israel's history, then, the issue of land will be at the forefront of national consciousness, for it represents, in many ways, the spiritual state of the nation.

The promise of land in Deuteronomy, then, presents the people with a decision. Yahweh has established a covenantal relationship with them, and has made them a nation. Now he is setting a land before them – a land given by God where his people might experience life with him. The Deuteronomist makes it clear that this gift is free and should provoke gratitude, expressed in obedience. He also shows that the enjoyment of this gift is tied to the quality of the response. This ambiguity lies at the heart of the covenant relationship and therefore at the heart of the ethics of Deuteronomy.

Excursus: The promises in Genesis and Deuteronomy

It is worth pausing at this point to consider how the use of the promises to the fathers in Deuteronomy compares with that of other pentateuchal material, notably that in Genesis. We have seen how the land itself is bound up in the Deuteronomist's 'preaching for decision'. He exploits the tension between the unconditional dimension of the land as Yahweh's gift of grace and the condition of obedience placed on

---

[51] Entry and long-term successful occupation are repeatedly linked; see *e.g.* 6:1–3; 8:1–3; 11:8–9; 12:1.

occupying and enjoying this same land with Yahweh. The question facing us now is the extent to which this is unique to Deuteronomy.

To answer this question, we need to take a brief look at the 'promise material' in Genesis. The crucial texts for the developing understanding of promise in Genesis are 12:1–9; 15:1–21; 17:1–27; 22:17–18 (but see also 28:3–4; 13–15; 35:11–12). For the sake of brevity, however, I will limit this discussion to the key text of Genesis 12:1–9.[52]

The first notable theological feature in Genesis 12 is that, as in Deuteronomy, Yahweh's *promise* of blessing is without condition, and yet the *enjoyment* of further blessing is linked to obedience; in this case, Abram's relocation (verses 1–2). Again we see that God acts in grace, and man is expected to respond. This is the case in each reference to the promise in the Abraham cycle.[53]

At this simple level, then, there seems to be nothing particularly distinctive about the Deuteronomic understanding of the promise to the patriarchs. The same tension between law and grace is characteristic of Genesis.[54]

Looking at the promises made to Abram in a little more detail, we can see two distinct elements:

1. Blessing *for* Abram
    Provision and protection (2ab, 3a)
    A great name (3ba)
    Nationhood for his offspring (2aa)
    A land for his offspring (1b, 7)

2. Blessing *through* Abram
    In a general sense (2bb)
    For those who bless him (3a)
    For all the 'families (*mišpᵉḥōt*) of the earth' (3b)

The guarantees of provision and protection are clear enough. The promise to 'make your name great' is more unusual. Ruprecht detects a basic oriental royal ideology here, which is reflected not only in the

---

[52] See bibliography in Wenham 1987: 264–265. See also Wolff 1966; Crüsemann 1981; Alexander 1982; Perlitt 1969. There is general agreement that there is early material in Gn. 12, but its extent is hotly debated. See *e.g.* Kilian 1966; van Seters 1975; Maag 1960; Ruprecht 1979a; Westermann 1974; Seebass 1983; Emerton 1982.

[53] Chapter 15 is more complex than chapter 12, yet it is clear that Abram's reward is a consequence of preceding actions. Verses 6 and 18 establish a cycle of initiative–response–blessing. A similar pattern occurs in chapter 17.

[54] Skweres shows that Deuteronomy knew much of the Genesis material (1979: 232–233).

promise of a name of renown, but also in those of nationhood, divine oversight and mediation of blessing (1979b: 452; also 2 Sa. 7:9, Ps. 72:17).

The blessing in verse 2bb is not easy to interpret.[55] It is usually taken either in a passive sense (where Abram is the archetype of a man blessed by God), or in an active sense, with Abraham acting as a source of blessing.[56] Wenham, partly on the basis of Zechariah 8:13, suggests that a situation is envisaged where people will say, 'Make me as blessed as Abraham' (1987: 276).[57] This would have the advantage of making verse 3b a development of verse 2bb rather than a repetition, but remains uncertain.

Controversy also surrounds the translation of verse 3b itself, and especially the Niphal form of *brk*.[58] Opinions differ as to whether the sense is passive ('be blessed'), middle ('find blessing') or reflexive ('bless themselves'). In a sense, there is little to be won or lost here. Abram is clearly the mediator of blessing, and the nuance of the 'mechanism' stressed in verse 3b does not greatly affect the meaning.[59] Whatever the precise intent of the writer in using this form of the verb, it is clear that it brings the series of promises to an expansive climax – Abraham has already been blessed, provision has been made for the blessing of those of his acquaintance, and now the sphere widens to encompass the whole earth.

Genesis 12:1–9 contains all the elements of the Genesis promise. The sequence is blessing for Abram himself, then for his family who prosper and are given a land. This is accompanied or followed by a universal dimension to blessing through him. The other occurrences of the promise develop or emphasize certain elements. As we proceed through Genesis we find that the preoccupation with seed is universal, and the interest in land grows steadily, while the mediation of blessing is never prominent.

In Genesis, then, the blessing of Abraham through his family is the major theme and the land a minor theme (although of growing importance), whereas in Deuteronomy we find this reversed (Alexander 1993: 269–270). Deuteronomy knows of a promise of population

---

[55] Also Is. 19:24.

[56] The versions and older commentators favour the passive; Wolff 1966, Westermann 1974 and Keil 1864 the active.

[57] The use of Abraham's name in a blessing, or acknowledgment that Yahweh has blessed Abraham, then leads to blessing Abraham himself, and on to verse 3b.

[58] It occurs only here and in 18:18 and 28:14.

[59] Wenham summarizes the debate (1987: 277–278). See also the discussion below of the patriarchs as mediators of blessing.

growth and national prosperity for Israel, but it is presented as largely fulfilled. The promise of land fills the Deuteronomic frame. But it should be emphasized that the nature of the covenant promise is essentially the same in the two books. If there is something 'new' in Deuteronomy, it is not at the level of the basic view of Yahweh's relationship with the patriarchs and Israel.

Rather, we should understand that the unique insights of the Deuteronomist into the nature of the covenant relationship are, in the early part of the book at least, of an ethical rather than an expressly theological nature.

For Moses in Deuteronomy, the main role of covenantal preaching is to move the people to obey, whether through the exposition of the indicatives or proclamation of direct imperatives regarding the land. In Deuteronomy, the covenant between Yahweh and Israel demands action in the present. This is the particular genius of the book, whether it shows itself in the form, in the language or in the content.

Conclusion

The aim of this preliminary reading of the book was to establish the impact of the covenantal atmosphere of Deuteronomy upon the book's ethics. This is apparent at four distinct levels, each of which, in its own way, highlights the decision which faces Israel on the edge of the land.

Deuteronomy is not a treaty document, but draws on the covenant metaphor in a structured exposition of Israel's relationship with Yahweh. The primary ethical consequence of this relationship is that Israel faces a decision. Yahweh has instigated a relationship; Israel must respond in obedience.

The proliferation of vocabulary urging Israel to obey makes available a vast range of language and metaphor which sharpen this call to choose, as does the pointed review of national history, begun in chapters 1 – 3, but recurring throughout the book.

But it is perhaps the use of the promise tradition, and in particular the concept of land, which provides the Deuteronomist with his most powerful tool. It is not so much that he develops new concepts (when compared, say, to Genesis), but that he exploits existing theological ideas to great homiletic effect. The distinctive contribution of Deuteronomy to the concept of Yahweh's relationship with Israel is the description of the ethical responsibilities it produces.

In form, content and vocabulary, Deuteronomy presents the covenant as a relationship with ethical consequences. This short chapter has demonstrated this at a relatively superficial level. In the more detailed exegetical study which occupies the rest of this book, I will attempt to unpack the ethics of Deuteronomy within this covenantal framework. But before we go any further, it is worth reflecting on some of these observations in a biblical-theological context.

Perhaps the two crucial issues in the Deuteronomic view of covenant and its relationship to ethics are the relationship between law and grace on the one hand and the relationship between the partial and complete fulfilment of promise on the other. I would suggest that both the issues and the Deuteronomic answers would not look out of place in the pages of the New Testament.

Deuteronomy insists on the priority of grace. Israel's religion, as is memorably and insistently argued in chapter 7, is a religion of grace from beginning to end. Yahweh initiates the relationship, and Yahweh facilitates the ongoing enjoyment of relationship. The place of law in relation to land is simply to ensure that the enjoyment of what God has already given can continue.

There is also a delicate balance between acknowledging the inheritance of Israel even in advance of the conquest, and insisting that their obedience must be open-ended, as the possibilities of fulfilment of promise stretch off into the future. This sounds remarkably like the New Testament assertion that while Christians already have been given all things in Christ now, the full implications of that remain hidden in the future. In both cases, the future which awaits God's people is the ultimate ethical incentive.

While one would hesitate to ascribe Pauline soteriology and eschatology to Deuteronomy, it is hard to resist the temptation when the correlation between this book and the apostolic teaching is so close! I shall, however, have more to say on this as I go on.

Chapter Two

Ethics and journey

Having established the importance of the covenant metaphor in Deuteronomy, we now turn to another image which shapes the book's message – that of 'journey'. I have already developed this at some length elsewhere (McConville & Millar 1994), so this discussion can be kept relatively brief.

While there are important 'journeys' to be made within the collection of laws (*e.g.* the journey to the sanctuary in chapter 12), it is in the 'framework' of Deuteronomy, chapters 1 – 11 and 27 – 34, that the idea of 'Israel on the move' is most important. This chapter will be devoted to explaining how the writer uses the language of journey to sharpen further the call to decision which lies at the heart of the book.

The journey begins (chapters 1 – 3)

For many years, the opening chapters of Deuteronomy have caused problems for those trying to interpret the book. In fact, for a long time the only real consensus among academics, at least, was that these chapters did not actually belong to the rest of the book. This position became popular at the end of the nineteenth century, and was adopted by such notables as Wellhausen (1889) and Steuernagel (1894; 1900).[1] But there has always been one major problem with this view. It could never adequately explain how the book reached its final form. It was in this context that Martin Noth produced a book called *Überlieferungs-geschichtliche Studien* (*The Deuteronomistic History*), which brought about a paradigm shift in Deuteronomic studies.

Noth broke new ground by arguing that chapters 1 – 3 have no connection whatsoever with the book of Deuteronomy. He saw them as the introduction not to Mosaic laws, but to the history of Israel which follows in Joshua – 2 Kings, which he called the 'Deuteronomistic history', that is, history written from within a 'Deuteronomic'

---

[1] The suggestion was first made by Kleinert (1872: 6, 31, 36). S. R. Driver was one of the few to maintain that chapters 1 – 11 should be regarded as a unity (1901: lxvii).

theological tradition.[2] Any connections with the rest of the original book are either accidental or cosmetic. For example, Noth argued that the historical details in these chapters are included simply to help the reader to understand the narrative of Joshua which follows (Noth 1981: 52).

Noth's work has had a massive influence. The vast majority of writers have accepted the principles of his approach, and simply fine-tuned his conclusions (Preuss 1982: 77). This, however, does not mean that Noth got it right. In fact, there are several crucial flaws in his work. His arguments rest on two key assertions: he insists both that Deuteronomy 1 – 3 have no real connection with what follows and that their 'theological' significance is limited to introducing characters or events in the Deuteronomistic narrative. On close examination of the text, both of these assertions are highly dubious.

Contra Noth, I would suggest that there are strong conceptual and rhetorical links between chapters 1 – 3 and the rest of the book, and in addition, that they are an integral part of the message of Deuteronomy as a whole, rather than the introduction to another body of literature.[3] In fact, I would go further and say that the fundamental importance of these chapters for the book's overall structure and message has been overlooked. For it is *here* that the journey of Israel begins; this is where the nation gets on the move. It is here, in these chapters, that the basic theological and ethical categories of the book are introduced. Without this material, what follows scarcely makes sense. In the rest of this chapter, I hope to justify these far-reaching claims.

It is not novel to claim that these chapters contain much theological material. The seeds for my interpretation of these chapters were sown by work done in 1960 by Norbert Lohfink, who seems to have been the first to recognize that the literary characteristics of these chapters hide a definite theological agenda.[4] He argued that old stories are retold to

---

[2] 'One quickly finds persuasive evidence that 1:1 – 4:43 has nothing in common with the Deuteronomic law but is directly related to the Deuteronomistic history. From this we conclude that Deuteronomy 1-3 (4) is not the introduction to the Deuteronomic law but the beginning of the Deuteronomistic historical narrative and that this narrative begins therefore at 1:1' (Noth 1981: 29). See also Mayes 1980: 67–69.

[3] Noth is reductionist in his characterization of alternative views. He argues that as chapters 1 – 3 have no connection with the 'lawcode' (his view of how 4–11 fit into this is unclear) they must be Deuteronomistic. The only other possibility admitted is that we have a double introduction. But chapters 1 – 3 need not be *directly* related to the law code to be Deuteronomic.

[4] See Lohfink 1960a, whose work is developed in Moran 1963b and Plöger 1967. I have discussed the literary-critical issues surrounding the study of chapters 1 – 3 elsewhere (McConville & Millar: 1994: 18–23).

make theological points. So the failure of the people to prosecute a 'holy war' takes the nation back towards Egypt on an 'anti-exodus' journey.[5] The conquest of Transjordan, by contrast, is held up as an example of the way things should be done (Plöger 1967: 20–22). It becomes clear that chapters 1 – 3 relate to the theological concerns of the book of Deuteronomy, especially 'holy war', 'decision' and the journey of Israel, rather than to the Deuteronomistic history *per se*.

It should, of course, be said that Lohfink himself does not explicitly criticize Noth's scheme; but the implications of his study are quite clear. He has begun to show that there are important connections between chapters 1 – 3 and the rest of the book, and that they are clearly the result of mature theological reflection, which is essentially *Deuteronomic* in character. There is much more to be said, however, especially concerning the journey which Israel makes.

The account of the journey to the land in chapters 1 – 3 is dominated by *places of failure* and *the road to success*. The opening chapter is concerned with places of failure in the experience of Israel. In the first four verses, the reader is introduced to the time and place of Moses' discourse. This hardly seems terribly significant, but on closer examination it introduces some of the key theological ideas in Deuteronomy. Israel stands in the Arabah in Moab, overlooking Canaan, but she cannot afford to forget where she has come from. The apparently banal parenthesis of verse 2 is a pointed reminder that the nation has been here before.[6] Eleven days has turned into forty years, but Israel is once more at a place of decision, and has the opportunity to correct an old mistake. This time, there is every reason for them to succeed. Not only do they have Moses' words ringing in their ears, but the conquest of Sihon and Og is still fresh in the national memory, and

---

[5] Lohfink 1960a: 119. See also Moran 1963b: 334–337; Segal 1967: 91.

[6] 'Moses reminded the people that they had completed the journey from Horeb ... to Kadesh in eleven days that he might lead them to lay to heart the events which took place at Kadesh itself' (Keil 1864: 281). See Davies 1979 for a discussion of the geographical data. The usual view is represented by Weinfeld, who argues that it is a gloss (1991: 129), and by Perlitt, who dismisses it as an irrelevance to the narrative (1991: 14–15). Rabbinic traditions and the Targumim show more interest in this geography, using it to make a specific theological point: 'If the Israelites had had the merit, they would have entered the land in all of eleven days' [journey from beginning to end, instead of forty years]. But because they fouled up through their deeds, the Omnipresent turned forty days for them into forty years.' *Sifre to Deuteronomy* II.1.E (quoted in Neusner 1987); 'He rebuked them for having sinned in the wilderness and having caused provocation in the plains opposite the Sea of Reeds; at Paran they talked irreverently about the Manna, and at Haseroth they caused provocation about the meat, and because they made the golden calf.' *Targum Onqelos to Deuteronomy 1:1* (quoted in Grossfeld 1988). Also Miller 1990: 22.

provides a paradigm for successful advance. Again we are told that the people of God stands at a significant place of decision (verse 5). The question is, 'Will she obey?'[7]

There is little doubt what the Israelites should do. Yahweh's speech, remembered in 1:6–8, set out a straightforward programme for immediate advance from Horeb straight to Canaan. All that happened subsequently was a diversion from the ideal, and not to be repeated. Now Israel must do what she failed to do in the past – she must go straight into the land, trusting in God.

It is a little puzzling to find that these stirring words are followed by a fairly detailed account of Moses' devolution of political, judicial and spiritual authority.[8] When one sees that this 'devolution' lies at the root of the wrong decisions which follow, however, all becomes clear. The failures which follow cannot be seen as the failures of Moses alone.[9] Moses, while sharing in the responsibility for the action of the nation, is not blamed for what happened in the wilderness: 1:9–18 lays the responsibility for what follows squarely at the feet of the people as a whole, represented by the new devolved leadership.

This lays the foundation for the Deuteronomic version of the 'spy-narrative' beginning in 1:19. The emphasis here is placed firmly on the decision made by the whole people under their newly appointed leaders (1:22) not to enter the land. This failure is painted in the grimmest terms, as the nation chooses a 'vast and dreadful' desert rather than a good and pleasant land. Even the divine cajoling of 1:29–33 cannot persuade them to move forward. In the words of 1:26, Israel rebelled (*hmrh*) against God. Kadesh Barnea is thus presented as an important 'place of failure', where Israel made a bad decision and lost the opportunity to enter the land.

It is important to see, however, that this is not simply a history lesson. These chapters are, in fact, a sermon to those who have emerged from the wilderness experience, and are once more on the verge of the land. According to 2:14, those who have made it to Moab (with the exception

---

[7] Noth sees this as disturbing the syntax, and 'contrary to Dtr.'s intention mentions the law at this early stage and hence sees Deuteronomy 1–3(4) as a speech introducing the law' (1981: 46 n. 3). This is unsatisfactory: the use of 'torah' does not demand that chapters 1 – 3 are an introduction to the laws (Braulik 1970: 64).

[8] Many see these verses as an intrusion aiming to venerate Moses (von Rad 1966a: 38; Mayes 1981: 119; Perlitt 1991: 61). Noth argues that 1:9–18 deals with command structure in the army of the conquest (1981: 31, 51).

[9] I take Ex. 18:13–27 and Nu. 11:16–25 to refer to separate incidents where administrative and 'spiritual' support was given to Moses (Wenham 1981: 108). This passage is making a theological observation from Israel's experience which is pertinent to the narrative to follow, rather than harmonizing the tradition.

of Moses, Joshua and Caleb) were not actually present first time round, as the entire generation had died on the way. That is what makes 1:26 so fascinating. Here Moses claims that his listeners share the responsibility for the earlier rebellion at Kadesh, and now are being given the opportunity to put things right.[10] The place of failure revisited becomes an important junction on the road to success.

Such a reading makes sense of Caleb's otherwise puzzling appearance in 1:36. Caleb is held out as the man who made the right decision, and therefore becomes an appropriate role model for the new generation in its attempts to redress the failures of the past. In contrast, Moses is implicated in the rebellious decision of the Kadesh generation, and cannot continue as the leader of the nation in its journey on into the land. Like his peers, he must die outside the land, while a new start is held out to the people if they follow Caleb's example and submit to Joshua's leadership (Olson 1994: 18).

If any further proof is needed that the journey to the land depends entirely on divine sponsorship (which, in turn, is dependent upon obedient decision-making), then it is found in the closing verses of chapter 1. Once the wrong decision is made, Israel can do nothing to redress the situation, no matter how hard she tries. The direct route to the land is no longer an option (see *e.g.* verse 40). Instead national progress stalls at Kadesh, and then moves into reverse, as Yahweh instigates an anti-exodus. Israel, however, is not forced to retrace her steps for nothing. As chapters 2 and 3 show, Moses sees God as acting to bring Israel to a new 'Kadesh', where, in his grace, a new generation will face a new decision. Chapters 2 and 3 describe this journey that was necessary to bring Israel again to the place where it all went wrong. Eventually, after many years languishing in the desert, Yahweh begins to lead Israel along a new road to success.

The majority of Israel's experiences in the wilderness are passed over without comment, as the narrative moves straight to the turning-point of Israel's fortunes in 2:1–3. Then Israel suddenly rediscovers that obedience ensures success. Now the journey, initiated in 1:6–8 by Yahweh, gets under way once more. The text of chapters 2 and 3 is packed with journey language, and Israel is seen to fulfil her calling as she 'sets out', 'moves on' and 'crosses over'. In contrast to the static conclusion to chapter 1 and the 'static' beginning to chapter 2 (aimless wandering in the hills of Seir), Israel is now on the move towards

---

[10] There have, of course, been many attempts to put this down to variant traditions. This is simply unnecessary, and does not pay sufficient attention to the rhetorical aim of these chapters.

the land, and when Israel is on the move, Israel is obeying Yahweh.

Israel's remedial journey takes her not this time to Kadesh but to Moab, and the Deuteronomist is quick to point out that there are theological lessons to be learned along the way. This distinctive, pastoral perspective accounts for the significant discrepancies between this version of the Israelite itinerary and that given in Numbers 20 – 21 (Mayes 1981: 134–145). The focus here is on what Israel can learn from the nations through which she passes.

Special emphasis is placed on God's procurement of land for the Edomites, Moabites and Ammonites. Both in Moses' words and the 'antiquarian footnotes' of verses 10–12 and 20–23, the failure of the Israelites to enter the land at Kadesh Barnea is shown up by the willingness of her neighbours to take possession of Yahweh's 'gift' to them, giants or no giants.[11] Israel must face this before she goes any further, for as 2:14–15 make plain, it is a matter of life and death. God has seen them safely through a difficult period (verse 7), but he has done so in order that they might learn from their mistakes, and do the right thing when they come back to the edge of the land.

As the journey back to the land reaches the Transjordan, we are presented with a powerful paradigm of what obedient decision-making can achieve. The kings of Heshbon and Bashan, Sihon and Og, in contrast to Edom, Ammon and Moab, refuse to allow Israel to pass, as their progress to Canaan gathers momentum (2:24, 27–29; 3:1). The events which follow become a 'dry run' for the land proper, and demonstrate beyond any doubt that Yahweh is able to deliver the victories he promises.[12] This prelude to the conquest proper then calls those at Moab to choose to obey Yahweh today in the light of the success that obedience had brought in the relatively recent past (3:21–22).

As we approach the end of chapter 3, the buoyant optimism of the defeat of Sihon and Og is tempered by the definitive refusal of Moses' request to enter the land (on the grounds of national disobedience under his leadership; Olson 1994: 28–29). Failure has serious consequences. The geographical detail with which chapter 3 closes does little to lift the atmosphere, as Israel is left 'near Beth Peor', which, according to Numbers 25, was another place of national failure (or apostasy, in this case). Unlike Kadesh Barnea, however, this was presumably within the experience of all who listened. Israel cannot afford to repeat the

[11] There is surely some irony intended here – national rebellion has led to Israel initially failing where other nations succeeded (see also Ezk. 36:16).

[12] Bächli 1962: 77–78. Thus there is no echo of Moses' reluctant concession in Nu. 32 to those wishing to remain in Transjordan, nor is there any sense of foreboding, as if those remaining outside Canaan were repeating the mistake of the Kadesh generation.

mistakes of the past. Yahweh had graciously allowed them to reach this point, despite a record which was far from unblemished. Now they must take their chance or the consequences would be disastrous.

The traditional interpretation of the opening chapters of Deuteronomy has isolated them from the theological and ethical themes of the rest of the book. I have shown this to rest on assumptions which cannot be sustained. The 'prologue' introduces two foundational concepts which are essential to Deuteronomic theology. The first is that Israel is a nation on the move – engaged on a journey with Yahweh. This journey began in Egypt, and is still in progress at Moab. This journey involves every member of the Mosaic community, and the community's faithfulness to the covenant of Yahweh is mirrored by its course. The second concept cannot be separated from the first, as it asserts that the past experience of Israel holds the key to enjoyment of their covenant relationship. If Israel is to enter the land and live at peace in it, then the lessons of the past must be absorbed into the national consciousness.

At the outset, the theology of the book (and therefore the ethics) is imbued with a dynamic element. Relationship with Yahweh involves changing obedience in changing circumstances. This is much more than a treaty-like list of obligations. For Israel, a life of obedience is life on the move towards the land. This development of the journey motif, of course, is only preliminary. It is not described in such detail to have it grind to a halt at Moab. At the end of chapter 3 we are left in suspense concerning the nature of what is to come, but we know that, come what may, the journey must continue.

As I have already pointed out, the people of Israel standing at Moab are not simply *observers* of this journey, but are addressed as *participants* in it. Moses insists that the past involved his listeners (1: 7, 9, 18, 21). Every aspect of the ensuing journey, every decision, every battle involves every person in Moses' audience. These chapters are insistently immediate and inclusive, demanding the instant attention of everyone listening. This is not only salvation history, but an exposition of the *way* of salvation in the present and the future, based on the national experience of the past. The events and places of the past coalesce with those of the present so that Israel may walk in the ways of Yahweh. This 'journey' means more to the Deuteronomist than a simple transition from the life of the wilderness to the paradisal agrarian existence set before them in Canaan. The 'journey' is a pregnant metaphor for life with Yahweh.

If chapters 1 – 3 introduce this concept, then it is chapter 4, which is probably the most profound chapter in the book, that develops the journey metaphor in a most powerful way.

Places on the way (chapter 4)

If chapters 1 – 3 concentrate on the beginnings of the journey of Israel, then chapter 4 focuses on places on the way. The places which most interest the Deuteronomist are Horeb and Moab, and, in this most complex chapter, he binds these two key moments of decision together in the consciousness of Israel.

This is an unusual chapter, even for Deuteronomy, in that the words of Moses are punctuated by changes in number (see *e.g.* verses 3–4, 19–20, 21–22, 23–26, 34–35). Much ink has been spilled in trying to account for this (Knapp 1987: 21–29; Preuss 1982: 84–86). The most thoroughgoing account of this phenomenon is given by Braulik (1977: 54–56; 1978a), who has shown that whatever the change of number signifies, it cannot be used as the basis for detecting different compositional layers in the chapter. He suggests that the rough division of the chapter into plural (verses 1–28) and singular (verses 29–40) reflects an attempt to confirm that Yahweh's promise can survive even the exile. Within these sections the key concerns are flagged by a change in number. For instance, multiple changes in verses 23–26 (verse 23: plural-singular; verse 25: singular-plural-singular; verse 26: singular-plural) serve to heighten the stress on the final warning against idolatry (1978a: 149).

Braulik's further observations on the meaning of the chapter as a whole are fairly typical of recent scholarship (1977: 53–93). He reads the chapter as an exilic attempt to revise Israelite theology in the wake of the destruction of the temple. God's presence is 'relocated' in heaven, and wisdom replaces law as the key to obedience. Such new ideas are linked to the earlier revelation at Horeb to enhance their authority for the exiles in Babylon (see also Lohfink 1964: 169–175).

This approach has some good points – it is important to recognize that Israelite theology is 'moving on' in this chapter – but these are outweighed by its weaknesses. It is simply not necessary to assume that the exile provided the impetus for this new theological initiative. The concept of divine presence here seems to have much more in common with the exodus/wilderness traditions than with later temple ideology.[13] Nor is it clear that this is an attempt to imbue 'wisdom' with the authority of 'law'. But the most telling weakness of such studies has been the failure to take proper account of the chapter in its context in the book of Deuteronomy as we now have it. It seems a rather obvious

---

[13] For a thorough discussion of presence see McConville in McConville & Millar 1994; I. Wilson 1992; 1995.

point, but far too often this chapter has been torn from its context prior to interpretation. As a result, I believe much of its significance has been overlooked.

I would suggest that Deuteronomy 4 needs to be read in the context of the journey of Israel which has begun in chapters 1 – 3. A parallel is drawn between the events of Horeb (and in particular the theophany) and the moment of national decision at Moab. In the process, the journey facing Israel takes on a new significance, and is extended into the distant future. The journey to the land becomes a model for ongoing life in the land. Understood in this way, chapter 4 is an integral part of the rhetoric of Deuteronomy, as I shall attempt to show.

The key to unravelling this complex chapter is the manner in which two 'places on the way', Horeb and Moab, are carefully superimposed. The present events at Moab are intricately linked with the past events at Horeb by linking the content of the revelation at each place.

As Moses shifts from narrating the past to addressing his contemporaries, a crucial phrase is introduced in 4:1 – *ḥuqqîm ûmišpāṭîm* (laws and statutes). This little phrase occurs five times in this chapter (4:1, 5, 8, 14, 45) and at other crucial points in the book (5:1, 31; 6:1, 20; 7:11; 11:31; 12:1; 26:16, 17). In itself, it is rather innocuous, and outside Deuteronomy it has no special significance. Within this book, however, it is extremely important – as one may have guessed from the fact that it not only dominates this chapter but frames chapters 5 – 11 (often called the *parenesis* or exhortation) and the laws of chapters 12 – 26.

The first thing to notice is that despite being heralded with a flourish in 4:1, it is very hard to see what these 'laws and statutes' actually are. There is certainly nothing in chapter 4 which warrants such a description, but then this is part of the point. Chapters 1 – 3 outlined the clear-cut decisions which Israel had faced on her journey from Egypt. Now chapter 4 begins to define the decision which Israel will face at Moab, and every day of her life in the land – the decision to obey *ḥuqqîm ûmišpāṭîm*. In 4:1 the question is raised: 'What are these laws and statutes?' The rest of the chapter begins to provide the answer.

The *ḥuqqîm ûmišpāṭîm* appear again in 4:5 and 4:8, and these verses take us to the heart of the ambiguity surrounding the phrase in chapter 4. The verb in 4:5 is most naturally taken as past tense – 'the laws and statutes which I taught you'– and seems to refer back, presumably to the Mosaic teaching at Horeb.[14] But in 4:8, it is quite clear that the

---

[14] It may, however, be possible to read the verb here with present force (a 'declarative perfect') – see GKC §106i; Mayes 1981: 150; Waltke & O'Connor: 488; but this is

reference is to the teaching that Moses is in the process of delivering at Horeb. The *ḥuqqîm ûmišpāṭîm* then, are seen to have both a past and a present/future reference, but we are not much clearer on the precise nature of these laws.

In verse 14, the ambiguity persists. Especially when read with 5:30, it seems that after the divine communication of the Decalogue, 'at that time' Moses was commissioned to add the *ḥuqqîm ûmišpāṭîm* at some further juncture. It is clear that the laws and statutes are linked to the revelation at Horeb in some way, we are still none the wiser as to what they actually are.

The rest of chapter 4, as we shall see, is essentially a meditation on the events of Horeb. Israel is reminded of the revelation of God there and the response demanded of her (4:40).[15] But at the conclusion of the chapter in 4:44–45, some of the mist surrounding the *ḥuqqîm ûmišpāṭîm* begins to clear. The laws, statutes and commands (*'ēḍûṭ*) are explicitly identified with Moses' teaching on the verge of the land.

We can now see that, in the context of Deuteronomy, this is theology 'on the move'. The journey so carefully described in chapters 1 – 3 now prepares to traverse the borders of Canaan itself. As part of this transition, Moses brings a new set of laws to Israel for a new set of conditions. The author carefully juxtaposes Horeb and Moab. As God spoke through Moses at Horeb, so now he is speaking through him at Moab. At Horeb, the content of this revelation was to enable Israel to progress obediently to the land, now at Moab, the focus of the revelation will be on living successfully in the land, as new laws are given for a radically new context. As in chapters 1 – 3, Israel must be prepared to obey. One little historical detail, easily missed, brings this sharply into focus. In 4:3–4, Moses alludes once more to the events at Beth-Peor (see 3:29), now, as in Hosea 9:10, called Baal-Peor. This loaded reminder in 4:3 drives home to the Israelites that even at this new place of revelation, they are in danger of rejecting Yahweh. Moab is the new Kadesh: Israel cannot afford to let it become the new Baal-Peor.

It is not just the similar content of the revelations at Horeb and Moab, the *ḥuqqîm ûmišpāṭîm*, which is used to bring home the

---

without parallel in Deuteronomy. Note also that *r^e 'ēh* (see) occurs in a similar context in 1:8, 11:26, 30:15 and possibly 32:49. It is a prominent feature of the journey narrative of 1 – 3: 1:21; 2:24, 31; 3:27. The use in 4:5 (and 4:3) binds chapter 4 to this introductory section.

[15] It is interesting that in 4:40, where one might expect *ḥuqqîm ûmišpāṭîm*, we find *miṣwâ* instead.

importance of the decisions facing Israel at Moab. These two epochal moments are tied even more closely together by the Deuteronomist's subtle use of time. Moses preaches to the generation at Moab, as if they actually are at Horeb (Deurloo 1994: 46).

This first emerges in 4:9–10, where the people are called to remember 'the things that you have seen with your own eyes', and specifically 'the day you stood before Yahweh your God at Horeb'. The glaring problem is that if we take 1:35 and 2:14 seriously, none of them *did* stand before God at Horeb. But I believe that the author intended his readers to see beyond the obvious anachronism to the theological point behind it.[16] Moses is calling Israel to *an act of corporate, imaginative remembrance* as the insights of the past are brought to bear on the decisions of the present and future.[17] In doing so, he binds the events of 'that day' at Horeb (verse 10) to the unfolding events of Israel's 'today' at Moab (verse 8). In a sense, every day of Israel's past is drawn into 'today', as the present and future decisions of God's people are shaped by the formative moments at Horeb and Moab.

Gerhard von Rad first drew attention to the recurrence of *hayyôm* (today) in Deuteronomy:

> It is the common denominator of the Deuteronomic homiletic as a whole ... It cannot be maintained that this is merely an effective stylistic device which the Deuteronomist has chosen to make more vivid what he has to say. On the contrary, it is a quite fundamental feature of Deuteronomy (1966b: 26).

The preaching of the book is marked by an 'emphatic contemporaneity' as Israel is repeatedly and powerfully called to make the right decision 'today'.[18] Whether at Kadesh in chapter 2, Horeb and Moab in chapters 4 and 5 or even outside the land (chapter 30), Israel always faces crucial decisions *hayyôm*. Clearly, 'today' encompasses past, present and future decisions faced by Israel in all manner of places. As DeVries helpfully points out:

---

[16] In any case, many of the Israelites would have died anyway, even if 1:35 and 2:14 are late additions. The point remains that for the Israel of 'today' the events of Moab are to be equated with those at Horeb. See Deurloo 1994: 43; Lohfink 1991a: 23.

[17] See Brueggemann 1985: 1–27; Bächli 1962: 71–73.

[18] See *e.g.* 4:8, 26, 38, 39, 40; 5:1, 3; 6:6; 7:11; 8:1, 11, 18, 19; 9:1, 3; 10:13; 11:2, 4(?), 8, 13, 26, 27, 28, 32; 12:8(?); 13:19; 15:5, 15; 19:9; 26:16, 17, 18; 27:1, 4, 9, 10; 28:1, 13, 14, 15; 29:9, 11, 12, 14, 17; 30:2, 8, 11, 15, 16, 18, 19; 32:46.

As we analyse the use of the present *yôm*, we soon see that a basic distinction needs to be made between the day that is historically present in existential distinctiveness and the day that is present in gnomic discourse or in cultic regulation. The latter refers to a 'today' that is continually repeated and hence continuously present (1975a: 45).

Israel's 'today' at Moab in Deuteronomy 4 is informed by the past, particularly at Horeb, and shown to be crucial to their future in the land and beyond.

I have suggested that Deuteronomy builds on the concept of Israel's ethical journey. This journey begins in Egypt, passes through Kadesh and the wilderness to Moab, and is about to move on to Canaan. This picture can be augmented by adding that the journey of Israel inevitably consists of a series of 'todays', when the same basic response must be made to Yahweh. Israel must continue to obey *ḥuqqîm ûmišpāṭîm*.

So the decision to be made at Moab takes on a new significance. For not only is it the key to entering the land, but repeating this decision is the key to living successfully in the land. Thus, in a way, the entire future of Israel is encapsulated in 'today at Moab'. Each stage of national life – crossing the Jordan, pausing at Shechem and the far reaches of her experience in the land and out of it – can be negotiated only by responding in the same way as 'today at Moab'. Every stage of the journey can be comprehended and successfully negotiated at Moab, the place of decision. In this chapter, therefore, it is made plain that Israel must take on board and respond to the revelation at Moab in exactly the same way as to that received at Horeb, not only in the present, but at all times, as her covenant relationship unfolds.

This reading is simply confirmed by the Deuteronomic version of the events at Horeb in the rest of the chapter. Verses 11–14 stress the presence of the assembled nation, as at Horeb. There is no difference between the 'you' who stood at Horeb and the 'you' who are now on the verge of the land awaiting further exposition of the law.[19] Just as they heard the voice of God from the cloud, so now they are to pay heed to the words of Moses preached at Moab. Unlike the inhabitants of the land which they are about to enter, Israel's worship and experience must be defined by the divine word (verse 15), underlined by the absence of any visual phenomenon. The climax of this part of the argument comes in verse 20. Because of Israel's election by Yahweh to

---

[19] 'The later generations should listen to the law as if they themselves, rather than their forefathers, stood at Horeb to receive God's commands' (Noth 1952: 11, my translation).

be the people of his inheritance, demonstrated in the exodus, their worship in general (and their decision at Moab in particular) is to be determined by the Horeb theophany. (This is further developed in chapters 7, 9 and 10.)

So far, the impact of memory on Israel's *present* actions has dominated the discussion.[20] At 4:25, however, we find something new, as the focus moves on to the implications of Horeb and Moab for the future of the nation. Israel is not merely to reach Moab and stop, either literally or metaphorically. She must keep moving on, continually remembering the mighty acts of God and responding to him in obedience. Moab is not merely a place to pause to look back, but the point at which Israel is to live in the future.

Chapter 4 makes it plain that the lessons of Moab do not merely provide the gateway to the land, but encapsulate the enduring preconditions of existence in the land. If Israel moves away from the revelation at Moab, then disaster will quickly follow (verses 25–29a). Moab, then, is not a moment to be experienced and then left behind, for the future of Israel is bound up with this paradigmatic moment. Even if Israel is expelled from the land (verse 29), the only way back is through repentance and a new commitment to the *ḥuqqîm ûmišpāṭîm*, or, to put it metaphorically, the only way back is via 'Moab'. For it is here that the divine word is heard, enabling true obedience (Lohfink 1964: 86). Only if this 'journey of repentance' is undertaken is return possible.

Moab is presented as the place where the past and future of Israel coalesce in a single moment, the place where the decision to follow Yahweh must be reaffirmed in every generation. The remainder of the chapter serves only to underline this. Whatever the complexities of verses 32–40, they celebrate the primacy of God's revelation at Horeb and now, by extension, at Moab, and call for a confessional response (verse 35). The unexpected list of the east bank cities of refuge in verses 41–43 earths the call for response in the land to be possessed, with the east bank experience presented as a 'dry run' for the conquest proper. This fits well with the summary in 4:44–49. The recapitulation of the dispossession of Sihon and Og and the extent of the land speak of the possibilities before Israel. Yet the reminder of Beth-Peor maintains tension by reintroducing the possibility of apostasy. Once again the formula 'These are the commands and statutes ...' recurs. This

[20] 'In the Bible, memory is rarely simply psychological recall. If one remembers in the biblical sense, the past is brought into the present with compelling power. Action in the present is conditioned by what is remembered' (Blair 1961: 43). See also Brueggemann 1978: 53–58; 1985.

continues to push Israel on towards the decision, even if the precise content of this decision is still tantalizingly withheld.

Deuteronomy 4 then, displays both theological innovation and continuity with chapters 1 – 3. Its primary concerns are to demonstrate the inseparability of the preaching of Deuteronomy and the revelation at Horeb, and to urge Israel to commit itself to following the way of obedience today at Moab, and every day in the land of Canaan. This way of obedience, usually designated by the *ḥuqqîm ûmišpāṭîm*, has not yet been clearly defined. For that we must move on to the rest of the book, as the national journey so carefully introduced in chapters 1 – 3 moves on into the present and the future.

The journey into the land (chapters 5 – 1.1)

We have seen that the opening four chapters of Deuteronomy show that Israel has reached a crisis point in her short existence. At Moab, God presents an opportunity to reverse the disastrous repercussions of the refusal to enter Canaan from Kadesh Barnea. Now, as at Horeb, Israel has the chance to respond obediently to the revelation of Yahweh. Chapters 5 – 11 preach this opportunity, repeatedly calling God's people Israel to move on into radical obedience with far-reaching consequences.

The study of these chapters has tended in recent years to become bogged down in literary analysis (see Preuss 1982: 93–96). In fact, the only theological issue to be tackled with any vigour has been the relationship between chapter 5 and what follows.[21] This preoccupation with literary matters has resulted in the neglect of the *content* of these chapters. Thus a holistic approach has much to offer here.

The basic goal of these chapters is to encourage Israel to go in and possess the land, or, in the terms we have been using, to continue the journey, started in Egypt, into the land of promise itself.

Chapter 5 picks up almost where chapter 4 left off. Now, it seems, Israel is to discover what exactly the *ḥuqqîm ûmišpāṭîm* consist of, as 5:1 introduces the preaching which stretches to the end of chapter 11 as the 'laws and statutes'. In fact, we find that the phrase recurs in 11:32,

---

[21] Lohfink's *Das Hauptgebot* was the first (and the most influential) such study. Many of its inadequacies have been pointed out (even by Lohfink himself), but its combination of literary, redaction and form criticism set the tone for much that followed. It is impossible to do justice to his argument here, but Lohfink's conclusions can be reduced in essence to the theory that early covenantal material was used by the Deuteronomist to expound the 'Hauptgebot' of 6:5. While the findings of *e.g.* Seitz (1971) and García López (1977–78) differ, their methods remain essentially the same.

the last verse of this section. But there too, the phrase refers, not to what has gone before, but to what is coming next in chapters 12 – 26. It seems then that we should not expect to find the 'laws and statutes' in their entirety in chapters 5 – 11, for they stretch on throughout the heart of the book. But we must begin by tracing the development of this idea in these six chapters.

The announcement of 5:1 is followed almost immediately by Moses' repetition of Decalogue, revealed by God at Horeb. The words which he will declare (5:1) are first underwritten by the words which God has already spoken in the hearing of all the people. This fits well with what we have seen in chapter 4, where the incipient preaching of Moses was linked to the earlier divine pronouncements. God has spoken; soon Moses will speak. While the two revelations are distinct, the ultimate authority and origin of these words is the same – they are all *ḥuqqîm ûmišpāṭîm* which come from God. This is reiterated in 5:31. The Decalogue is presented as the beginning of a process of declaration, but not as the end. For life in Canaan, something new is needed. This new thing is given as Yahweh continues to reveal his will at Moab in the Deuteronomic legislation.[22]

At 5:31, then, we are still waiting for the *content* of the new revelation, and this gradual unfolding continues into chapter 6.[23] The first verse of chapter 6 shows conclusively that the Decalogue in chapter 5 cannot be the final word on the law for the Deuteronomist (see also 6:20 and 7:11). The *ḥuqqîm ûmišpāṭîm* go far beyond this.

It is in the context of the revelation of new law for a new life that we must read the Shema in 6:4. For Deuteronomy, keeping the *ḥuqqîm ûmišpāṭîm*, whatever they may be, is not just a matter of external obedience, but an expression of heartfelt covenantal loyalty to Yahweh. These ringing words logically take their place at the beginning of the 'new' material to go under the rubric of *ḥuqqîm ûmišpāṭîm*. The decision to love Yahweh without constraint is then the dominant theme of the following chapters.

As we shall see, chapters 5 – 11 by no means exhaust the content of the 'laws and statutes'. For it is not only this passage of preaching which is bracketed by references to *ḥuqqîm ûmišpāṭîm*. This pivotal phrase also occurs in 12:1 and in 26:16–17 (twice). The laws too, it seems, are to be understood as part of this new divinely appointed teaching at Moab. When we see that 11:32 and 12:1 are intricately

---

[22] This dynamic is emphasized by the addition of the singular *hammiṣwâ*. See also Brekelmans 1985: 167.

[23] Lohfink shows a chiastic structure bridging chapters 5 and 6 (1963: 151; 1989a: 9).

linked to one another (Seitz 1971: 39; McConville 1984: 34), it is clear
that the preaching of chapters 5 – 11 and the 'preached law' of chapters
12 – 26 are brought together under the heading of *ḥuqqîm ûmišpāṭîm*
(see Cholewinski 1985: 97). Even at this early stage in our studies, it is
obvious that the constant decision which Israel will face on her national
journey is defined by the core of the message of Deuteronomy. An
unbroken thread runs through chapter 4, the Decalogue in chapter 5, the
preaching of chapters 6 – 11 and the laws of chapters 12 – 26. This
takes us close to the heart of Deuteronomic theology.

Having recognized all this, we must return to some of the details of
chapters 5 – 11, which reinforce the conclusions set out above,
beginning with 5:2–3. These are crucial verses, for here the link
between Horeb and Moab is at its clearest. Moses goes as far as to say
that the covenant made at Horeb was actually with the present
generation, not with their fathers at all. The events of Horeb and Moab,
for Moses, involved the same people, the same God and essentially the
same revelation. This generation is not to think of the covenant at
Horeb as a mere memory, but as *a memory which is actualized in the
present at Moab.*[24] Miller comments:

> This verse expresses a kind of hermeneutical formula for the
> book. The time gap and the generation gap are dissolved in the
> claim that the covenant at Sinai, the primal revelation that
> created the enduring relationship between the people and the
> Lord, was really made with the *present* generation. The covenant
> is not an event, a claim, a relationship of the past; it is of the
> present. The time between the primal moment and the present
> moment is telescoped, and the two are equated (1990: 67).

Then, in 5:4, Moses claims that the central element of the national
experience at Horeb was Yahweh addressing the nation 'face to face'.
There is no explicit mention of a direct revelation of the Ten
Commandments to the whole people 'face to face' in Exodus 20, which
concentrates on Moses' mediating role (noted here in verse 5).[25] But the
Deuteronomist is not attempting to paint a detailed picture of the
theophany at Sinai. The 'mechanics' of the encounter are irrelevant.
The point is that Yahweh spoke to the people in a way which no-one
could deny, and then subsequently Moses conveyed his words to the

---

[24] See von Rad 1966a: 55; Braulik 1986b: 49; Buis and Leclerq 1963: 63.

[25] There is no necessary contradiction between the Deuteronomist's theological
account and Ex. 20 (note that the temporal reference of Ex. 20:18–22 is uncertain). See
Nicholson 1977.

people. Precisely the same pattern is repeated at Moab – God speaking to Moses, and Moses conveying the authoritative teaching to the people.

Forty years (and an entire generation) may have passed, but in the divine economy *all* Israel has experienced theophany, hearing the voice of God at first hand, and now must continue to respond to the words of Moses, his spokesman.

This is reiterated in verses 22–27. Yahweh spoke to *all* Israel decisively from the fire and cloud declaring the commandments to them, and 'then said no more'. This distinct revelation was then succeeded by communication via Moses, the mediator. Now at Moab, again the pattern is replicated. At both places Israel hears the voice of God. At Horeb, Israel encountered Yahweh in an intimate and overwhelming way, and requested a mediated revelation instead (Ex. 20:19). Moses teaching at the edge of the land is the continuation of this mediated revelation.

Deuteronomy 5 suggests that the experience of the Israelites at Moab subsumes and augments that at Horeb. Not only were this generation 'at Horeb', but they have seen much more of Yahweh in action since. In response to this, they must obey the divine word as transmitted by Moses (5:32–33). Taking the nation back to meditate on the Horeb tradition has the effect of presenting them with a further choice – not only do they have to decide whether or not to enter the land (as at Kadesh Barnea), but they must choose the foundations upon which they build their new life in the land in the light of their encounter with Yahweh himself.

Chapter 6 sees a shift in the focus of Moses' preaching from the past to the future. The first five chapters emphasize making decisions on the basis of past experience. Now, as the new revelation begins, the possibilities and problems of the future begin to dominate the frame.

Moab is the fulcrum of the history of Israel in the view of Deuteronomy. The past, present and future of the nation are intimately tied to Moab, the place of decision. We have already seen that Moab is the *place of recapitulation*. In chapters 1 – 5, Moab is carefully presented as the culmination of Israelite history, as missed opportunities are reversed and Yahweh speaks again. As the place of recapitulation, Moab could be described as both the place of revelation (the new Horeb) and the place of action (the new Kadesh Barnea). In chapter 6, Moab also becomes a *place of anticipation*, as further dimensions to the decisions facing Israel are spelled out. 'Today' Israel is given the chance not merely to undo the mistakes of the past, but to realize the potential of an exciting future. As the place of anticipation, Moab is the place of entry to the land, the place at which Israel must stay 'spiritually' to occupy the land and the place to which she must return in her spiritual journey if she is to return to the land after apostasy (see especially chapters 4 and 30).

These various aspects of the role of Moab can be represented in the diagram below.

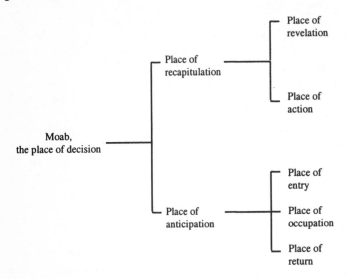

Chapter 6 links the concepts of Moab as holding the key to entering the land, and also to a successful occupation of it. The former is shown by the injunctions to 'obey these statutes *so that you may go into the land to inherit it*' (6:1, 18, 24).[26] But we may not simply make Moab the door to the land, for its significance stretches on into the future. This is made clear in 6:1–3 (see also 11:8–9), where the writer moves naturally from entry to continued occupation as a result of keeping the *ḥuqqîm ûmišpāṭîm*. The motif of long life inevitably extends the decision from the present moment to a perpetual lifestyle in the future. Life for Israel is to be life at Moab, even when firmly rooted in Canaan.[27]

Alternatively this could be expressed in terms of life on the move. Israel's journey does not stop on 'settling' in the land. They are always on the verge of realizing new possibilities, when they continue to act

[26] See also *e.g.* 8:1, 7–8; 9:4–6; 10:11; 11:8–9, 22, 23; 16:20. Also Pss. 37:11; 22; 29; 34; Pr. 2:21–2; 10:30.

[27] See *e.g.* 4:25; 8:10–20. Forgetting Yahweh is to forget the decisions faced at Moab, rejecting the life of decision for a life of proud complacency. Poulter's discussion of chapter 8 shows this well (1989: 115–117).

obediently (see 6:24–25; 7:12ff.; 8:10ff.; 11:13ff.). Thus Moab stands at the theological intersection of the Deuteronomic doctrines of promise and obedience, as well as at the temporal intersection of past and future. It is in here, at Moab, the place of recapitulation and anticipation, the place of promise and obedience, that the Shema must be heard.

The call for Israel to 'listen' in 6:4, comes at the climax of two chapters which have been dominated by the verb *šm'*.[28] Only when we take this seriously can we feel its full impact. The opening verses of chapter 6 bind the entry to and enjoyment of the land to an appropriate, obedient response to the word of Yahweh, heard by Israel at Horeb and now declared by Moses at Moab. The Shema makes it clear that 'listening' is the basis of any such response.

This command to 'hear' simultaneously takes Israel back to Horeb and forward into Canaan. As Israel 'heard' Yahweh speak at Horeb, now Israel must go on 'hearing' the words of Moses at Moab. This new call to 'hear' is a command to credit Moses' new words with the same divine origin as the Decalogue itself, which is expounded and reapplied for the new conditions of conquest and occupation of Canaan. Only through such listening can the fulfilment of the promise be experienced (6:10–11, 18).

Chapter 6, then, makes the transition from the identification of Moab with Horeb to the implications for the future of Israel in Canaan. The preaching of chapters 7 – 11 spells out immediate demands and long-term necessities arising in the new situation, as the journey continues in the land itself.

This is not the place for detailed exegesis of these chapters, but it is useful to highlight some of the key elements of the teaching presented there in the context of this ongoing journey of decision.

The first decision Israel was to face on entering and occupying Canaan was, quite simply, what to do about the Canaanites. Chapter 7 consists of a thorough treatment of the problem.[29] This is given such a prominent position because Moses insists that unless the right decision is taken regarding the inhabitants, the occupation of the land is doomed from the start. Verses 1–5 set out the action which must be taken (see also chapters 12 and 13; Ex. 34:13–17), and verse 6 the rationale. Verses 11–16 emphasize that this is to be understood, in the light of chapter 6, as a response to the revelation at Moab. This is the only sure way to success in the land.

---

[28] This link is implicit in Deurloo 1994: 44 and Braulik 1986b: 55, but is not discussed.

[29] See Preuss 1982: 101–103 for an overview of work on this chapter.

The stereotyped opening of chapter 8 maintains the same theme. Moses continues to preach that the way to experience the fulfilment of promise is obedience to what was heard at Moab.[30] Verses 1–5 remind Israel of the educative events of the wilderness, and verses 7–10 of the potential of the future. Then a powerful plea to remember Yahweh at all times is introduced in verses 11–18 (echoing 6:10–19). The stern warning of the consequences of failure to heed the injunctions at Moab brings the chapter to a close.

The repetition of the command to 'hear' in 9:1 undergirds a meditation on past failures of Israel in 9:1 – 10:11, which is rather like chapters 1 – 3. Now, however, the application to the Israel of today is much more pointed. As he calls Israel to advance fearlessly into the land in 9:2–3, Moses ironically asserts that even Anakites pose no problem to Yahweh. There is no reason for Israel to repeat the mistakes of Kadesh Barnea, nor, for that matter, those of Horeb. Even there, Israel did not respond to Yahweh as she ought. Five times in this long section Moses refers to 'forty days and forty nights' on Horeb (9:9, 11, 18, 25; 10:10). In the context of the stubbornness and apostasy of Israel, the frequent reminders of Moses' intimate fellowship with God stand in sharp contrast to the forty years of discipline experienced by the nation in the wilderness.

The golden calf incident sounds a warning that even a place of revelation has the potential to become a place of apostasy. As if this were not enough, set in the middle of the narrative, in 9:22–24, is a litany of Israel's propensity to rebel: Taberah, Massah, Kibroth-hattaavah and ultimately Kadesh Barnea itself are surely enough to warn God's people. In the short distance (1:2) between Horeb and Kadesh, the Israelites had managed to compound the apostasy at Horeb with a repeated refusal to trust Yahweh's provision, whether of comfort (Taberah), water (Massah), manna (Kibroth-hattaavah) or even of the land itself. Moab was potentially a place of great evil, as well as of great blessing.

In 10:1–11, we read of another chance for Israel. Despite the most serious rejection of Yahweh, he revealed his word to them once again. Just as God had given Israel a second chance, a new revelation at Horeb, so he would do again at Moab – where, after the rebellion of Kadesh, Israel receives another chance to enter the land. Moab shares

---

[30] Poulter's detailed redactional and rhetorical analysis of the text basically supports this view: 'The "here and now" of the text and, therewith, of the audience it addresses, is conceived as a day of decision ... "Today" is a time of solemn proclamation and earnest listening. Essentially the audience are placed in the tension between the demand of today and the promised blessing of tomorrow' (1989: 117).

not only *revelation* with Horeb, but also the demonstration of Yahweh's grace and forgiveness in providing his people with another chance to hear his word and experience the fulfilment of his promise.

The heavily marked command in 10:11 precedes the short summary of chapters 9 – 10 in 10:12–22. Now Yahweh commands Israel to move on once more in response to the new start he has given. This cannot be accidental. Surely Moses intends that Israel at Moab, on seeing that Yahweh has given them another chance, must resume their journey of obedience.

Chapter 11 summarizes all that Moses has said so far, and gives a stirring call to respond to this part of the message. 'Today' at Moab is presented as the culmination of the events in Egypt and the wilderness (verses 2–6). Israel must listen to God's word through Moses and walk on into the land of promise, unlike Dathan and Abiram, who in Numbers 16:12–14 rejected Moses' leadership and called *Egypt* a land of milk and honey (Brown 1993: 138). Again, the Moab generation is involved in events long past and therefore has every reason to learn the lessons (11:7). In verses 8–17, it is stated once more that obedience to the divine revelation at Moab holds the key to successful entry to and occupation of the paradise of Canaan. Verses 18–25 return to the language of chapter 6 to underline the importance of absorbing the Mosaic preaching and acting upon it for the entire course of the nation's future.

The section concludes with a graphic illustration of what it means to live at the point of decision both inside and outside the land. First, in verses 26–28 the choice before the people at Moab is characterized as one between blessing and curse. This is then translated physically to a new situation within the land itself at Shechem (verse 29). Here, in the heart of the land, Israel is to re-enact the decision of Moab. These twin peaks would for ever stand before Israel as a reminder of their dilemma on the verge of the land, and of the continual obligation to decide for Yahweh. Israel must choose blessing if they are to enjoy life with Yahweh in the land.

Now we have seen that the basic insight of chapter 4 (that the content of the revelation at Horeb is linked to the Mosaic preaching at Moab) is developed at some length in chapter 5. Moab is the place where God can be heard to speak again as he spoke at Horeb. Chapter 5 is, in turn, linked inextricably to chapter 6, and in particular to the Shema, as the focus shifts from the past to the future. Moses' preaching hammers this home, forcing the Israelites to realize that their reaction at this new place of revelation has even more significance than at the mountain of God. Now the conquest and settlement of Canaan are at stake, as well as the development of their relationship with Yahweh. Dispossession of the Canaanite nations, cultivation of the land and future residence in Canaan all hinge on the obedience defined at Moab. As the preaching moves to its climax, it becomes increasingly apparent that Moab is the place which subsumes all previous places in Israel's past and controls every dimension of Israel's future.

Moab becomes the key place in the journey of Israel, opening the way for a life of blessing in the land – a life of remembering the acts of Yahweh and responding to them, a life of perpetually choosing the way of obedience – living as permanent nomads, long after they have settled down.

The journey of exile and return (chapters 27 – 34)

The closing chapters of Deuteronomy have proved more elusive than the rest of the book. They are often taken to be a jumble of unconnected (and even irrelevant) fragments. I hope to show, however, that they play an important theological role in the journey of Israel depicted in the book, and thus to shed a little light on some of the more obscure passages. I shall consider the text in nine short sections.

1. The stones and altar on Mount Ebal (27:1–10)

After the conclusion of the laws, Israel, according to chapter 27, must enact a specific ritual on Mount Ebal. It has often been suggested that this chapter interrupts the narrative flow from chapters 26 to 28, and should be omitted.[31] Others have tried to uncover links with Joshua 24. But no such drastic solution is necessary. As 11:29 announced, Shechem is just the next place on the itinerary of the journey of Israel. Here, the decision spelled out at Moab is enacted in a graphic way in the land proper. All the puzzling (and probably ancient) details serve to depict this crucial decision.

In fact chapter 27 does seem to pick up where chapter 11 left off, as we might expect. Once more we are moving in the sphere of a 'concrete' response to 'all the commandments' preached at Moab.[32] Now the 'elders of Israel' are given a special responsibility to ensure that these details are carried out.[33]

This is not an easy passage to interpret, and much confusion has

[31] Many find this attractive because of problems chapter 27 raises for a Josianic setting. See Anbar 1985: 304–307.

[32] See 5:31; 6:25; 8:1; 11:8, 22; 15:5; 19:9; also 6:1; 7:11; 11:28.

[33] This mirrors 1:9–18. There devolution established the culpability of all the people; here it underlines the future responsibility of elders and people in the land.

arisen from the odd placement of verse 8. It seems that the initial command to set up the stones is completed in the repetitive verses 2–4.[34] Yet we return to this theme in verse 8. It has also been argued (rather pedantically) that Ebal is more than a day's journey from the crossing-point into the land (*cf.* verse 2). But neither of these problems can obscure the point. Moses' concern is not with the twenty-four-hour period beginning with the crossing of the Jordan, or even with the details of the inscription. His words rather demand that the 'day of decision' of Moab becomes the 'day of response' in Canaan. The transition between the 'todays' of 27:1 and 27:2 involves the extension of the 'day of decision' to life on the west bank, in keeping with the dynamic view of 'Moab' described above. I have already suggested that life in the land is to consist of a 'settled nomadism'; it is to remain the 'day of decision', even when the fulfilment of promise begins to unfold. Mount Ebal takes its place in the succession of places in Israel's journey to the land where obedience is what God requires. The journey continues into the land.

I should, however, make some comment on a couple of other significant details here before I move on. First, it is clear that the command to make the altar draws heavily on Exodus 20:24. Along with the 'law stones' in verse 8, this establishes a relationship between Ebal and Horeb (as well as Moab). If this is the case, verse 8 may be positioned for rhetorical effect to make this connection clear. Even more interesting, however, is the command to sacrifice in 27:7. The language and sentiment here are thoroughly Deuteronomic, as the people rejoice before God (see chapters 12 and 15). God's people on the move are commanded to underline their decision through sacrifice.[35]

The section 27:1–8, therefore, provides a fitting response to the lawcode. The focus shifts from Moab to a future place of commitment, also linked to Horeb, the first place of obedience in the land. This may explain the introduction of the 'levitical priests' in 27:9–10, who are to function as the guardians of this new Mosaic legislation. However these verses are to be read, the call to Israel to 'hear' at this point is striking. Once again, Israel is called to listen to and act on God's commands. Here this is further strengthened by the unique demand for silence, which precedes it. Once again it is plain that obedience 'this day' will

---

[34] The reference of the phrase 'all the words of this law' in verse 3 is perplexing, but the point is clear; the Moab revelation is to be written on stone just as at Horeb.

[35] If Dt. 12 is regarded as demanding a Jerusalem cult, then this is a major problem (C. J. H. Wright 1996: 279). This potential difficulty disappears if one takes into account the journey motif, which is central to the theological outlook of the Deuteronomist, including the way we read chapter 12, as we shall see.

have definite implications in the future, as the journey moves on to Shechem, whose significance as the next point of decision in the life of the nation is expounded at some length.

2. The levitical curses at Shechem (27:11-26)

In some ways, this section is quite obscure. It is unusual in that there are no blessings to go with the curses, and it is much more specific than other such lists (it demands obedience to definite elements of the preaching at Moab and/or Horeb).[36] The corporate response to the Levites, who now take their place as guardians of the preached law, is also unique, but it is hardly unexpected in a book which features national decision so prominently. In fact, once more, while some details may remain elusive, it is quite obvious how this passage fits into the flow of the book as a whole.

Just as the early part of chapter 27 featured detailed prescriptions for obedience, the levitical pronouncements spell out the inevitable consequences of disobedience, of making a wrong decision. After the tribes assemble on facing peaks, listen to and respond to the annunciation of these 'legal curses' by the Levites, it is made abundantly clear that disobedience after this point must be culpable, for, in the light of verses 14–26, it must inevitably be wilful.

So in this chapter we have three separate rituals – inscribing the law on stones, building an altar and the levitical rehearsal of 'legal curses'. The purpose in each case is exactly the same: to enable Israel to recapitulate the experiences of Horeb and Moab at Shechem. The divine demand for obedient response is to be fixed in Israel's national consciousness in this most vivid way immediately after they enter the land.

3. Blessings and curses at Moab (28:1–68)

After Moses lays down the details of the levitical cursing ritual, in chapter 28 he presents his own extended list of blessings and curses. Perhaps the most interesting feature of the lists, from our point of view, is the way in which, especially after the curses take up the specific subject of expulsion from the land in verse 21, the dominant motif becomes a return to Egypt. This echoes the 'anti-exodus' theme of the opening chapters, but here it is metaphorical rather than literal.

This is introduced explicitly in verse 27, but memories of Egypt lie behind much of what follows: the death of livestock (verse 31), anger

---

[36] See Schottroff 1969: 94; Blank 1950–51; Bellefontaine 1975; Schulz 1969; Lewy 1962.

and anguish under oppression (verses 32–33), affliction with boils (verse 35), failed harvests due to locusts (verse 38) and loss of offspring (verse 41). In verse 46, the function of the curses in the life of the nation is to act as a 'sign and a wonder'. This phrase occurred in 4:34; 6:22 and 7:19. In every case it referred to the plagues in Egypt (see also in Ex. 7:3; 8:23; 10:1, 2; 11:9, 10). This is a new journey of reversal, culminating in a renewed exposure to the painful reality of life 'in Egypt' (verses 47–48).

This is reiterated at the conclusion of the list of curses. First, in verses 50–52, the gracious provision of chapter 8 is systematically withdrawn and overrun. Then verses 59–60 assert with biting irony that the failure of Israel to 'cleave' to Yahweh will result in the plagues of the 'new Egypt' 'cleaving' to Israel. This idea of a 'return to Egypt' is not the only one present in this list of curses, but it is an important one. It is, of course, a fairly obvious one. Yahweh's solemn undertaking to bring the nation of Israel back to Egypt in sorrow via the road by which they left is a recapitulation of the nation's experience in the wilderness. The journey from Egypt to Horeb, Moab and eventually Shechem will be followed by an instant return to Egypt direct from Shechem, if Israel refuses to obey. As in chapter 27, the ideas of the early part of the book (here chapters 1 – 3) are taken up again and reapplied to the future of Israel in the land, whether experienced as blessing in Canaan, or as curse back in 'Egypt', where the journey began.

4. *The covenant at Moab (28:69–29:29)*

There is much to say regarding the form of this part of the text, and its similarities to other ancient covenants (See Baltzer 1970: 34ff.; Lohfink 1962a), in line with the conviction expressed elsewhere that all such forms have been shaped to the theological agenda in Deuteronomy. I shall limit myself to discussing the content.

One only has to look at the first verse of the chapter in most English versions (28:69, MT) to hit a problem in interpretation. Some older commentators (including Driver) argued that 'the words of the covenant' refers to the preceding chapters. I, however, prefer to read it with the majority of commentators as introducing chapter 29, with its numerous allusions to covenant. While chapters 29 and 30 have much in common, I think there is sufficient evidence for reading chapter 29 as a distinct entity (*contra* Lohfink 1962a; Rofé 1985a).

However one reads it, 28:69 is striking for its juxtaposition of Moab and Horeb. Despite all we have seen so far, only here is a 'covenant at Moab' explicitly designated and laid alongside that at Horeb (see Preuss 1982: 158). This is unique in the Old Testament, but in the context of Deuteronomy it is little more than the logical culmination of the detailed parallel which has been developed throughout. The revelation at Moab is presented not as *replacing* Horeb in the life of Israel (*pace* Preuss), but as *augmenting and upgrading* it for the new conditions of life in the land of Canaan. If Israel is to avoid the journey of reversal, then they must abide by the conditions set out at the new Horeb; they must keep this 'new covenant'.

This 'new covenant' however, stands in complete continuity with that cut with Israel at Horeb. This is made explicit in 29:1–3. As in chapters 1 – 11, the whole nation is addressed as if every member had been present at every stage in her history, and here, in particular, suffered the oppression of Egypt. The same is true of the idealistic representation of the wilderness years (see also 8:4), the conquest of Sihon and Og and the occupation of Transjordan (verses 4–7). This presentation of the journey of Israel is in effect a selective account of the opening three chapters, culminating in an injunction to adhere to the stipulations of this covenant (verse 8).

Verses 9–14 expand on the central theme of response to the covenant – the same covenant made with Israel at Horeb. The language is that of reiteration or renewal rather than replacement.[37] The covenant at Moab is presented as fulfilling both the promise to Abram in Genesis 15 and the declaration of Exodus 19:5 that Yahweh will be Israel's God and she will be his people.

As we have seen elsewhere in the book, *hayyôm* plays an important part in determining the meaning of the text. All the events of chapter 29 are bracketed by two 'todays', in verse 3 and in verse 27. I am not convinced that verse 27 reflects a later perspective. Rather, this chapter is carefully enveloped between these two 'todays' to show that the whole future of Israel in the land, prior to the divine intervention envisaged in chapter 30, is essentially life under the covenant at Moab – an endless succession of 'todays', where Israel must repeatedly respond to the Mosaic preaching.[38] This emphasis on 'today' is reflected in verses 9, 11, 12 and 14. Today is the day for Israel to decide, although, in the light of 29:3, Israel's prospects do not appear very promising.

So this covenant at Moab gathers up all of Israel's history and brings them to a climactic moment of decision. Learning to live at this moment

---

[37] 'The chief clues for understanding this second covenant are found in recognizing the boundary character of Deuteronomy, the place of this covenant in the structure of the book, and Deuteronomy's concern for actualizing in the present moment the relationship between God and Israel and the demands and consequences of that relationship' (Miller 1990: 200).

[38] I am indebted to Paul Barker for his stimulating suggestions on chapters 29 and 30.

– learning to keep this covenant – will be the key to a successful occupation and ongoing life with Yahweh in the land.[39] In verse 17, for example, apostasy is not envisaged on the day of Moses' preaching, but on some 'today' in the future in the land (also verse 27). There is something timeless in this covenantal response, for the covenant at Moab is not primarily about ritual, but about the wholehearted ethical response demanded of them today and for all time to come.

If Israel fails to take this covenant seriously, it will not be a case of their moving forward while the nations look on, but of the nations forming a sorry parade to witness the desolation in Israel (verse 21), which can be compared only to that of Sodom, Gomorrah, Admah and Zeboiim. Instead of the nations' declaration of Israel's derivative superiority in 4:5–8, we now see them asking for an explanation of Yahweh's punishment of his own people.

5. Return from 'Egypt' to the land (30:1–20)

Chapters 27 – 29 have majored on the possibility of another anti-exodus, a journey back to a new 'Egypt'. Chapter 30 reasserts the grace of Yahweh and the amazing possibility of that journey of reversal being itself 'reversed'. If the journey out of the land may become a reality, so too, through repentance provoked by Yahweh himself, may a journey back to the land of promise.

It is here that Deuteronomy envisages another 'new covenant' emerging, which, like that in Jeremiah or Ezekiel, is much more far-reaching than the covenant at Moab. A time is described when Israel repents, and makes a new journey back to the land (verses 4–5). But rather than resulting from any change on Israel's part, this issues from an eschatological circumcision performed on Israel's hearts. God himself does for Israel what they had failed to do for themselves (see 10:16). Now, finally, Israel can live in obedience to the *ḥuqqîm ûmišpāṭîm*, loving Yahweh with heart, soul and strength. Once more, as Israel moves forward again with Yahweh, the curses are turned on the enemies of Yahweh and his people enjoy the paradise of his benefits. As Israel moves back to Yahweh in repentance (*šûb*), so they begin to return to the land (*šûb*) in a final eschatological climax to the journey of the people of God.

There are several prominent ideas within the overall message of these verses. The first is that of the heart. This is surely a deliberate echo of

---

[39] Braulik notes that 28:69 – 29:1 mirrors 5:3 (1992: 214). The future is linked to the present in the same way that the present was linked to the past. The Horeb generation and the exiled generation of chapter 30 are linked through the Moab generation. See also Deurloo 1994: 45.

chapter 6. In verses 2 and 3, it is a change of heart in Israel which issues in the return to the land. The same change of heart is described in verse 10. This, of course, flows from Yahweh's circumcision of their hearts in verse 6 (contrast 29:3).

Once more, *hayyôm* is an important term. On the day when Yahweh intervenes to change the human heart, all Israel will be able to obey wholeheartedly what Moses has proclaimed 'today' (verses 2 and 8). The time reference is a little ambiguous – it is difficult to tell if *hayyôm* refers to the day *after* Yahweh's intervention, or the day of Moses' preaching at Moab. Either way, it is clear that the obligation to live out each day in obedience to Yahweh is Israel's primary concern.

This ambiguity is also reflected in verses 11–14. The 'command which I give you today' echoes verses 2 and 8. This may mean that verses 11–14, as Braulik argues, contain the command to be issued on a future day of decision, after the return and the circumcision of the heart (1992: 218–219). If, however, verses 2 and 8 are taken to refer to Moses' preaching in the present, then the command is given before Israel has the wherewithal to obey.

Verse 14 may support the former reading; in language reminiscent of 6:6; 11:18 and most strikingly 4:5–8, it is declared that this *dābār* (word), like God himself, is very near, even on their lips and *in their hearts*. This seems to square most easily with the situation after God's intervention.

Our problems, however, do not disappear when we come to verses 15–20. For if much of verses 1–14 appears to be addressed to Israel on some future 'day of decision', in the rest of the chapter we come very much back into the present. The two parts of the chapter use the same ideas (see verses 6 and 20), yet by verse 16 we seem to have reverted to a time when blessing and curse have not been experienced, where Yahweh can still be rejected (verse 17) and where the emphasis on *hayyôm* (verses 15, 16, 18 and 19) brings us back to the hearers' present.

I suggest, therefore, that chapters 29 – 30 presents a series of 'days' which lead up to a day when Yahweh will circumcise the hearts of Israel, enabling them to respond to him (30:1–14). This is then juxtaposed with a renewed call to obey in the present (30:15–20). (I discuss this in more detail in the final chapter.) Moses' oration reaches a powerful climax as he expresses the decision facing Israel: it is a choice between life and death, good and evil. He lays this choice before Israel, summarizing the content of the blessing/curse material in chapter 27 – 29, and calling them to 'choose life'. Only if Israel chooses life, today, tomorrow and on into the future, can they hope to experience intimacy with God in the land which he is giving to them. Only as they listen and obey, only as they love God, will this life open up before them.

Chapter 30 has much in common with chapter 4 (see *e.g.* 30:1–3 and 4:29–31), and if chapter 4 acts an overture to the book, then chapter 30 is the finale. Here many of the themes introduced in chapter 4 reach their *dénouement*.

6. *The succession of Joshua (31:1–8)*

The relationship of chapters 31 – 34 to what precedes them is a little like that of chapters 1 – 3 to what follows. They do form an important part of the whole Deuteronomic scheme, but primarily in terms of tying up loose ends (as the opening chapters introduce important theological ideas), chiefly the passing of Moses and succession of Joshua, which occupies 31:1–8.

Like chapters 1 – 3, verses 2–8 focus on the journey which Israel must continue to make. The authority of Joshua's appointment rests on the assurance that under his leadership Yahweh's presence will remain and the journey of Israel will continue. The idea that this presence controls Israel's advance is so dominant that the mention of Joshua (verse 3b) almost seems an afterthought. Joshua's personal commission is simply an assurance that God's sponsorship of the journey will continue under his leadership. Obviously, there is much in common with Joshua 1 here (see Lohfink 1962b: 82–83), but it is the theological concerns of Deuteronomy which are to the fore.

7. *Writing and reading the law (31:9–13)*

Moses' instruction to write down the law and read it to the nation *en masse* at regular intervals (in keeping with the laws set out in chapters 12 – 26) ensures that his teaching at Moab remains at the heart of the national consciousness, guarded by the levitical priests (see also 31:24–29). It supports the repeated injunctions to remember what Yahweh has done and what Israel has learned at each stage of her journey. It encourages Israel to re-enact the decisions of Horeb, Moab and Shechem.

In keeping with the rest of the chapter, this section is extremely brief. It is simply recording the words of the dying leader, rather than offering comment on them. It is almost as if by now all has been said.

8. *Moses' swan-song (31:14 – 32:44)*

Yahweh's final words to Moses return to the issue which raised its head briefly in chapter 30: can Israel obey, and is she prepared to do so? Yahweh, in the most striking revelation of the future in the whole book, makes it clear to Moses that Israel will experience blessing and curse in turn, because ultimately their stubborn nature will prevail (Cholewinski

1985: 107). The song (and indeed the book as a whole; verse 24) is given to point the nation back to Yahweh in its time of rebellion.

Much has been written about the Song of Moses, but discussion has generally centred on its form rather than on its content (Preuss 1982: 166–168). The most common approach is to read the chapter as an example of a 'divine lawsuit'.[40] It is extremely difficult, however, to tie this poetic (and rather vague) material to either a specific form or a context, and, on balance, it is more useful to read this chapter as a didactic poem, which shapes contemporary forms to serve the unique purposes of Deuteronomy (Thompson 1974: 297). In fact, there is nothing in its content that excludes it from being exactly what it claims to be – a hymnic composition from the very earliest national traditions of Israel on the verge of the land, as Moses looks rather pessimistically to the immediate future and beyond to the hope of eventual restoration.

It is important, however, to recognize that the theological material in the song does cohere well with the central themes of Deuteronomy. The song's main thrust appeals to Israel to come back to the point of decision, to reverse the direction of her journey in a time of apostasy. Verses 10–14 are a poetic representation of the progress of Israel from Egypt through the wilderness to the land. Their failure to learn from this journey leads them to fall foul of the dangers spelled out in chapter 8, and exposes them to the wrath of Yahweh. Lohfink has shown that there is an axis in verses 26–27 on which the whole song revolves (1962a: 53). The first half of the song deals with Israel's failure to live a life of covenant faithfulness in the distant and recent past, and the resultant curses which fall on them. Then in the rest of the song the possibility of a return to blessing gradually emerges; Yahweh is still essentially for his people. There is a way back to the land through repentance.

The Song of Moses is not the most complete expression of Deuteronomic thought. Its central message, however, although couched in poetic form, is that Israel faces a decision in the present and in the future which will determine the course of her national life. In this, it is in complete agreement with chapters 1 – 11 and 27 – 31.

9. *The death of Moses (32:45 – 34:12)*

The last, ominous words of Moses to Israel (32:45–47) pick up the theme of 30:15–20, urging Israel to obey at any cost. The climax of the patriarchal blessing of the tribes of Israel (33:26–29) depicts Israel finally settled in the land, secure and obedient because of covenant

---

[40] G. E. Wright 1962; Baumann 1956; Mayes 1981; Mendenhall 1974. Others have tried to tie it closely to ancient wisdom (von Rad 1966a; Boston 1968).

faithfulness. The journey is at an end. Moses' work is done. This eschatological consummation for Israel leads naturally to the account of the death of the great leader.

The exclusion of Moses from the land is a dark theme which runs through the whole book (see Olson 1994), serving to adumbrate the consequences of disobedience for the people in the most powerful way. Even here, where one eye is on the future security and satisfaction of God's people in the land of promise, this death serves as a warning of the consequences of disobedience. Moses dies at the point of decision, because of past failure. Israel, under her new leader, is left to make the decision on her own, aware of the fate of the man who knew Yahweh intimately. Even the death of Moses provides further impetus to the call for Israel to obey.

Even in these closing chapters of the book, which, at first glance, seem to bear little relation to the sustained preaching of chapters 1 – 11, the same theological concerns are visible. Here the journey of Israel reaches its climax. Here the lifetime of decision facing Israel receives its fullest exposition, as Horeb, Moab, Shechem and the entire land are drawn together as the locus of Israel's response to God. Here the choice between a life of intimacy with God, constantly moving forward in the land of promise, and the death of a return to Egypt is presented in the starkest terms. Now Israel must simply obey, committing themselves to covenant faithfulness to Yahweh, deciding to love him and live for him alone.

Conclusion

Deuteronomy makes it very clear that Israel is to be a nation on the move. The journey begun in Egypt must continue to Moab and beyond into the land. Even as they enjoy life with God in the land, to use the categories of Hebrews 11, Israel must remain 'strangers and pilgrims'. For paradoxically, it is in this movement that the secret of successful settlement is to be found.

The 'framework' of this book (chapters 1 – 11 and 27 – 34) makes it plain that there is an important dynamic element in living as the people of God. Walking in the ways of Yahweh means living obediently in the face of changing circumstances. Israel is not called simply to stick with what they heard at Horeb, but to go on listening to God's word, as it is unfolded to them in Moab and then in the land, equipping them to love God wholeheartedly in their rapidly changing context. The authority of the divine word remains the same, but the application varies as the journey goes on.

This, of course, is all intensely practical. These are matters of life and death. This theological preaching has only one goal – to encourage Israel to embrace life with God in all its fullness by listening to and responding to the divine word. All this preaching and theology ultimately serves an ethical agenda. Israel must embrace this message by loving Yahweh with heart, soul and strength, as she lives out the *ḥuqqîm ûmišpāṭîm*. This cannot merely be the whim of a moment, but must be the commitment of a lifetime, choosing to obey not just 'today' but for a lifetime of 'todays', as she awaits the eschatological intervention of God which will finally bring her journey to an end.

Chapter Three

Ethics and law

If the framework of Deuteronomy (chapters 1 – 11 and 27 – 34) establishes that Israel faces a life of decision in the land of promise, then the laws provide the details of what a loving response to God looks like in practice.

Studying the collection of laws in chapters 12 – 26 exhaustively would be a massive undertaking, which I could not hope to do adequately here. It is important to narrow the focus of this chapter, so that what is pertinent to this book is not buried by a mass of exegetical detail. I shall not attempt to unearth the original setting of these laws, or to clarify every detail of the text. Instead, I intend to focus on the *theology* of these laws, which, here more than anywhere else, will also take us into the realm of ethics. In particular, I hope to discover the extent to which the theological perspective of the framework, which gives meaning to the laws in the context of the book, is actually reflected by the laws themselves.

Before we can begin to examine individual laws, there are some preliminary methodological issues to be addressed.

Methodological issues

Before one can begin to study Deuteronomy 12 – 26, two basic questions must be given some attention. The first is the relationship of these laws to the history of Israel, and the second, their relationship to other such collections, both inside and outside the canon.

The laws of Deuteronomy and the history of Israel

For many years, most scholars have seen some of the laws of Deuteronomy, at least, as arising in the context of a reform movement in Israel in the seventh century, during the reign of Josiah. The celebrated passage in 2 Kings 22, where Josiah 'finds' the book of the law, is read as an attempt to give credence to this newly produced 'Jerusalem propaganda'. The main purpose of this literature was to support efforts to 'centralize' Israelite worship in the temple by stamping out unorthodox sacrifice. From now on, the cult would be confined to 'the place which Yahweh chooses for his name'.

This view, however, is not without its problems. It has not been easy to square attempts to promote one sanctuary (usually thought to be Jerusalem) with a willingness to allow slaughter of animals and other rites in the country and an apparent lack of interest in priestcraft. Nor has it been clear how these ideas fit into the overall scheme of the book. The usual solution has been to see the text as we have it as the result of attempts to reconcile conflicting opinions.

Wellhausen's (1889) original discrimination between the 'P' source (which presupposed a central sanctuary) and earlier 'D' material demanding centralization in an attempt to clean up the cult has been developed by many others. Von Rad, for example, argued that the spirit of the laws concerned with centralization was completely foreign to the book (1953: 67). Clements, Nicholson and Weinfeld all suggest that the tensions arise from a religious debate in the Israelite community. For Nicholson, northern covenantal ideas and the southern Zion tradition come into conflict (1967: 103–106). Clements and Weinfeld see the tension as the product of self-criticism of the Zion tradition in the south, 'demythologizing' earlier ideas.[1] More recently, Halpern has characterized this material as a marriage of prophetic ideas, Deuteronomic thought and social reform, brought about by political expediency in the face of the Assyrian threat (1991). The innovations in Josiah's time, for Halpern, went far beyond the national religion, but aimed to bring about a social revolution by undermining persistent clan and kinship patterns rooted in patriarchal society. These laws set out to instigate a new individualism in the interests of 'progress' and national security. The old ways are depicted as Canaanite idolatry (*e.g.* Dt. 13) in an attempt to denigrate the former polity and protect the emergent order from any resurgence of such structures (Dion 1991: 147–49, 196–206). On this view, Deuteronomy is essentially a piece of state-sponsored propaganda, concerned to uphold the new order.

None of these suggestions, however, succeeds in integrating the theological concerns of the so-called centralization laws with the rest of the book. The passages in the Deuteronomic laws where this passion for centralization is clearest are chapter 12 (general injunctions against Canaanites; regulations for slaughter – the altar law); 14:22–29 (the

---

[1] Clements 1965a; Weinfeld 1972: 51–58. Weinfeld comments: 'It is interesting to note that the very book which elevates the chosen place to the highest rank of importance in the Israelite cultus should, at the same time, divest it of all sacral content and import' (1972: 197).

tithe); 15:19–23 (firstlings); 16:1–17, 21 (festivals); 17:8–13 (judicial law); 18:1–8 (provision for priests and Levites); 26:1–15 (conclusion to the laws – firstfruits and tithes). So we must begin by making some comment on the meaning and purpose of these laws.

These laws are linked, in the first place, by the prominence of what we could call the 'place' formula, that is, the variants on the phrase 'the place which Yahweh your God will choose for his name to dwell'.

The first significant element of this phrase is *māqôm*, the place itself. In keeping with the interpretation of these laws as demanding a central sanctuary, much energy has been devoted to discovering the particular place (or places) the Deuteronomist may have had in mind. Most writers have taken it to refer to a single physical sanctuary (usually Jerusalem, but alternatively Bethel, Shiloh or Shechem), but a few have allowed that it may denote either several such sanctuaries in operation at any one time or a succession of central sanctuaries.[2]

Recently Gordon McConville and I have proposed a different solution (McConville & Millar 1994), in which the meaning of the place formula is consistent with Deuteronomic theology as a whole. In our discussion of the framework, we have seen the preoccupation of Deuteronomy with the journey of Israel. Now, in the laws, the careful use of the place formula defines the journey which is to be made within the land itself. The journey to Yahweh's place is part of the perpetual, loving response which Israel must make in the land.

Therefore, the *identity* of the place is virtually unimportant. It is the movement of Israel to that place which is significant for the Deuteronomist. There is no need, then, to perceive the reticence to identify this place as part of an attempt of a later writer to cover his tracks. It is perfectly in keeping with the Deuteronomic concern to preserve the freedom of Yahweh as the transcendent God who knows no limits, while insisting that, in his grace, he has chosen to make his presence known at his own place.[3] It is worth developing this a little.

---

[2] *E.g.* von Rad 1966b: Bethel or Shiloh; Eissfeldt 1956: Shiloh; Dumermuth 1958: Bethel; Rowley 1967: Shechem. Welch (1924) and Wenham (1970; 1971) proposed simultaneous sanctuaries, whereas Noth (1981) and Craigie (1978a) posited a succession of single sanctuaries.

[3] 'As Israel was to be distinct from the nations in not choosing its own king, so too with the altar. They were not to worship at any place, a place of their own choosing, but at the place which Yahweh would choose. The contrast is plain in 12:2, 5. It is the choosing by Yahweh which distinguishes Israel's place of worship from the nations' place. Here is confirmation that the altar-law, like that of the king, is primarily a manifestation of the theme of Yahweh's choice. The frequency of the occurrence of the altar-law in comparison with other manifestations of the same principle should not deter

When we examine how *māqôm* is actually used in the text, especially in chapter 12, some interesting phenomena emerge. Even in verses 1–5, the word is used in three different ways. In verse 2, *māqôm* refers to Canaanite shrines and sanctuaries. In verse 3, the situation is less clear; the alternatives are to take the singular to refer in a general sense to the places of verse 2, or the land of Canaan as a whole (*cf.* 26:9 and Je. 7:3–7). If indeed *māqôm* in 12:3 is the land, then the first reference to the place which Yahweh will choose in verse 5 is, in effect, the choice of a special place within a special place. This slightly tortuous argument is important, because it establishes what is virtually a sacramental relationship between the land and Yahweh's place. It is the place in Yahweh's land where his benefits, and above all his presence, are to be enjoyed (14:23–25; 15:20; 16 *passim*; 18:1–5; 26:1–11). *māqôm* is used consistently to present the place chosen by Yahweh as the land in microcosm. It is here that the milk and honey of the land are to be consumed before Yahweh. It is here that Israel faces her pre-eminent decision in living for God. This connection between the place chosen by Yahweh and the land is developed in the rest of the laws.

The *māqôm* in the land is one in a succession of significant places of decision (Kadesh–Horeb–Moab) in the journey of Israel. Elsewhere in the book, Yahweh brings Israel to the place which he has chosen (1:31, 33; 9:7; 11:5; 29:6). Now Israel must respond by making their own way to this new chosen place (11:24). The verb *b'* is used to draw attention to this. In the material surrounding the laws, the Hiphil form of the verb is used only of Yahweh's action, in 'bringing' Israel to the land. When we reach the laws themselves, the 'bringing' is to be done by Israel in response (12:6, 11; 23:19; 26:2, 9–10).[4] Now the focus has shifted from the journey to the land to the journey to the sanctuary. Now that they have reached the land, the onus is on Israel to keep travelling to the sanctuary. The place formula, then, is a literary and theological device. It is set in the context of the journey into Canaan and Israel's ongoing 'journey' within the land itself. This journey involves going to worship at the place within the place, where the full benefits of the covenant

---

us from this conclusion, frequent repetition being a feature of Deuteronomy in general' (McConville 1984: 31–33).

[4]'Our investigations have shown, therefore, first that the collocation of *b'* and *māqôm* in Deuteronomy is not confined to the altar-law, and second – and more importantly – that the force of the combination in chapters 1 – 11 contrasts neatly with that in 12 – 26. It is possible to show, furthermore, that the contrast between the two kinds of usage has been deliberately produced, when at certain key points in the text they are very pointedly brought together' (McConville 1984: 33–34). In fact, chapters 12 – 25 are tied to 11 and 26 by a grammatical chiasmus involving 'going'.

relationship were to be enjoyed. This leads us to the second important element in the 'place formula' – the presence of Yahweh.

It has long been argued that the 'name theology' in these laws (where the *name* of Yahweh is said to dwell at the sanctuary) was an attempt to suppress any thoughts of the real presence of Yahweh at the sanctuary (as part of the religious and political reforms we discussed earlier). The classic statement of this is provided by von Rad, whose work has been expounded at length by Weinfeld and others.[5] It is argued that the Deuteronomist replaced old anthropomorphic ideas about God with the abstract notion of transcendence, so Yahweh is thus no longer present at the sanctuary.

This view, however, has recently been severely criticized by Wilson (1995) and McConville (McConville & Millar 1994). Wilson demonstrates that throughout Deuteronomy, from the rehearsal of the wilderness events onwards, there is actually a *heightened* interest in the divine presence. This is particularly evident in the use of the phrase *lipnê YHWH* (before Yahweh), which consistently implies the actual presence of God in the Old Testament (Jenson 1992: 112–114). Wilson's exhaustive study of occurrences in the laws of Deuteronomy puts the matter beyond any doubt (1995: 131–217). The presence of Yahweh at the sanctuary is real and actual.

This confirms what we saw in 12:1–5. The primary motive for going to the place is not simply conformity in worship, but to meet with Yahweh himself. It is this reality that lies at the heart of the covenantal relationship. 'Rejoicing before Yahweh' is much more than enjoying the produce of the land – it is revelling in the relationship with the Giver of the land.

I believe that this is a fundamental tenet of Deuteronomic theology. If Yahweh is not actually present at the place, then there is no qualitative difference between it and the cultic places to be destroyed. The difference in the Canaanite places and the place chosen by Yahweh would then be reduced to one of sponsorship, with the new sponsor demanding a change in venue. This is surely not what the Deuteronomist has in mind. The ways of the Canaanites are always presented as brutal and empty. True worship requires the presence of Yahweh.

In Deuteronomy, the land is, above all else, the locus for relationship with Yahweh. The place chosen by Yahweh is the place *par excellence* within the land. It is here, at the sanctuary, that the promised intimacy

---

[5] Von Rad 1953: 37–44; Weinfeld 1972: 192; Mettinger 1982: 45–48. I. Wilson provides an excellent summary of the various interpretations (1995: 1–8).

with Yahweh is most evident, and enjoyment marking the Deutero-nomic covenant most intense.

The role of the laws of Deuteronomy in Israelite history, then, may not be that which is most often assumed. Rather than a political role, purifying a corrupt religious system, the *primary* function of the laws seems to be to ensure that Israel keeps on the move, and avoids the stagnation which must inevitably lead to spiritual bankruptcy. The prominence of the 'place which Yahweh shall choose' confronts Israel with a further decision, or perhaps a decision within a decision, regarding a journey to be made within the land. They are to maintain a nomadic spirit of dependence upon Yahweh in the land, physically represented by the periodic journey within the land to meet with God at the place of his choice. Such a reading of the laws brings them much closer to the preaching of the framework, while at the same time throwing into question any attempt to link them to a religious or political agenda at the time of Josiah.

The Deuteronomic laws in their ancient near-eastern and biblical context

The collection of laws in Deuteronomy is not unique, even within the biblical corpus. There are substantial similarities between collections of biblical laws, including Deuteronomy 12 – 26, and the cuneiform laws of Mesopotamia.[6] While comparison of the content of individual legal sentences is useful, it is the techniques by which these laws are linked to form a so-called 'law code' and the functions of such collections in national life which may shed most light on the role of the laws in Deuteronomy.

Interest in drafting techniques in Mesopotamian law among biblical scholars was precipitated by Wiener's work on the arrangement of the Deuteronomic laws in Deuteronomy in 1926. His rather vague ideas were developed in a more rigorous way by Petschow, in his study of the Code of Hammurabi (1965). He highlighted five major principles by which Hammurabi's laws were arranged: chronology; progression in class or worth of objects; frequency; contrast of case and counter-case; factual and juridical similarities. Lohfink (1971a) and Braulik (1985: 258) have shown examples of each of these in Deuteronomy. Rofé has covered much of the same ground in his application of the methods of his teacher Cassuto to the study of the Deuteronomic law (1988). He uses six broad categories of connection which, he argues, are commonly used in the arrangement of biblical

---

[6] See *e.g.* Epsztein 1986; Paul 1970; Driver & Miles 1952–55.

texts: associative; topical; chronological; ending with consolation; length; concentricity.

The similarities between biblical and non-biblical law codes stretch beyond the way in which successive laws are connected. Shalom Paul's seminal study shows that both the Book of the Covenant and Deuteronomy 12 – 26 share a basic prologue–stipulations–epilogue structure with collections of cuneiform laws (Paul 1970; Otto 1993a).

But despite these basic similarities, biblical law is fundamentally different from contemporary legislation. Paul has highlighted ten distinctives of Israelite law: the classification of all crime as sin; the jurisdiction of the law over all of life; the divine prerogative in legislation and administration; the unmediated entrusting of the law to the nation as a whole; the open administration of justice; an essentially didactic purpose; the sacredness of human life; individual culpability; class equality; humane treatment of slaves (1970: 37–39). For Paul, 'the prime purpose of biblical compilations is sanctification' (1970: 41). The biblical laws are theocentric in essence and expression, and as such are necessarily of a different genre from most comparative material (Phillips 1981).

Fishbane's massive discussion of legal traditions in Israel clarifies the situation still further. His most significant theoretical observation concerns the puzzling range of subjects addressed in the biblical law collections. He helpfully points out that none of these collections, whether taken individually or combined, 'sufficiently cover the numerous areas required for an operative and positive lawcode' (1985: 91). In particular, he cites the silence concerning marriage, death, contract and direct damage to property (see also Daube 1961: 257). It is argued that the character of the biblical laws is not consistent with providing either a comprehensive polity for the nation or an exhaustive handbook of judicial procedure. Fishbane concludes that 'biblical law collections may best be considered as prototypical compendia of legal and ethical norms rather than comprehensive codes' (1985: 95).

Israel's collections of law stand out, then, from those of her ancient contemporaries. Fishbane concurs with Paul in asserting that the distinctives of the biblical collections are their avowedly *revealed* nature, and the presentation of the legal and ethical prescriptions as normative for covenantal life. The laws of Israel are inevitably shaped by their Yahwistic origin and covenantal context. This is precisely what one would expect in Deuteronomy. Before we proceed, however, we must consider the relationship between the biblical collections of law themselves.

This, of course, raises the question of the history of traditions in the

Pentateuch as a whole, which is much too large an issue to be discussed in any detail here It is safe to say that there is *some* resemblance between the Book of the Covenant and the Deuteronomic legislation, but it is hard to go beyond that. Eckart Otto has recently attempted to show that one stage in the complicated literary history of the laws is a Deuteronomic revision of the Book of the Covenant to call Israel to purity and obedience in the land in response to the lordship of Yahweh (1993b: 261–278; see also Lohfink 1984: 326–327). But even this helpful study is forced in places, and ultimately does more to highlight the pitfalls than to tie down the history of legal traditions in Israel.

The situation is no different when we examine the relationship between the 'Priestly' laws, contained primarily in the Holiness Code of Leviticus, and those of Deuteronomy. The traditional view of 'P' as a later 'correction' of 'D' (as represented by Cholewinski, who argues for a 'straight-line development' from the Book of the Covenant to Deuteronomy to the Holiness Code) does not command the unqualified support it once did.[7] We can, it seems, do little more than acknowledge the complexity of the issues involved and then concentrate on Deuteronomy itself. There is, however, one last question which we should tackle in this context, which is generated by the shape of the text of Deuteronomy itself. That is the relationship between the Decalogue (chapter 5) and the collection of laws in Deuteronomy 12 – 26.

There have been many attempts to discern some coherent order in these chapters (Preuss 1982: 113). Steuernagel's designation of cultic laws, *tô'ēḇâ* laws, ancient laws, judicial laws, humanitarian laws, war laws and unclassifiable individual stipulations remains a common working hypothesis (Steuernagel 1900; L'Hour 1963; 1964; Rofé 1987). Carmichael has tried to link many of the laws to narrative, elsewhere in the Pentateuch and in the Deuteronomistic History.[8] Unfortunately, none of these attempts has been altogether successful. In fact, A. C. Welch so despaired of finding any coherence or logic in the sequence of material that he wrote: 'While any order into which the laws may be placed is sure to be unsatisfactory, none can be quite so bad as the order in which they appear in Deuteronomy today' (1924: 23). Over half a century later, however, Kaufman proposed an interesting way forward. He suggested that

---

[7] Cholewinski 1976. Contrast *e.g.* Weinfeld 1972; 1991; Fishbane 1985; McConville 1984.

[8] Carmichael 1967; 1974; 1985. Preuss, however, pours scorn on his method (1984: 108–109). Kaufman says his structure is 'totally devoid of reason' (1978–79: 108).

... not only is the arrangement of the laws in Deuteronomy highly structured but ... that structure is both consonant with and dictated by the role of the Deuteronomic Law within the framework of the book of Deuteronomy. Furthermore, and no less important, within this overriding structure the individual laws are arranged according to the general principles characteristic of other ANE legal corpora (1978–79: 108).[9]

This structure, in fact, corresponds to the 'Ten Commandments' in Deuteronomy 5. This is an attractive proposition, not least because it accounts for the presence of chapter 5 in the text. It also is consistent with the interpretation of chapter 5 offered in the previous chapter. Kaufman's basic proposal is that the text can be divided as follows:

I–II   Right worship (12:1–28)
III   False oaths (13:1 – 14:27)
IV   Sabbath (15:1–18; 16:1–17)
V   Authority (16:18–20; 17:2–20; 18:1–22)
VI   Homicide (19:1–13, 20; 21:1–9, 22–23; 22:8)
VII   Adultery and illicit mixtures (22:9–11; 22:13 – 23:1; 23:3–15, 18–19)
VIII   Theft and property violations (23:20–26; 24:7)
IX   Fair treatment of fellows (24:8 – 25:4)
Xa   Coveting neighbour's wife (25:5–12)
Xb   Coveting neighbour's property (25:13–16)[10]

There are two major problems with this scheme. Nowhere in chapters 12 – 25 is the Decalogue actually quoted, nor are the connections with it always terribly clear. He resorts to special pleading in coping with the latter objection (trying to argue that the author perceived connections where we cannot), and to the former he responds that there is a lack of allusion to the Decalogue because it is everywhere assumed. It must be said that neither of these responses is terribly convincing. That, however, does not detract from the detail of much of his work, where, drawing on Petschow and Paul, he shows that many of the laws fall within this Decalogue order. Kaufman concludes that the Deuteronomic

[9] Luther and Calvin hinted at this without developing it (Braulik 1991: 11–15). *Cf.* Breit 1933: 31–34; Schulz 1969; Lohfink 1989a: 24–28.

[10] His numbering system is confusing. He uses the Jewish, Anglican and Reformed numbering of the commandments, while arguing that the text supports the Roman and Lutheran view, that is, seeing separate prohibitions of coveting a neighbour's wife (Xa) and property (Xb), but only one on worshipping Yahweh (I–II).

law is a unified whole, crafted on a Decalogue pattern, which was composed for its present context in the book, and therefore must be interpreted as such. Even if at times he claims too much, this is an important insight (1978–79: 147).

Georg Braulik, who has done most to bring this idea of a Decalogue order to the attention of scholars, is significantly indebted to Kaufman, although he is quick to criticize the methodological deficiencies in his work. Braulik divides chapters 12 – 25 in a similar way, but claims rather less for his scheme than Kaufman. He admits that in much of chapters 12 – 18 the correspondence to the Decalogue is somewhat vague, and that in chapters 19 – 25 the picture is obscured by the intermingling of the sixth and seventh, and seventh and eighth, commandments respectively. Deuteronomic concerns, he argues, are much less evident here.[11] He calls the Decalogue a *Grobraster*, a rough framework for the laws, and also departs from Kaufman's approach in trying to uncover the redactional history of the text (See 1985: 71 and 1991: 23).

Braulik and Kaufman do reach essentially the same conclusion on the relation of the Decalogue and the laws in Deuteronomy as the book stands: the order, and the theological understanding displayed in the laws, are dependent on the Decalogue in chapter 5. Whether one is convinced by Kaufman's holistic reading or Braulik's more traditional redactional study, their combined arguments for seeing a Decalogue pattern in the laws are powerful (Preuss 1982: 111–112). They have, at the very least, succeeded in showing that a case can be made for reading chapters 12 – 26 as a literary work.

This brief discussion of the main issues involved in studying the collection of laws has proved most interesting. A theological reading of the laws does seem viable, in principle at least, as does the possibility of discerning some kind of order, or deliberate arrangement, which is in keeping with the theological and ethical concerns of the rest of the book. This can be justified, however, only in the light of exegesis, to which we now turn.

Exegesis of Deuteronomy 12 – 26

12:1–31

The interpretation of chapter 12 has exerted more influence on the understanding of Deuteronomy than any other. This profoundly

---

[11] Braulik 1985; 1986b; 1988b; 1991; 1992. He differs from Kaufman on chapter 13 (first commandment not third) and 14:22–27 (second not third).

theological chapter is the clearest call for Israel to worship 'at the place which Yahweh shall choose'. The chapter poses some literary-critical problems (Mayes 1981: 222; Merendino 1969: 56–57), but nevertheless it is obvious that we are now confronted with a sustained polemic against the immediate threat of Canaanite religious practices as portrayed by the Deuteronomist.

The opening seven verses set the scene for what follows. Verses 2–3 demand the destruction of idols, and verses 5–7 prescribe the appropriate way to worship Yahweh in the land, namely 'at the place which he shall choose'. The assertion that Israel must not act in the same way as the Canaanites ties the two together. Verses 2–4 form part of an *inclusio* (with verses 29–31) which gives the whole chapter an anti-Canaanite cast. The structure of the chapter is as follows:

1	Heading
2–4	Introduction: Canaanite worship
5–28	Israelite worship
29–31	Conclusion: Canaanite worship

The heading links the laws to the preaching which precedes it, through the phrase *ḥuqqîm ûmišpāṭîm*, which now, at last, are spelled out.

Destroying the Canaanite shrines (12:2–4, 29–31)
Like the Book of the Covenant (see Ex. 20:22–26), the laws in Deuteronomy begin by warning of the danger of idolatry, although here the emphasis is not on refraining from making idols but destroying the Canaanite sanctuaries which filled the land. There is nothing special or inherently magical about these places, but they are symbolic of the whole Canaanite way of life (12:4). By destroying them, Israel repudiates every practice and attitude that departs from a pure Yahwistic faith (*cf.* 7:5).

This anti-Canaanite polemic is restated in the plainest terms at the end of the chapter, which serves to strengthen this message. The particular temptations which Israel would face in Canaan must be resisted at any price (*cf.* 6:18; 7:1–11). Failure to do so will result in the death of the nation, as compromise in this area denies the very nature of Israel as God's people.[12]

---

[12] The actual practice of these nations (*e.g.* the extent of child sacrifice) is not important here. These laws are a continuation of Moses' preaching, and not necessarily concerned to give a 'fair' representation of Canaanite culture.

In verse 31, we find the first occurrence of the prominent term *tô'ēḇâ*, which is common in contemporary wisdom literature.[13] It seems quite clear, however, that the Deuteronomist has taken this term and used it in a novel way to serve his own specific purposes. In the Deuteronomic context it denotes an action violating the covenant by adopting Canaanite practices:

> In practically all cases in Deuteronomy it has a cultic sense, and expresses a strong anti-Canaanite sentiment and a Yahwistic exclusiveness. The cultic and nationalistic use of the phrase is not, however, its original sense, but represents a secondary adaptation of what was in origin a wisdom phrase (Mayes 1981: 189. See also Bächli 1962: 53).

Worship at the place which Yahweh shall choose (12:5–28)
The large panel dealing with the worship of Yahweh falls into three sections:

5–7	Introductory injunction: 'Not high places but Yahweh's place'
8–12	Theological reflection
13–28	Parenthesis dealing with qualifications

After the denunciation of Canaanite worship in 12:4, the positive corollary follows at once in verse 5 (the same pattern is present in verses 8–9, 13–14, 17–18). The place that Israel is to seek is the one chosen by Yahweh. This new place must be free from any associations with Canaanite idolatry and is established by Yahweh's initiative. It is at *Yahweh's place* and not any of the Canaanite sanctuaries that worship must be offered (verse 6). The aim is *not* to identify this place, but to urge Israel to conform her worship to the divine command. Yahweh has chosen Israel as his people. Now he will choose where he is to be worshipped. It is the responsibility of Israel to respond.

The absence of interest in the location of Yahweh's place is mirrored by the vagueness marking the Deuteronomic treatment of the sacrifices to be offered (verse 6). The imprecise vocabulary is due to a wholly different agenda to that of, for example, the Priestly material. The writer is at pains to guard the purity and distinctiveness of Israel's worship in

---

[13] *E.g.* in the *Instruction of Amen-em-opet* xiii.1, in *ANET* 426.

a potentially dangerous environment, rather than to spell out the minutiae of sacrificial practice.[14]

Verse 7 introduces a further distinct element. Enjoyment of the shared sacrificial meal is stressed. Commentators have some difficulty with the last part of verse 7 and many want to delete the final phrase, which is in the singular (*e.g.* Merendino 1969: 26). This is unnecessary. In Deuteronomy, the land is the place where God's people can enjoy the blessing which he has given them (as in 7:11-16 and 8:7-10). The change in number is a rhetorical device which highlights this. At the place which Yahweh shall choose, Israel is to eat as a sacramental participation in the total joy of life in the land which he has given (also 12:27; 14:23; 15:20; 16:1).

In the scant treatment of sacrifice in 12:5-7, it is very noticeable that there is no role for the priests, particularly as they are so generously provided for in other ways. But this omission is neither the result of lack of interest nor a programme of reform which aimed to marginalize the priesthood (for the priest has an important role, *e.g.* in chapter 26). The part the priest has to play is simply irrelevant to the preaching of the Deuteronomist; Moses is not addressing the priests, but the people, who must choose to worship God his way.

On reading these verses, it is interesting that one does not get the sense that this is some radical departure from current practice; in fact, it all seems rather matter of fact, and not at all what one would expect from reformist propaganda. There is little concern to regulate at all, but simply to ensure national obedience in the face of new temptations. If there is a reason for playing down the role of the priests, it is simply to emphasize that Israel is one nation serving one God in one land. But, the method of approaching Yahweh is not the main concern; obedience is.

This is reiterated in 12:8-14, where the worship required by Yahweh is given a firm theological grounding. The emphasis is the same as in chapters 1 – 11, but the response required befits a new life in a new land. The current sacral arrangements (whatever they were) become redundant (verses 8-9). Now Israel must *be careful about places* (verse 10-14).

In future, individuals would inevitably find themselves a long way from the new place of God's choice, and be tempted to use one of the surrounding 'sacred' places for the sake of convenience. But giving in to the temptation of such 'convenience sacrifice' would inevitably violate Yahweh's covenant relationship with his people. True worship

[14] Von Rad 1966b: 92; Carmichael 1974: 36; McConville 1984: 52.

could take place only in the presence of the true God, sharing the enjoyment of the sacrificial meals in the sanctuary. Israel must not stop at any place, but travel on to the place which Yahweh had chosen.

In these verses, the theological themes of journey and enjoyment of Yahweh's presence at this place of places take precedence over cultic details. There is a certain carelessness in phrases like 'all the choice gifts which you have vowed to Yahweh', and the lists of those sharing in the celebration (verses 7, 12).[15]

Verses 13–14 contain one of the strongest statements of the Deuteronomist's insistence that all sacrifice must take place where Yahweh chooses, and not 'at any place which you see'. In keeping with chapters 4 – 5, Israelite worship is to be defined by the ear rather than the eye. Whether the intention is to worship the gods of Canaan or the God of Israel, if it is offered at a heterodox place, it is tantamount to idolatry.

What follows is basically a list of concessions made to ease the likelihood of an individual falling foul of the temptation of 'convenience sacrifice.' In verses 15–16, the concessive clause allows for slaughter (zbḥ) for food at any time and in any place without recourse to the sanctuary (Milgrom 1976: 1–2). It is generally agreed that slaughter was construed as a sacral act in earliest times, so this is usually referred to as the introduction of 'profane slaughter', as zbḥ is stripped of cultic significance (e.g. Weinfeld 1973). The allusion to the gazelle and the deer shows that this is a modification of earlier practice, as restrictions are relaxed.[16]

It is too simple, however, to describe the main purpose of these laws as desacralizing slaughter. If that were the case, then surely it would be unnecessary to be so careful with the blood. Yet a clear mandate is given for killing game away from the sanctuary.[17] I would suggest, then, that this modification of an earlier law, rather than a move towards

---

[15] Also 'whole-offerings' stands for all the sacrifices in verse 13. 'Choice' may be a play on the appropriate response to Yahweh at the place which he will choose (McConville 1984: 32). This explains why the Levites are omitted from verse 7, but included in verse 12 in the light of Yahweh's treatment of Israel.

[16] De Vaux 1961: 406–456. The change to so-called 'profane slaughter' probably began earlier than is usually allowed; see 1 Sa. 14:32–35 (McConville 1984: 44–48).

[17] 'Pouring out the blood like water' is normally taken to imply that one is to treat the blood as if it had no intrinsic sacral significance. I question whether there is in fact any evidence for this. Parallel uses of the phraseology occur in 2 Sa. 14:14; Pss. 22:15; 79:3; Jb. 3:24; La. 2:19. In each place the thought is of dissipation, rather than a precise manual process. Pouring out like water [on to the ground] implies that the blood is not to be used, but rather allowed to soak into the earth and drain away. The equation is not between blood and water, but between the pouring away of both liquids. In addition, in an arid climate, it seems unlikely that water would be regarded as something to be disposed of lightly.

secular slaughter, is simply a practical way of protecting Israelites from the temptation to use other sacred places and preventing the misuse of blood. It is a theologically motivated change, designed to prevent inadvertent idolatry in the new land.[18]

In marked contrast to the relaxing of the legislation on slaughter, allowing for the abundance of Canaan and providing suitable safeguards against defilement, verses 17–19 remind the Israelites of the obligation to bring certain offerings to the place designated by God. Two reasons are given for this requirement: that a meal can be enjoyed in the presence of God and that the landless Levites should not be neglected. The seriousness of the latter is evident when we see that the expression 'take care that you' is normally reserved for remembering the events of Horeb (4:9), the exodus (6:12) and even God himself (11:16). Remembering the Levites is just as important, for this is a mark of a proper loving response to God within Deuteronomic theology. If they are neglected, and prevented from joining in the celebration in God's presence, then God's relationship with the entire nation would be affected, in keeping with their failure to obey the laws and statutes.

We return to the changes in animal slaughter in verses 20–25. This is repetitive, but that is probably to be expected when a new practice is being introduced. Verse 20, which mentions distance from the chosen place for the first time, has been taken as contradicting verse 15, where there are no such limits. But if verse 15 is concerned to reduce the likelihood of Israelites using a local high place rather than the temple for the sake of convenience, then it was already assumed that the situation would arise only at some distance from Yahweh's appointed place.

It is then made explicit that this extension applies to *all* animals, including those acceptable for sacrifice (12:21–22). The lengthy instructions on handling the blood (verses 23–25) show that this is an *exemption* rather than an abolition. This is practical legislation which enables the theological heart of the cult to be preserved in a new situation in the land. This is reiterated in the reminder of verses 26–27 that, where it is practical to make the journey to the sanctuary, things continue as normal. The extensions and exemptions of this chapter do not undermine the sacrificial system.

The lack of interest shown by the writer in the details of the various offerings, save the acknowledgment that burnt offerings go completely

---

[18] The change from the plural (verses 1–12) to the singular (verses 13–15, 17–31) may be intended to attract attention (as in verse 7). The 'intrusion' of the plural verse 16 is very odd. Neither the version of the law in Leviticus (see 17:10–11) nor the parallels in 15:23 or 12:23 are in the plural. If there is an explanation for this, it may be that once more the switch to the plural form is to highlight the second concessive clause.

to God, while the others provide the menu for the feasting, is typical. It may have been novel to allow the use of some of the priest's portion to go in the common pot, ensuring that the liberality of God was a reality in the minds and experience of the community (McConville 1984: 68–87; 88–98), but it is hard to say, for Deuteronomy has no interest in priestly percentages.

The summarizing call to obey in verse 28 is remarkably like the recurring demands for obedience scattered throughout chapters 6 – 11, and, like 5:22, uses the phrase 'all these words' (cf. too 5:1 and 12:1). This may be an attempt to tie this chapter to the Decalogue. Whether or not that is the case, we can say with some assurance that the controlling factors in this chapter are theological and rhetorical rather than legal in any narrow sense. The same concerns remain as Moses turns now to preach law.

Kaufman and Braulik argue that the chapter is a unity, directly linked to the first 'word' of the Decalogue.[19] They divide the text in slightly different ways. While Kaufman restricts the opening section of the expanded Decalogue to chapter 12, Braulik includes chapter 13. The details of their discussion of chapter 12 are, however, essentially the same. Both require the chapter to be read as prescribing the love of God and refraining from making idols. This is plausible without being compelling.

It is more important, however, to see the intimate connection between the preaching of all of chapters 5 – 11 and the opening chapter of the laws. This is clear not simply in the use of *ḥuqqîm ûmišpāṭîm*, but in the emphasis placed on continuing the journey of obedience within the land by repudiating all things Canaanite. God must be worshipped in accordance with what he says.

It must be said that the main concern of the chapter is *not* that worship, currently diversified, should be centralized. Nor is there any real evidence of a political attempt to subvert the role of the priesthood and elevate the 'state'. The emphasis in the chapter as a whole is that Israel must obey Yahweh in this as in all other things, with certain realistic exemptions. Then the one people will be able to worship the one God in the one place which he has chosen.

13:1–18

The preoccupation of chapter 12 with idolatry and the possibility of the Israelites falling into sin now gives way to the necessary reaction to

[19] It is necessary to follow a Roman and Lutheran division, or the 'second' commandment (verses 2–4, 29–31) precedes the 'first' (verses 5–28).

apostasy arising from the actions of *agents provocateurs* among the people of God (Dion 1991: 147–149). There is a progression from the upper strata of society downwards. First, the text deals with charismatic leaders who undermine national obedience to Yahweh. Next, the problem arises in the body politic of Israel. The case of one member of a family leading the others astray is followed by the pollution of whole cities by the deliberate action of a few hardened apostates.[20]

The prominence of the 'word' in this chapter is not often noticed. The use of *dābār* in 13:1 links these laws to chapters 5 – 11 in much the same way as the 'laws and statutes' in 12:1. Verses 1 and 19 of chapter 13 set the whole chapter in the context of obedience. This is not surprising, as both chapters are concerned to ensure that the nation goes on listening to the word of God (Kaufman 1978–79: 126), rather than to the human word.

Listening to a prophet (13:2–6)

Most of these words could have come straight from chapters 6 – 11. Specifically, 13:3 recalls 6:5, but the tone and language throughout are typical of Moses' earlier preaching.[21] One can see why this has been called 'preached law'. The concentration on motive here is far greater than in any other biblical collection.

It is interesting to trace the development in the motive clauses justifying the punitive action in the chapter. In this first section, dealing with apostasy among leaders, the motive for radical action is essentially that of cleansing, that the evil may be purged from Israel.[22]

Listening to your brothers (13:7–12)

Irrespective of the text read in verse 7, the people in mind are those closest to any particular member of the community of Israel. Apostasy must be punished quickly and severely, even among one's own flesh and blood (and *a fortiori* within the whole nation).

It is striking that this law anticipates such apostasy occurring as a deliberate rejection of Yahweh by his people, rather than by accident or due to wrongheaded zeal (as in chapter 12). Because of this, the sin of

[20] Merendino 1969: 81. Dion shows that each consists of a protasis spelling out the eventuality, an apodosis prescribing the reaction, and a concluding motive clause (1991: 162–166). See also Mayes 1981: 231–237 on the strange alternation between singular and plural in this chapter.

[21] See 4:29; 5:32; 6:4, 13–14; 8:6; 10:12–13, 20; 11:1, 13, 22; *et al.*

[22] L'Hour points out similar language in 17:2–7; 19:11–13, 16–19; 21:1–9; 22:13–21; 22:23–27 (1963: 3).

the apostate in the family is met with the fiercest response, including the prohibition of mercy or equivocation.

Instead of a simple demand for the cleansing of the evil, verse 12 introduces the idea of punishing the apostate as a deterrent to the rest of the nation (see also 13:15; 17:12–13). It is also noticeable that the Hophal (passive) form of verse 6 is replaced by an emphatic, active construction in verse 10. Apostasy among leaders is a corporate responsibility, but among family members rebellion is to be dealt with by those closest to its source. While this may be a family matter, it has national ramifications, and must be treated with great seriousness. Allegiance to Yahweh transcends even the closest family ties.

Listening to an infiltrator (13:13–19)

Those condemned here are literally 'sons of Belial'.[23] This is a strong denunciation of men from within Israel who are peddling apostasy. The progression from the previous paragraph is not only in the identity of the people concerned, but also the extent of their deeds. We have moved from the secret enticement of verse 7 to purveying idolatry beyond one's family and kin group. The denunciation of the instigators of this rebellion springs from the terrible consequences of their actions (see also verse 12). The same treatment must be meted out to these 'Canaanized' Israelites as was prescribed for the original inhabitants of Canaan in chapter 7. The application of the ban within Israel (verses 18–19) is the final stage in the progression of motive clauses; this time, if Israel is to maintain her relationship with Yahweh, then his anger at the entire apostate town must be sated by its utter destruction.

So there is a double progression in chapter 13 – of people who rebel, and of the motivation for punishing the apostasy with death. The false prophets must die to purge Israel, for a corrupt leadership will inevitably lead to a corrupt people. Murmurings against Yahweh by an ordinary Israelite must be punished by his immediate family, for even family ties cannot be allowed to endanger that covenant. If apostasy at this 'grass-roots' level was to go unchecked, the nation would slide rapidly into the ways of Canaan. Hence, the stress is on the death of the apostate as a deterrent which is imperative for national survival. The destruction of any town which succumbs to advances of the fifth-columnists rounds off the series neatly by placing it firmly in the context of Yahweh's implacable opposition to the Canaanites and their

---

[23] BDB suggests 'worthlessness'; Dahood proposes 'the swallower' referring to Sheol (1966: 105). Kaufman designates them 'outcasts', emphasizing the movement in the chapter from the inside out (1978–79: 126).

worship of Baal. So serious is this type of mass apostasy that it cannot merely be stopped, but demands a restoration of a proper standing with Yahweh through propitiation.

There is a deep-rooted coherence in chapter 13. Like chapter 12, it is profoundly theological, and, along with chapter 12, it legislates to guard the heart of Israel's covenant relationship with Yahweh.[24]

Kaufman makes the novel suggestion that this chapter should be linked to the third commandment (1978–79: 125). He asserts that the twin crimes set out in chapter 13 are 'speaking' against God and 'listening' to voices other than his, which are both considered to be apostasy.[25] The play on *šm'* here is very like that in chapters 5 and 6, and makes Kaufman's argument quite attractive; the focus on listening in 13:4–5 is strikingly similar to 6:4–5. It does appear that the general instruction to listen to Yahweh's Horeb/Moab revelation is now given a specific content for life in the land. In this chapter, Israel speaks only to urge others to follow the way of the Canaanites. Israel must learn that it is Yahweh's prerogative to speak, and her responsibility to listen to Yahweh alone. These chapters do move in the same thought-world as Moses' earlier exhortation, although the preaching has progressed to the concrete realities of life in the land.

14:1–21

A holy people (14:1–2)

The section 14:1–2, in line with the progression of chapter 13, addresses the nation as a whole. It sets the tone for the chapter, telling Israel why she should be different. In contrast to 8:5 and 1:31, where the nation is Yahweh's son, now each individual is called a child of God (also 32:5, 19).

The denunciation of mourning rites (verse 1b) is relatively common in the Old Testament and provides a natural transition from the previous material on capital punishment for apostasy.[26] Israel is barred from this common practice presumably to show that their God has power even over death. The reminder that Israel is God's treasured possession (7:6; also 26:18) reintroduces a key element of Deuteronomic theology – the election of Israel – as a motivation to obey, and this is quickly followed by a long list of prohibitions. These two verses establish a pattern of indicatives followed by imperatives which is repeated throughout the laws.

---

[24] This is some way from the first/second commandment, *contra* Braulik 1991: 262.

[25] 'Speaking': 13:3, 4, 5, 6, 7, 12, 13, 14, 15, 19; 'listening': 13:4, 5, 9, 12, 13, 19.

[26] See Am. 8:10; Is. 15:2; 22:12; Je. 16:6; 41:5; Ezk. 7:18. Also Lv. 19:28; 21:5.

Food laws (14:3–21a)

In the terse introduction to the food laws, *tô'ēḇâ* is used in the distinctly Deuteronomic way which we saw in chapter 12, condemning 'Canaanite' behaviour (rather than dealing with primeval taboos). Israel is to be different in her diet simply because it reflects her holiness. The nation must speak through her cuisine as well as her cult.

The composition of the list of acceptable fare here is very similar to that of Leviticus 11.[27] The differences are mostly in the position of individual animals, although the general progression within the regulations is identical (animals to be eaten, prohibited large animals, fish, birds and insects). The primary concern in Leviticus is the ritual purity of Israel *per se*, whereas the context in Deuteronomy promotes this diet as part of a positive corollary to the lifestyle of Canaan.

Verse 21a returns to the theme of Israel as Yahweh's people. Verses 1 and 21a form a neat inclusion for this material, and confirm the theological motivation of this section.

A kid and its mother's milk (14:21b)

Verse 21b is not quite so easy to account for. For a start, its positioning seems decidedly odd. But parallels in the Book of the Covenant may be of some help here. In Exodus 23:19b and 34:26b, this same prohibition comes at the end of a series of laws on bringing firstfruits to the sanctuary, and seems to represent rebellion rather than obedience. The Deuteronomist may be using 'boiling a kid in its mother's milk', in the same way, perhaps as a metonym, standing for the nexus of pagan practice which Israel must resist.

Unfortunately, it is almost impossible to verify this. If Maimonides' claim that an actual Canaanite practice lay behind this verse (III.48, followed by Milgrom 1963 and Goldberg 1984 among others) could be proven, it would carry this view. But as it is, neither this position nor that which reads this verse in the light of a Ugaritic reference to cooking in goat's milk (but, crucially, not *mother's* milk) is entirely convincing, so the origins of this verse remain a mystery.[28]

The precise background, however, is not the most important issue for us. Irrespective of its origins (which in view of the exodus parallels are

[27] Moran argues that Lv. 11 is later (1966); Milgrom claims the opposite (1991: 698–704). See Houston 1993: 83–93; Firmage 1990: 177–182.

[28] Craigie summarizes the issues (1978a: 277–278). For ANE parallels, see Keel 1980. Haran argues that as milk ferments quickly in the ANE, this command was initially a matter of culinary common sense. Now it outlaws rapid slaughter of mother and kid, demanding cruelty (1979: 24–35), but there is no mention of the mother being slaughtered too.

almost certainly pre-Deuteronomic), the Deuteronomist has used a phrase which seems to have been fairly common currency to urge God's people to live differently.

If this is the function of verse 21b, then it may help to explain the position and role of the tithe law at the end of chapter 14. Chapters 12 – 14 have been concerned with the potential contamination of Israel's life by practices of the current occupants of the land. Such syncretism would inevitably disrupt Israel's covenant relationship with Yahweh. Verse 22 of chapter 14 seems to mark a move away from a negative preoccupation with the evils of Canaan to a lengthy exposition of the festivals and polity which Israel must observe in the land; its idolatrous inhabitants fade from view for some time. If this is the case, then 14:21b may well act as a staccato reminder of the teaching of the previous chapters, while showing that we have reached a natural break in the subject matter.

In this chapter, a concern to avoid contamination mingles with the necessity of Israel's national life making a positive statement to the watching world. For the first time, the Deuteronomist appears to make use of earlier material, although he has given it his own distinctive theological slant.

Both Kaufman and Braulik take the presentation of forbidden actions and foodstuffs to be connected in some way with the third commandment. For Kaufman, who takes this chapter with chapter 13, the link is through the theme of apostasy, which, once more, is possible without being entirely convincing. It does seem, however, that this material, including even 14:21, has been carefully arranged to mark the transition from the predominantly negative 12:2 – 14:21 to the more positive injunctions of the next series of laws.

14:22 – 16:17

This long section deals with the periodic observances which are crucial to the successful occupation of the land. The positive emphasis in these chapters reflects the wording of the Deuteronomic version of the fourth commandment (5:12–15), where the motivation to keep the sabbath (and participate in the national festivals) is the enjoyment which is experienced before Yahweh in the place of his choice.

The tithe (14:22–29)

The section 14:22–29 could easily have been considered with the rest of chapter 14 (with which it shares a concern for eating; as a whole, chapter 14 has a rhetorical structure: 'Do not eat ... but eat'), but it is also an integral part of what follows (McConville 1984: 80–81; Patrick

1985: 111). It therefore joins 14:21b in providing a smooth transition from one phase of the argument (largely negative) to the next (largely positive).

Most work has been devoted to comparing the Deuteronomic version of the tithe with other legislation, but, as usual, I shall focus on the theological role of the laws within the book.[29] The tithe reaffirms that Israel is entering a land which is a gift to them from its ultimate owner, who continues to hold the deeds. Israel is to acknowledge this (verse 23, see also 7:13) by eating the tithe only at the 'place which Yahweh shall choose'. In 14:1–21, the election of Israel determined what she should eat; now the focus shifts to when and where to eat.

The family's enjoyment of a meal in Yahweh's presence is the distinctive of the ritual laws in Deuteronomy; only here is the tithe to be eaten in a joyful celebration. This is the tangible fulfilment of Yahweh's promise of a land flowing with milk and honey. Irrespective of cultic practice before or after, Deuteronomy insists that the cult gives the chance to revel in the fulfilment of the promise. This theological idea dominates chapters 15 – 16.[30]

The special provision for the Levites (14:27–29), as in chapter 12, is peculiar to Deuteronomy. Throughout these laws, along with aliens, orphans and widows, the way in which the Levites are treated provides an index of Israel's obedience. Self-preoccupation can have no place in the life of Israel. Enjoyment of the land leads to enjoyment of the meal at the sanctuary, which in turn demands an imitative response of generosity to those who have no direct access to the blessings of the land. Yahweh gives to Israel, and Israel gives to the excluded, in the stead of Yahweh. In a very real sense, the Levites, widows and orphans represent Yahweh to Israel. This is very close to Jesus' message in Matthew 25:34–46.

Laws of release (15:1–23)

It is surprising that there is no sabbath legislation in the Deuteronomic collection. It has often been suggested that the laws of release stand in its place. This is partly because of the motivation attached to the fourth commandment in 5:14 – 'remember that you were slaves in Egypt' – and partly because this chapter is dominated by a 'sabbatical' pattern. Now that the nation has arrived in Canaan, it seems that the Sabbath

---

[29] Eissfeldt 1917; Weinfeld 1972: 190ff., esp. 215–217; Milgrom 1976 and McConville 1984: 68–87 all provide lengthy discussions of the tithe in Israel.

[30] This theological reading undermines the argument that the Deuteronomic version tries simply to abolish the fallow year in favour of a triennial tithe (Kaufman 1978–79: 129–130; Carmichael 1974: 81–83).

principle goes beyond a universal right to rest one day in seven, but allows each Israelite to be free to enjoy the rest which Yahweh has given in the land (Hamilton 1992: 105–117).

The legislation deals in turn with the case of 'a neighbour or brother' who has mortgaged land, a 'brother Hebrew' (probably a landless member of the community who is not an ethnic Israelite) who has sold himself into slavery and finally 'firstlings'.[31] This is essentially the progression within the fourth commandment itself, which is typical of ANE legal material.

The opening prescription protects the individual responsibility and autonomy of each Israelite within the covenant framework. Even in the sphere of the collection of debts it is the 'brotherhood' of Israel which is the controlling ethical factor. Brotherhood is an important Deuteronomic theme and is crucial in this chapter.[32] There is a qualitative difference in the eyes of Yahweh between those who belong to his covenant people (*rē'â*, 'companion', and *'āḥ*, 'brother') and those who do not (*nokrî*, 'foreigner') (verse 3), which shows in how they are treated. It is unacceptable to return those who have been freed by Yahweh to conditions of economic bondage, whereas those who have no knowledge of redemption, while they should not be exploited, have no right to the economic advantage and property which is bound up with the deliverance from Egypt.

The idealistic tone of verses 4–6 is virtually unmatched in Deuteronomy. They describe a utopian situation where Yahweh blesses Israel's obedience to the degree that there are no poor in the land and all enjoy the fullness of his gift. Israel's place among the nations is one of pre-eminence. The pattern of no brother accruing lasting debt is extended to the nation achieving the status of a self-sufficient 'world bank'. This financial autonomy is mirrored by supremacy in international relations, with Israel always acting as a suzerain and never as a vassal.

The real problem seems to be caused by the presence of verse 11. We should not, however, be too quick to dismiss this as a contradiction. The reflections on poverty must be read in the context of the year of release. This legislation is not designed to eradicate poverty as such but to ensure that the phenomenon of the 'poverty trap' never arises in

---

[31]C. J. H. Wright shows that the first case is that of landowning Israelites being 'freed' by the return of mortgaged land and the second of a 'Hapiru', a landless member of the community who was not an ethnic Israelite. *Cf.* Ex. 23:10–11 (1990: 147–148, 167–173, 249–259). This is essentially the view of Braulik, who sees an elevation of the Hapiru from slave (Ex. 21:1) to the status of brother here (1986a: 15–16).

[32] See 15:2, 3, 9, 11, 12. *Cf.* 15:12 with 2:4, 8.

Israel, either for the ethnic Israelite or for the landless 'brother Hebrew' (verses 10, 14). Yahweh has not redeemed Israel to allow individual members of the community to languish in poverty, thus questioning the point of his redemption in the first place. Verse 11 is then both a realistic admission (that there will always be Israelites in financial difficulties) and an implicit reminder of the necessity of generosity and the careful observation of the year of release, lest Israelites are abandoned and stripped of hope. This is probably the best example of the tension which often arises in Deuteronomy between the goal which the Mosaic preaching aims for and the reality which it expects.

Verse 12 moves from a landowning Israelite to 'a brother Hebrew' who is forced to sell himself into slavery. The principle of imitative generosity is now extended: from lending freely to one in trouble, to giving freely to the Hebrew released at the end of his six years (maximum) of slavery. This again shows the Deuteronomist's concern that there should be no poverty trap in Israel. The provision for re-entering free society ensures that no vicious cycle of continuing slavery is allowed to develop. Liberality marks the provisions at every stage. In contrast to Exodus 21:1-6, no mention is made of the family of the Hapiru. Presumably this is because the new status of 'brother' enjoyed by the landless workers makes such regulations redundant. Legislation to allow a Hebrew the option of staying in 'service' of his own accord is added in 16–18, providing a contingency measure when self-sufficiency or economic stability in the long term seems to be an unattainable goal. As in the fourth commandment, all this new generosity springs from the powerful paradigm of Yahweh's exodus action (verse 15) and the necessity of obedience for enjoyment of the land. It is quite plain that these laws are structured in such a way as to call Israel to obey; they are indeed preached (Hamilton 1992: 26).

The transition to the 'firstlings' maintains the movement of the chapter through the strata of human society to animals.[33] Whether the Deuteronomist gave laws a new emphasis or composed new legislation, here the law of firstlings serves a theological and rhetorical purpose. There is a parallel between the treatment of Israelites and non-Israelites in the year of release and the treatment of whole and blemished animals in the law of firstlings which binds the chapter together (McConville 1984: 95).

The legislation in 15:19–23 is a condensed and stylized account of

---

[33] McConville has already shown that the form of this law reflects the theological concerns of the Deuteronomist and cannot be easily used to reconstruct the history of the practice in any straightforward manner (1984: 88–98).

sacral practice. The details of the sacrifices are typically general (see *e.g.* 12:15–18) and subordinate to basic principles of Deuteronomic theology. It is interesting that mutilated animals, while not fit to be sacrificed, can be eaten by anyone *subject to the normal restrictions on the disposal of the blood.*

The Deuteronomist draws on (probably familiar) traditions, using a certain degree of literary and theological artistry to emphasize that life in the land should be marked by freedom, which has its roots in Israel's exodus experience.

The festivals (16:1–17)

Discussion of the festivals in Deuteronomy has focused on the fusion of two festivals in verses 1–8: Passover and Unleavened Bread. There are several difficulties here. Verses 3 and 8 are apparently contradictory; the unparalleled command to take the Passover sacrifice from the flock or herd and to cook it (*bšl*) appears to contravene Exodus 12; the details of the ritual itself are far from clear. These problems have generally been interpreted as the result of an attempt to regulate a (Canaanite) Massot ritual and a family Passover meal by combining them and bringing them to the central sanctuary.[34]

There is, however, one major problem with this approach. It provides no explanation of *why* these rituals were combined, nor does it do justice to the careful, chiastic arrangement of verses 1–7 around the salvation-historical statement of verse 3b (Halbe 1975a). There is also some doubt as to the supposed Canaanite origins of Massot (Halbe 1975b). In fact, on closer examination, the argument that the primary purpose of this passage was to merge two originally separate rituals is actually quite weak.[35] It is much better, with McConville (1984: 112–123), to read this passage as a theological fusion of two of the major themes in Deuteronomy: the significance of the exodus for Israel's life in the land, and the enjoyment of that life with Yahweh. The solemnity of the exodus memorial (Passover) and the vigorous enjoyment of the land in Massot (see Ex. 13:3–8 and Jos. 5:10–12) are carefully brought together. This is the essence of Deuteronomic theology: the exodus and enjoyment of the land must go hand in hand.

[34] The account of the separate origins of the semi-nomadic Israelite Passover and the agricultural, Canaanite Massot in de Vaux is widely accepted (1961: 489–492). The text is typically divided: verses 1–2, 5–7, Passover; verses 3–4, 8, Massot (Mayes 1981: 254). But a supposed desire for 'centralization' does not explain the combination of the rituals.

[35] Mayes 1981: 255; J. B. Segal 1963: 111; McConville 1984: 100–107. McConville demonstrates the complexity (and fluctuation) of the relation of the two feasts throughout the OT.

This is another example of the indicative–imperative pattern which the Mosaic preaching has followed throughout. Yahweh redeems and gives the land; Israel enjoys the land and worships. The allusion in verse 1 and the emphatic reference to the seventh day of rest in verse 8 (which simply separates the seven days of verse 3–4 into six plus one) set this in a sabbatical context. The enjoyment of the land is then expressed in terms of eating unleavened bread and of sabbath rest.[36]

The seventh day of Passover-Massot leads neatly into the seven weeks prior to the feast of Weeks. The themes of enjoyment and remembering the exodus still dominate (verses 11–12; also Lv. 23:40), but when we come to the three verses dealing with Booths (verses 13–15), they are so dominated by the note of joy that scarcely another detail is given. These short passages, like 16:1–8, are further examples of the theological way in which the Deuteronomist presents cultic material. Whatever the festival event, Israel is to remember the exodus and enjoy the fruits of her relationship with Yahweh, as the people of God gathers at the place he chooses (verses 16–17).

Those verses, 16–17, mark the end of a section where Deuteronomy draws selectively on the cultic tradition of Israel to reinforce the message of chapters 1 – 11 in the context of religious observance in the land.[37] This is one area where the Decalogue scheme has much to be said for it. The Deuteronomic version of the Sabbath in 5:12–13 reflects the link between the exodus and the intended enjoyment of blessing and rest in Canaan developed in chapters 15 and 16. But the most important feature is that, in every case, the detail of the rituals plays second fiddle to the theological agenda, as the centrality of the exodus experience, and the ensuing freedom, prosperity, rest and enjoyment are stressed again and again, most eloquently of all in the solemn centrepiece of the chapters – the Passover-Massot festival.

This may be 'law' but it is clearly law with a theological message. God's people are not only confronted with the practicalities of decision, but urged to make the right choice on the grounds of the past, present and future, in a way which is entirely in keeping with chapters 1 – 11.

It is worth pausing at this stage to reflect briefly on what we have seen in the first four chapters of the laws. These chapters have much in common. The emphasis throughout is on theological and ethical

---

[36] *bšl* here is used generally (contrast the cooking in water in Ex. 12). The sacrifices refer to food eaten during the week, not to the Passover itself. This reflects carelessness about cultic details.

[37] See McConville 1984: 119–121 on the omission of firstfruits.

matters. In chapter 12, the focus is on worshipping Yahweh in his way, rather than simply adopting the practices of Canaan. This serves to underline his sovereignty and the uniqueness of his relationship with Israel. The flip-side of responding to Yahweh's initiatives by worshipping him is repudiating the worship of other gods. Thus dealing with apostasy occupies chapter 13, and the distinctiveness of Israel 14:1–21. At this point, more positive concerns begin to dominate. The freedom of Yahweh, expressed in chapter 12, finds a corollary in the freedom of Israel in chapter 15. The enjoyment and rest which the promised land gives are shown to be central to observing the festivals. These three themes of freedom, enjoyment and rest are the direct result of the exodus, which must be engraved on Israel's corporate memory.

16:18 – 18:22

A new section begins at 16:18. For the first time we move beyond matters of 'worship' to justice. Now the injunctions address individual members or groups in society, rather than the people as whole.

The pursuit of justice (16:18–20)

Despite the change in subject matter, the emphasis on response is similar to verses 16–17. In the Hebrew text, there is a fairly obvious pun on *ntn*: Israel is to appoint (*ntn*) judges in response to Yahweh's giving (*ntn*) them the land. The role of these judges is to dispense *mišpaṭ-ṣedeq* (literally, justice-righteousness).[38] The play on these two concepts dominates verses 18–20 (*cf.* 6:24–25).

Neither *mišpaṭ* nor *ṣedeq* is a prominent term in Deuteronomy. *ṣedeq* occurs elsewhere only in 1:16 (although see 6:25; 9:4–6 and 24:13 for *ṣᵉdāqâ*) and the double use of *ṣedeq* is unique in the Hebrew Bible. *mišpaṭ* occurs in the singular only in 1:17; 17:8–10; 18:3; 19:6; 21:17, 22; 25:1. In each case, once more the context is of fairness in the courts. It seems that these verses are simply saying that things must be done properly in Israel. This acts as a heading for all the diverse stipulations to follow. The judiciary is to be a model for the nation, enacting the laws and statutes with *mišpaṭ-ṣedeq*. As the following laws show, it is the responsibility of the leaders of Israel to preserve the tone (and the health) of national life. They are to be the guardians of the nation's relationship with Yahweh in his land (Goldberg 1984).[39]

In some ways, then, 16:18–20 appears to act as a heading, or at least

---

[38] This combination is unique, but see Zc. 7:9; Pr. 31:9; La. 3:59; and also 1 Ki. 3:28; 1 Ch. 18:14; 2 Ch. 9:8.

[39] See also the elders' role in 17:2–13; 19:11–13; 21:1–9, 19–20, 22:13–21; 25:5–10.

provides a transition from the laws concerning Israelite worship to the rest of the laws.

Dealing with idolatry (16:21 – 17:7)

Surprisingly, the long discussion of authority in Israel begins with a return to the themes of idolatry and apostasy. Verses 21–22 of chapter 16 cover actions which Yahweh hates, and 17:1 that which is an abomination to him. Both passages refer to Canaanite practices in the usual way. Kaufman (1978–79: 134) has pointed out the transitional role of these verses. They introduce the breaches of covenant which the judges must deal with in 17:2–7, showing that the issues which dominated chapters 12 – 16 are still central. The question remains that of conforming to Yahweh's revealed will. Guarding the covenant relationship takes precedence over the more conventional matters (verse 8).[40]

The judicial system (17:8–13)

If any further evidence is needed that these laws are not attempting to reduce the power of the priesthood, it is found in verses 8–13. Difficult cases are to be taken to Yahweh's place, where the Levitical priests are to deliberate with the 'head of the supreme court' (the 'judge who is [there/in office] in those days').[41] Together, they are to enact the demands of chapter 13. In view of 16:18–20 and 16:21 – 17:7, where the judges are given jurisdiction over 'religious' matters, it is not surprising to find the Levites, the priestly guardians of the law, playing a part in the judicial process. For Deuteronomy, the important thing is that the one people live in obedience to the one God – and that is a responsibility shared by all the leaders.

The king (17:14–20)

It is an easy transition from the highest judicial authority to the question of kingship in Israel. Before considering the hypothetical *faux pas* of appointing a king, the 'king-law' reaffirms that the land is a gift from Yahweh. This establishes the pattern of Yahweh taking the initiative and Israel responding. Departure from this must lead to disaster – it is Israel's place not to instigate, but to obey. The request to appoint a king 'as all the other nations do', then, is doubly ominous – it is both a departure from the consistent anti-Canaanite tone of the preceding

---

[40] This eases the problem of the relationship of chapter 17 to chapter 13. In both places the presentation is tailored to a specific purpose: in chapter 13 to demand repudiation of apostasy and in chapter 17 to spell out the duty of the judges.

[41] Mayes summarizes literary-critical attempts to makes sense of these verses (1981: 268–269).

chapters and a purely a human initiative – and is implicitly condemned (Perlitt 1994: 182–198).

In verse 15, however, Yahweh takes the initiative once more. This king is to be chosen not by Israel, but by God. There is hope for the 'rehabilitation' of this human initiative, if they submit to Yahweh's choice of king, in the same way that they must submit to his choice of place.

The king is to be chosen from 'among your brothers'. This is important, because a new monarchy cannot be allowed to undermine the fundamental equality established by Yahweh's redemption. So rather than releasing the king from the normal obligations of the covenant community, the law reinforces them. Verses 16–17 insist that the king must lead Israel on her journey of obedience, rather than mimicking the ways of other nations and returning to 'Egypt'. Instead, he is to be the definitive Israelite. It is particularly striking in an ANE context, where the role of declaring and prosecuting war was the fundamental responsibility of the king, that this remains firmly in the hands of Yahweh (Halbe 1985: 55–75; Lind 1980: 155).

Verses 18–20 make it clear that in Israel the king's primary responsibility is essentially the same as that of each of his brothers – to obey the law. There is no call for Israel to submit to her king; the only responsibility cited is that of the king to Yahweh, and the reversal of the unwise question is complete.

This law has been used repeatedly to argue for either a pro-monarchical (usually southern) or anti-monarchical (either northern or demythologizing) agenda in Deuteronomy. But a theologically sensitive reading of the text justifies neither. It is part of the Deuteronomic concern to establish a leadership in Israel which ensures that relationship with Yahweh flourishes. The law is for godly kingship and against ungodly kingship. This tells us little or nothing about the setting of the book.[42]

The Levite (18:1–8)

In 18:1–8, legislation concerning priests succeeds the king-law. Deuteronomy is peculiar in its consistent reference to the 'priests who are Levites', and attempts to account for this have been many and varied. Discussion has focused on the purpose of the law and the unusual priestly terminology.

---

[42] Perlitt (1994: 182–185) provides the most detailed discussion of this issue, where he also reads the king-law as theological, rather than as part of a specific political agenda. I do not share his view, however, that the law is post-exilic.

On the former question, the consensus has been that 18:1–8 is a provision for Levites (whose livelihood was destroyed by the Josianic reform), who may have been discriminated against by the Jerusalem priesthood. The latter has proven more tricky, with some seeing the designations 'priest', 'Levite' and 'Levitical priest/priests who are Levites' as interchangeable, while others argue that it reflects a hierarchy within the priesthood.[43]

There may, however, be a theological explanation which once again addresses difficult questions of interpretation in the context of the whole book. We have seen how the Levites in Deuteronomy function as an index of Israel's obedience, as they are included in religious celebrations. Now the Levites themselves are held up as a model for Israel's relationship with God (Gunneweg 1965: 182). McConville refines this somewhat:

> His prosperity is realised in dependence. His dependence upon Yahweh is more conspicuous than that of his brethren, because he does not have private property in the same way that they do. His prosperity depends on the day-to-day factor of his brothers' continued obedient giving of cultic offerings ... the relation of Levi to Israel in Deuteronomy is such as to be an ideal representation of how the whole people should stand both to Yahweh and the land (1984: 151).

The landless Levites in Deuteronomy characterize the ideal relationship with Yahweh. Verses 1–2 remind Israel that while, for them, this land is the locus of their relationship with Yahweh, their goal is relationship with Yahweh himself. The function of Levi in the land is to remind Israel that her ultimate calling is not merely to enjoy its produce, but relationship with him. Enjoyment of the land is not forgotten (verses 3–5). But the Deuteronomist is pointing to a deeper enjoyment, which is the goal of Yahweh's action. Now we see that if the Levites are neglected, it is not simply a sign of disobedience, but of a falling away from the relationship which the Levites themselves model.

This eases the problem of the relation of the priests and Levites in verses 1–3. The Deuteronomist is aware of divisions of function within the tribe (see *e.g.* 10:6 and 31:25), but they are irrelevant to his message. He is concerned with the challenge of Levi as a whole to Israel as a whole. Verses 6–8, then, do not address the rights of

---

[43] See *e.g.* Emerton 1962 and G. E. Wright 1954 respectively, and the summaries of Abba 1977; McConville 1984: 124–135.

marginalized Levites at all. Having implicitly set out the consequences for the nation of neglecting the Levites, the writer turns to the needs of the Levites themselves. These verses ensure that *any* Levite who *wants to* move from his home to the new static centre in the land should be allowed to share in the inheritance of the whole people at the place chosen by Yahweh. In the same way as chapter 12 removes the need for 'convenience sacrifice', verses 6–8 ensure that there is no danger of 'disenfranchized' Levites leading the nation astray (Jdg. 17:1–10).

This passage deals with the priorities of the whole nation. For the tribe of Levi, the physical expression of their enjoyment of the gifts of the land is mediated through the obedience of the rest of the brotherhood.[44] Israel's spiritual appropriation of the inheritance can come only when she sees the landless Levite, with only the Lord himself to enjoy, and models her life on him. If either disobeys, the consequence is a disrupted covenant relationship.

The prophet (18:9–22)

Verses 9–13 return to the theme of apostasy, which tends to support reading verses 6–8 as a measure to avoid alienating Levites. As in 17:1–7, this passage is placed here to remind those in 'public office' in Israel, whether Levite, king, judge or prophet, that their primary responsibility is to resist the ways of Canaan. Verse 9 states the demands on Israel plainly. Israel's response to Yahweh's gift of the land cannot be to imitate the present occupants, whose actions are *tô'ēḇâ* and who stand under the judgment of God (verse 12). Instead, Yahweh is to be carefully imitated and obeyed (verse 13). This denunciation of Canaanite practice introduces the final authority figure, the prophet.

The message of this chapter is that divine guidance will come to Israel in a way which is refreshingly simple. Like the king, the prophet is to be a member of the 'brotherhood' (verse 18). It is only to him that Israel is to listen. The emphasis on *šm'* shows that the words of the prophet continue the process of Yahweh's speaking to his people on their journey. Yahweh was heard at Horeb, is heard at Moab and will be heard through the prophet. This is the significance of 'a prophet like you'. Yahweh promises to continue the process of revealing the 'laws and statutes' which are necessary for life in an ever-changing context. He will keep speaking; it is the work of Israel to keep listening.

This inevitably raises the question of verification (verses 20–22). Just as listening to apostates is prohibited, failure to listen to the prophet is

---

[44] The widow, orphan and alien are in an analogous position, but the Levites lend themselves to the theological exposition presented by the Deuteronomist.

condemned. The warning against failure to listen is followed by a warning against speaking presumptuously. Purporting to speak in the name of Yahweh is tantamount to apostasy. The criterion for judgment and the accompanying reassurance that 'such a prophet need not be feared', however, are cryptic. The implication for the prophet seems to be that, like the king, he is ultimately subject to Yahweh. For their part, the people are not to be overawed by extravagant claims of charlatans.

Despite the transition from the more overtly 'religious' legislation, the text is still dominated by theological preaching. At the heart of the *mišpaṭ-ṣedeq* which the judges and priests are to dispense is the need to guard the nation's relationship with Yaweh. The king is to maintain the distinctiveness of Israel and live a life of model conformity to the will of Yahweh. The prophet, while on an equal footing with the rest of his brothers, is the agent of Yahweh's continuing revelation. Only if this concern for covenant faithfulness is maintained will justice prevail in Israel. Only if justice prevails will Israel live long in the land in a right relationship with Yahweh.

At this point, connections with the Decalogue seem to become a little more tenuous. Braulik and Kaufman contend that this is essentially the fifth commandment, with parents replaced by authority figures; but this is hard to maintain, as the legislation is addressed to the leaders themselves, rather than to the people. But the Deuteronomist has carefully woven a coherent theological whole, which continues to advance his own spiritual agenda.

19:1 – 22:12

At the end of chapter 18, there is a distinct change in the nature of the laws. The 'preached law' we have seen so far peaks with the law of the prophet, and from this point both a rational order and theological purpose are harder to spot.

Having said that, there are several common threads running through 19:1 – 22:12. The most obvious is murder, which Kaufman argues links much of 19:1 – 21:9 as it deals with 'institutional matters', free citizens, criminals and finally animals (1978–79: 130).

Protecting the innocent and punishing the guilty (19:1–21)

This section legislates for the establishment of cities of refuge, designed to prevent the over-zealous pursuit of justice (4:41–43), and sets a humanitarian tone. But there is no question of these measures arising from mere philanthropy. Verses 8–10 and 13 set this legislation in a theological context. Proper use of these cities is a matter of obedience (verses 8–9) and of keeping the land free of innocent blood (verses 10,

13).[45] This is to be understood primarily in terms of interrupting Israel's relationship with Yahweh, since in Deuteronomy the locus for this relationship is always the land. The land is to be purged of innocent blood in much the same way as it is to be purged of apostasy.

This belief that defilement of the land interrupts Israel's relationship with Yahweh provides the transition to the next phase of the argument. For the Deuteronomist, it seems that moving a boundary stone (and thus stealing the land allotted in chapter 4) is serious enough to be laid alongside murder (verse 14). Infringement of land rights interferes with the inheritance given by Yahweh. Stealing land is an indirect attack on the individual's relationship with God and prevents him from enjoying the blessing of Yahweh which is his right. This common piece of ANE legislation has been invested with great significance: it is concerned not purely with the administration of justice, but also with the consequences of civil disobedience for the community's relationship with Yahweh.[46]

The necessary criteria for a sound conviction are set out in verses 15–19. The legislation is designed to pre-empt perjury, to purge the nation of this evil (thus preserving the nation's relationship with Yahweh; verse 19) and to provide a deterrent (verse 20). This is followed by a harsh statement of the *lex talionis* in verse 21. This seems to jar with the general humanitarian tone of the chapter, leading Mayes to argue that it bears no relation to its present context (1981: 290–291). This fails to take proper account of the underlying concerns of chapter 19. Perjury threatens the whole legal process. It promotes evil (freeing the perpetrator to act again), defiles the land and jeopardizes Israel's relationship with Yahweh. It undermines justice in Israel, the very *mišpaṭ-ṣedeq* demanded in chapter 16. The appropriateness of talionic retribution is clear. The necessity to purge and deter may suggest that, for the Deuteronomist, these crimes are potentially as serious as apostasy. Hence the vehemence of the condemnation is aimed to dissuade Israel from being too lenient, as a result of failing to appreciate the consequences of the crime.

Chapter 19 is dominated by the Deuteronomist's determination to present a model for life in Israel characterized by justice. This justice is essentially humanitarian, hence the cities of refuge and the laws of evidence precede the procedure for conviction. The innocent must be protected and the guilty brought to justice. Unnecessary deaths must be

---

[45] See Weinfeld 1973; Milgrom 1973. 'Defiling the land' implies an obstacle to tracing the humanitarianism to 'secular' royal wisdom, *contra* Weinfeld 1961.

[46] Driver gives parallels (1901: 234–235). The link between land and relationship explains this rare excursion into property law. See C. J. H. Wright 1990: 129–130.

avoided. This is the message of the chapter, more than that murder is wrong and must be punished.

The conduct of war (20:1–20)

The treatment of war in chapter 20 may, surprisingly, add some support to the suggestions of the previous paragraph. The fact that the laws on warfare follow a long section on the avoidance of shedding innocent blood are the first hint that Deuteronomy is not as bloodthirsty or jingoistic as is sometimes suggested. I would go as far as to suggest that these laws carefully circumscribe Israel's military action in such a way that the emphasis is still placed on avoiding unnecessary death.

Verses 1–4 make it plain that *any* war in which Israel is involved must have the divine sanction. The people of God are given neither a bland assurance of Yahweh's support nor a licence to slaughter.[47] Yahweh is not some local deity at the beck and call of Israel; he is not simply the sponsor of their wars. On the contrary, he chooses when to engage in battle. Any killing is justified only by the Lord's initiative, presence and prosecution. The role of the priest ensures that Israel does not lose sight of this (verses 2–4). The words of the priest underline the connection between Israel's wars and the rest of her life. Even on the battlefield, Israel must continue to listen, for even war, for Israel, is a matter of obedience.

The Deuteronomic flavour of these rules of war becomes even more obvious in verses 5–9. Even war should not inhibit the enjoyment of Yahweh's land, and an exemption from national service is extended to those who have not had the opportunity to enjoy his provision, be it house, vineyard or wife (verses 5–7). While this is remarkable in its sensitivity, the dismissal of anyone who lacks faith in the ability of Yahweh to secure victory (verse 8) seems more pragmatic and may simply be designed to preserve morale. Conversely, it might suggest that, for Israel, war is to be undertaken only as a matter of covenant faithfulness.

The twin panels of verses 10–15 and 16–18 clarify the picture still further. Verses 10–15 describe a paradigm for Israelite military action outside the borders of Canaan. The conduct of battle is governed by contemporary standards and military expediency; potential resistance is quashed and spoil taken. Women, children, livestock and so on are spoil

---

[47] This is in contrast to Babylonian thought, where Marduk is given 'Enlil' power in which his earthly representatives rule and act (Lind 1980: 146). Having said that, where Israel is the object of aggression, they could be confident that Yahweh would intervene on their behalf.

to be enjoyed as the provision of Yahweh. I would argue that the context makes it plain that these are wars which are deemed necessary for national security, rather than encouraging Israel to expand her power base. In any case, such wars have no ramifications for the covenant with Yahweh.

The situation in verses 16–18 is radically different. Yahweh has commanded that his judgment against the Canaanites is to be carried out to the letter by Israel. Failure to carry out his directives will put the covenant itself in jeopardy by allowing the seeds of apostasy to remain in the land. Abominable practices cannot be reformed; they must be rooted out. The terms on which the conquest is to be executed could not be made clearer.

Weinfeld has recently argued that this is a utopian reinterpretation of the ideas of expulsion or dispossession in Exodus and Numbers.[48] There is a progression of language in the Pentateuchal laws, and the concept of the ban is clearly a Deuteronomic innovation in line with persistent anti-Canaanite concerns. Whether the relationship between the laws is as Weinfeld suggests remains unproven, but it would not be surprising to find theological concerns controlling the legislation on war in the light of all that we have seen in chapters 12 – 19. I shall return to this in more detail in the next chapter.

Chapter 20 concludes with an unexpected 'environmental' concern. Israel is not to copy her neighbours by despoiling the land surrounding any city which they attack.[49] The fruit trees are spared because Israel knows that Yahweh has given the land for enjoyment, but it is shocking that the trees receive more mercy that the Canaanites. The radical treatment which must be meted out to the Canaanites, while necessary, is itself quite out of step with what God intends for life in the land beyond the conquest.

Dealing with unsolved murder (21:1–9)

In 21:1–9, we return to the idea that sin in the life of the nation affects the people's relationship with God This is a difficult passage, with many uncertain elements, including an obscure early ritual (Zevit 1976: 377–379).[50] The details of the symbolism need not detain us here, as the reason for the inclusion of this incident is clear.

The view that murder somehow interrupts the relationship with Yahweh is implicit in verse 1, where *^{a}dāmâ* (ground) replaces the more

---

[48] Weinfeld 1993. See in contrast Lilley 1993.
[49] In contrast to typical Assyrian procedure (Buis & Leclerq 1963: 145–146).
[50] L'Hour 1963: 20–22; Merendino 1969: 401–402; Finkelstein 1981: 30.

usual *'ereṣ* (land) to give graphic illustration of the nature of the defilement. The land/ground is still that given by Yahweh, but the soil itself is now stained by blood. Under normal circumstances, the judicial/cultic process atones for such crimes in Israel. When no culprit is found, this ritual ensures that there is no resulting rift between God and his people (verses 8–9). Again we see that preserving a right relationship with Yahweh is of primary importance.

Justice and family relationships (21:10–23)

Verses 10–17 seem to have nothing whatsoever to do with any of the surrounding material; it has nothing to do with killing, but deals with how to treat female prisoners of war.[51] After prohibiting the rape and/or exploitation of such women, a strict procedure is laid down for incorporating them into Israelite society. On the one hand, the woman is to be treated with dignity; on the other, she is to repudiate (and even mourn for) her pagan past, which is the significance of shaving her head, cutting her nails and destroying her clothes. If there is any connection with the preceding material, it is through the theme of the preservation of life.

It is no easier to see why 21:15–17, where we find the prohibition of disinheriting a rightful heir, comes next. It is possible that the Deuteronomist is representing such an act as akin to murder (as in 19:14), which would fit with a 'preservation of life' theme, but this is without parallel in the Hebrew Bible.

The 'case of the rebellious son', however, obviously deals with life and death. It presumably has some generic significance.[52] A contravention of parental authority is to be dealt with first by *both* parents and then judicially, where it is punishable by death. This limits the father's power significantly, but is in keeping with the Deuteronomic insistence that it is the responsibility of the community to guard Israel from such anarchic tendencies. The command to cleanse this wickedness from Israel as a deterrent draws the series of commands involving families to a close.

The injunction not to allow a body to remain suspended at the site of

---

[51] Rofé sees a connection with verses 18–21 through the idea of 'feelings' (1988: 272). Kaufman places verses 10–17 outside the Decalogue structure as the transition from war to family (1978–79: 133). Braulik assumes an 'associative' link with murder (1988b: 90).

[52] Bellefontaine makes the valuable observation that this is a metaphorical warning to the whole of Israel (1979: 25–26). Stulman shows the harshness of this law against its ANE background (1990: 624–625). Luke 15 is an analogous case of a son demanding his inheritance (wishing the father dead); Bailey 1976: 158.

execution overnight, used in the New Testament in connection with the crucifixion of Jesus, stands out from its context. The basic concern, that the national relationship with Yahweh should not be impaired by defiling the land, however, is not new, and, as before, implies that capital punishment is a contingency measure which enables intimacy with God to continue. The 'purging' must be done quickly, humanely and with the minimum of fuss.

One can see that the connections between successive laws are becoming more tenuous. While this section is not without its problems, there is a persistent concern to limit killing of all kinds in Israel and to ensure that where capital punishment is absolutely necessary, it is administered with justice and humanity.

Miscellaneous laws: kindness and mixture (22:1–12)
When we enter chapter 22, all sense of order seems to go out of the window, for these verses are both random and obscure.

The series opens in 22:1–4 by insisting that, as Israel is a 'brotherhood', every man must look out for his neighbour's animals and property. Verse 5 is one of the better-known stipulations of the Deuteronomic Code. The prohibition of cross-dressing probably concerns fertility rituals.[53] The recurrence of the *tô'ēḇâ* formula suggests a condemnation of 'Canaanite' behaviour. Its presence here is mystifying, especially when followed by a return to the humane treatment of animals (guarding the ecological balance) in verses 6–7.

The building-control legislation in 22:8 is remarkable only in the overbearing warning that negligence will bring 'bloodguilt upon your house'.[54] The four 'laws' of 22:9–12 again seem to bear little relation to their context. The first three seem to belong together, although it is hard to pin down the connection.

The unusual requirement that any crops sown together must be forfeited to the sanctuary implies that dabbling in unnatural practice results not in some taboo penalty falling on the transgressor but in the interruption of enjoyment of Yahweh's land (in this case by loss of the crops). The crops were not tainted in any way by the behaviour of the farmer, which suggests that the practice was outlawed simply because it was associated with the Canaanites. Verse 10 seems fairly straightforward, despite Carmichael's implausible attempt to read

---

[53] Steuernagel 1900: 81; W. H. Ph. Römer 1974: 217–219; Braulik 1992: 161.
[54] See Ex. 21:29ff.; 22:5ff. Rofé suggests that verses 6–7 and 8 are linked because birds lay eggs on roofs (1988: 274)!

a prohibition of sexual relations between an Israelite (the 'ox') and a Canaanite (the 'ass') into the text (1982: 394–395), but the background of both verse 10 and verse 11 is not easily traced. Houtman's efforts to read these things as breaches of the 'natural order' is not entirely convincing (1984: 226–228). So the origins of these sayings remains obscure. But that may not be terribly important. The fact that three such striking sayings have been placed together may possibly mean that their main role is structural, and that they act as a marker at the end of the section on justice. The aim of justice is to preserve Israel's unique relationship with God. She is not to plant, plough or dress in a way that compromises this distinctiveness.

This, of course, is highly speculative, but it finds some support in 22:12. The lack of explanation of this action suggests that this is an appeal to a well-known practice. If Deuteronomy is drawing on Numbers 15:37–41, then this saying calls Israel once more to obedience and holiness in the face of the 'Canaanite threat'. Perhaps 22:9–11 should be understood in the same way.

It is increasingly difficult to perceive any controlling factor in the content or arrangement of the laws, even though there is still substantial evidence of a theological mind at work and many common Deuteronomic themes re-emerge. In particular, the section lays down parameters for dealing with death in a way which does not disrupt Israel's relationship with Yahweh: preventing unnecessary vengeance and unsafe convictions; acting only with Yahweh's sanction in war; acting carefully in regard to unsolved murders, and even dealing with extreme family conflict.

It is impossible to make every part of the text fit some neat scheme, but the Deuteronomist's primary theological insight is unmistakable: he shows that murder interrupts relationship with Yahweh by the most serious infringement of the rights of others, which is surely in the spirit of the sixth commandment.

22:13 – 23:19

The next group of laws deals with aspects of sexual ethics, and has not surprisingly been linked to the seventh commandment. It is hard to detect any logic in the development of this passage, which deals largely with extreme cases.

Dealing with sexual misconduct (22:13–30)
Verses 13–21 address the case of a husband who accuses his wife of previous fornication. The legislation aims first to provide wives with

protection from unscrupulous husbands and then (verses 20–21) to deal with the wife if such allegations are proven true.[55]

It is difficult to unravel the workings of this law. Wenham has argued that the test seeks proof of pregnancy before marriage rather than of virginity (1972), and this may be so. In any case, if the girl is found guilty, she is to be put to death in order to preserve Israel's purity. If she is innocent, her husband is forbidden to divorce her and must pay a fine to her father.[56] Locher's excellent study shows that the Deutero-nomist has modified common legal ideas to emphasize the importance of the woman's honour, which set Israel apart from all other nations.[57]

For the same reason (verse 22), the same punishment is meted out to individuals involved in a 'simple' case of adultery. Verses 23–27 deal with fornication in the 'case of a virgin/young woman pledged to be married'. Regardless of circumstances, the man is to be put to death, whereas it is assumed the woman was raped, unless the act occurred within earshot of others. Verses 28–29 describe a different situation, where an unbetrothed virgin/young woman is involved. Here the con-cern is to protect the honour and welfare of the violated woman, rather than with 'purging the evil from Israel'. No death penalty is prescribed.

The section 22:13–29 displays many signs of being a unified whole (Wenham & McConville 1980: 248). Each case has a definition of the rights of the woman, the circumstances of the offence, the evidence needed, the appropriate punishment and a comment revealing the purpose. The unit falls neatly into halves dealing with married women (verses 13–22) and unmarried girls (verses 23–28). The case of flagrant adultery in verse 22 stands at the centre of this structure for emphasis. The solitary reference to incestuous relationships in verse 30 is strange. Either it is a primitive statement of consanguinity or it stands as representative of a much wider body of prohibitions.

Purity in Israel: the assembly and the camp (23:1–19)
Verses 1–8 make the transition from improper sexual relationships to their effect on relationship with Yahweh. At face value, exclusion of the emasculated from the assembly seems to add insult to injury. It is

---

[55] This is thought to be unique in the ANE; Phillips claims that it makes women criminally responsible for the first time (1981: 13–14).

[56] This is a double restitution of the fee set in 22:29. In effect, the father was being accused of the theft of the bride price (see Ex. 22:16). The scenario is not a legal case of husband *v.* wife. Presumably the wife's wilful act of marrying while pregnant warrants death. This does not then contradict 22:29.

[57] Locher 1986: 382–386. Stulman, however, argues that this is not humanitarian as such, but mirrors the demise of the power of the *paterfamilias* (1992: 61–62).

likely, however, that it is a reference to eunuchs or others involved in self-mutilation associated with Canaanite cults (Buis & Leclerq 1963: 154–155). The context also suggests that the legislation on the non-admission of bastards (*mamzēr*) to the assembly addresses those born of 'mixed' marriages rather than those born outside marriage in Israel. The lenient treatment meted out in 22:28–29 supports this, as does the following denunciation of Moabites and Ammonites. I will return to the issue of the admission of foreigners to the assembly in the next chapter.

Matters of war and asylum (23:9–16)

Verses 9–14 abandon sexual ethics to deal with appropriate behaviour in an assembly of war, and, in particular, improper toiletry habits. Verse 14 is the key to the section; Yahweh's presence demands holiness (here ritual cleanness). More than ethnic purity (verses 2–8) is required to maintain a right relationship with Yahweh. This is a rare allusion to matters of cleanness in Deuteronomy.

The runaway in 23:15–16 is a foreign slave crossing Israel's borders in search of safety. In stark contrast to contemporary legislation, asylum is to be granted (*e.g.* the Code of Hammurabi 15–20, *ANET* 166). It is hard to see a connection with the preceding verses.[58]

Sexual ethics (23:17–19)

The conclusion of this 'section' returns to the subject of sexual conduct. Prohibition of any form of prostitution, either 'common' or 'temple', neatly unites the physical and spiritual dimensions of sexual misbehaviour. Despite the presence of elements with no obvious relationship to sexuality, the central idea of this section is that justice and righteousness in personal relationships are fundamental to maintaining relationship with Yahweh.

The drift towards a more chaotic 'arrangement' is obvious, but a clear theme persists in these laws. Although there is less evidence of Deuteronomic 'preaching' than in earlier sections of the text (but see *e.g.* 23:4–5), the importance of acting in accordance with *mišpaṭ-ṣedeq* still comes across powerfully.

23:20 – 24:9

Regulating loans (23:20–26)

The initial statement is typically Deuteronomic: exacting interest on a loan from a brother Israelite violates the covenantal ideal of one people

---

[58] For Kaufman, 23:2–28 applies the prohibition of adultery to state affairs and the cult (1978–79: 186–190). This is hard to sustain at every point.

in one land worshipping one God, and will inevitably affect the relationship of God and his people.[59] Any reluctance to honour promises made to God (perhaps in haste or unwisely) has the same effect (23:22–24). This is equated with stealing from God. This would only become a problem in the wake of extravagant claims or gestures, which have no place in the down-to-earth world of the Deuteronomist.

The belief that the Israelite is ultimately a tenant on Yahweh's land comes to the fore in verses 25–26. All property rights belong ultimately to God, so any member of his people has the right to enjoy the produce of his land at any time and in any place. This Deuteronomic enjoyment is restricted, however, to prevent any attempt to deprive a brother of his rightful subsistence (verse 26).

Remarriage (24:1–4)

The prohibition of the remarriage of a twice-divorced wife to her first husband at the beginning of chapter 24 seems out of place here (although the theme of infringement of rights may provide the link with chapter 23). It is difficult to imagine the circumstances in which this law would be useful, and it surely cannot have been a regular occurrence.[60] So it may be that the Deuteronomist is trying to illustrate a wider principle: for instance, that relinquished rights cannot be reassumed in this way as that would amount to trying to undo a 'moral' act. It may simply be that this remarriage would have imperilled the position of the wife within both the family and the community. Jeremiah, in the only biblical parallel, is in no doubt that this is not a good thing to do (3:1). The motive clause here equates such behaviour with the ways of the nations (tô'ēḇâ). This would 'bring sin upon the land', breaking off relationship with Yahweh as before.

Miscellaneous laws: injustice and leprosy (24:5–9)

Verses 5–7 deals with depriving a fellow Israelite of his rights. Forcing a newly wed warrior into military service would, in effect, deprive him of the enjoyment of the new relationship which God has given him (see on 20:5). Removing a millstone in pledge would be robbing a brother of the means to support himself. This undermines both his dignity and his ability to enjoy the provision of Yahweh. The series reaches its climax

---

[59] See also Ex. 22:25; Lv. 25:35–37. Deuteronomy departs from contemporary practice: Fishbane 1985: 174–175; Neufeldt 1955: 355; Maloney 1974: 1–2.

[60] Thompson 1974: 244 and Yaron 1966: 1–2 read the law as preventing the first husband attempting to 'steal' his ex-wife, although this does not account well for the reference to the second husband's death. Wenham takes it as prohibiting incest (1979: 36). This is a little contrived.

in a strong denunciation of depriving a brother of freedom. This is a reversal of the exodus at a personal level and must be dealt with severely. This evil must be purged from Israel. In each case, the crime is construed in terms of depriving any brother Israelite of his rights. These rights are not defined in abstract, universal terms, but are the direct result of the action of Yahweh in establishing his special people in the land in relationship with him. Any infringement of these rights is a crime against the covenant.

The reference to the treatment of skin disorders, with its appeal to the historical experience of Miriam, is unexpected. It appears to have nothing in common with the surrounding material. Despite this, it is typically Deuteronomic in its historical allusion and reference to the Levitical priests. On closer examination of the text, we may be able to shed some light on the problem.

Miriam disobeyed Yahweh by refusing to submit to Moses (Nu. 12:14), and was punished by the infliction of a skin disease of some kind. Now she is presented as a paradigm of rebellion to Israel. The people must obey carefully in the matter of skin diseases, to ensure (by implication) that they are able to enjoy not only cleansing but all the delights of the land. The thinking of the passage runs as follows:

Miriam (enjoyment) → disobedience → 'leprosy'
Israel 'leprosy' → obedience → enjoyment

As in 22:12, the Deuteronomist uses an ancient tradition to underline the necessity of obedience.

With the possible exception of 24:1–4, the passage 23:20 – 24:9 is a cluster of stipulations on the theme of rights, concluded by the typically Deuteronomic reference to Miriam as a goad to obedience. It could possibly be seen as an exposition on theft. The most striking feature of this short section, however, is the variety of cases covered. There seems to be an increasing tendency in the laws to deal with the exception rather than the common case. Much that would seem of relevance to us is passed over (*e.g.* the single prohibition of incest in 22:30). It seems that a basic working system of justice and morality is assumed and that peripheral material is chosen to illustrate specific points.

24:10 – 25:4

Protection of the disadvantaged (24:10 – 25:4)

Kaufman has helpfully pointed out a broad progression here: brother–hireling–the poor–criminal–animal. These laws appear to have been reworked by the Deuteronomist to promote fair treatment for all in Israel.

The instructions on the management of loans to a brother aim, above all, to preserve his dignity (verse 11). In every case, he should be allowed to make restitution freely without coercion or violation of his sphere of authority, his home (*cf.* Ex. 22:26–27). If the brother is poor, care must be taken not to remove his means of keeping warm. At all times, Israelites should treat one another in a way which gives good reason to say, 'Righteousness be reckoned to you before Yahweh' (verse 13). This blessing shows that acting with righteousness is a condition of right relationships within the people of God, and consequently for a right relationship with God.

In 24:14–15, this is made explicit. Treating a down-at-heel brother or a resident alien badly by withholding his wages (putting self-sufficiency beyond his reach) is a violation of his God-given position, and jeopardizes the intimacy between God and his people. This prompts the emphatic assertion of individual responsibility in verse 16, which amounts to yet another appeal for justice and righteousness in Israel.[61]

The passage moves on to defend the disadvantaged – the orphan, widow and refugee. These people are not to be deprived of the basic necessities of life by grasping loan-sharks but, like the Levites, must be treated in the light of Israel's experience in Egypt (24:18, 22). Care for those with no hope of self-sufficiency even extends to deliberately maintaining inefficient harvesting techniques. The right of the landless and unwaged to enjoy the fruit of the land and gain subsistence from it must be guarded at all costs, for all Israel is redeemed to enjoy relationship with Yahweh in his land.

The passage 25:1–3 is the climax of the series. Even the dignity of a convicted criminal is to be preserved, for he remains one of the people of Yahweh (verse 3). Degrading a brother is a sin against Yahweh which cannot be tolerated. Verse 4 then continues the progression through the strata of society to animals. As in 24:8–9, it seems that the Deuteronomist may have inserted a short saying, which seems at odds with those on either side, to remind Israel of her responsibilities. This general appeal to act justly in the case of working an ox, may imply *a minore ad maius* the importance of Israel's acting with righteousness in all her relationships.

In 24:10 – 25:4, then, we see a carefully crafted section of the laws which display the acute theological awareness of chapters 1 – 11 and 12 – 18. Whether this section can legitmately be read as an exposition of

---

[61] See C. J. H. Wright 1990: 235; Driver 1901: 277–278. These are judicial rather than natural consequences, as in *e.g.* Ezk. 18. Wenham shows substitutionary punishment in Hammurabi's Code (1985: 39).

the ninth commandment remains a moot point. The exodus is again held up beside the enjoyment of Yahweh's land as the crucial category in Israelite decision-making. All false dealings are an affront to the purposes of God. Yahweh did not redeem his people from degradation in Egypt to see them degrade one another in the land.

25:5–19

The conclusion of the collection of laws contains unexpected and awkward material.

The Levirate (25:5–10)

First comes the case of a widow's brother-in-law who refuses to provide an heir for his deceased brother.[62] The main point is the prohibition of setting one's own desires above responsibilities to the immediate family and the community. The ritual vindicates the widow and results in the public humiliation of the man (Hoffner 1969: 48–51).

A violent woman (25:11–12)

In 25:11–12, a situation is envisaged where a woman's actions either disgrace a man or rob him of the ability to procreate (Eslinger 1981: 269). In the wake of the bold assertion of widows' rights in verses 5–10, I would tentatively suggest that verses 11–12 warn women against being carried away by the egalitarianism of earlier laws. This appears to be a comical situation, until the sole Old Testament prescription of punitive mutilation heightens the seriousness of such an action. This may be rather black humour, but the Deuteronomist's determination to legislate for the most bizarre circumstances is ultimately mystifying. The best one can do is to guess that it is supposed in some way to be the mirror image of verses 5–10.

Honesty in business and the Amalekites (25:13–19)

Verses 13–16 are more straightforward. Cheating a brother of his wealth for personal benefit is completely unacceptable within the nation of Israel. A connection with covetousness is not hard to discern here. The justification of these restrictions is cast in familiar terms: observance is presented as crucial to enjoyment of long life in the land and such behaviour denounced as tô'ēḇâ (Carmichael 1967: 198).

The short injunction based on Israel's encounter with the Amalekites returns to the themes of exodus and conquest, and eases the transition to

---

[62] On Levirate marriage in Deuteronomy, see E. W. Davies 1981; C. J. H. Wright 1990: 54–55.

chapter 26, the conclusion of the laws. The crime of the Amalekites was that of maltreating others to satiate their own desires, which is the antithesis of the *mišpaṭ-ṣedeq* which must define the life of Israel. The command to 'blot out Amalek from under heaven' urges Israel to disavow any such behaviour.

The Deuteronomist has gathered legislation concerning feuds involving wives with a short series demanding integrity in business. These are given a theological gloss and concluded by the Amalekite incident. While some of the details remain obscure, the Deuteronomist's insistence is very clear: Israel must live in obedience to Yahweh in a way which guarantees that the whole of society can enjoy relationship with him.

Chapter 26: the conclusion of the collection

Chapter 26 stands outside the basic structure of the law code. It is a carefully crafted conclusion to the laws, which has been shaped by the Deuteronomist to emphasize the theological concerns evident throughout chapters 12 – 25.

The first eleven verses provide a paradigmatic response not only to the grace of Yahweh, but to the revelation of laws which has preceded them. In 26:1, we return to focus on the first few days of occupation, and the necessity of acknowledging that the land is the gift of Yahweh from the very beginning.

Here, for the first time, we see legislation concerning 'firstfruits'. This has been withheld until now because it speaks so eloquently of Yahweh's ownership of the land, his redemption of Israel to live in it, and the need for Israel to live in response to his grace.[63]

Verses 1–2 combine entry to the land and the journey to the place of Yahweh's choice in a way reminiscent of chapter 12. At this place of places, Israel is to make her response to God. The basic affirmation to be made by the worshipper (verse 3) is that the land is the gift of Yahweh. (The priest is mentioned, but is basically irrelevant to the theological function of the chapter.) The longer credal statement running from verse 5b to verse 10a concentrates on the starting-point

---

[63] 'As Yahweh gives the land to Israel, so Israel gives back to him in response. Chapter 26 seems to have the function of returning to this theme, and bringing the legal corpus to a climax in doing so ... It is significant that the author of Deuteronomy chooses to achieve this climax and summation through a return to laws about cultic offerings, which have been absent from the legislation since ch. 16. This reflects, no doubt, the importance of the sacrificial worship of Israel, in the eyes of the author, as a vehicle for the expression of obedience to Yahweh' (McConville 1984: 120).

and destination of the journey of Israel.[64] The transition from landless rabble to landed nation is, in one sense, complete.

The absence of any reference to Horeb is confusing if one tries to see some covenantal ceremony here. I have argued, however, that chapters 12 – 26 are presented as updating the revelation at Horeb for life in Canaan. It is hardly surprising that the conclusion does not return to draw attention to the events at Horeb explicitly. Chapter 26 is concerned with the broad picture of the exodus and the transition from Egypt to Canaan. There is no need for details of the intermediate steps; Israel now has a new land and a 'new' law.

The characteristic reference to enjoyment of worship at the sanctuary in verse 11 supports the case for seeing these verses as a theological conclusion to the laws. The initial response to the grace of God concludes with a picture of the whole nation enjoying his provision of redemption. The produce of his land is eaten in his presence at the place which he has chosen.

Verses 1–11 enshrine the essence of the theology displayed not just in the laws but the whole book: Israel is to respond to God's grace in the way which he commands at the heart of the land which he has given. 'Firstfruits', then, is a token of the obedience to the laws and statutes demanded by the rest of the book.

In verses 12–15, the theme of obedience is picked up again, as a tithe ritual is appended to that of firstfruits. This is a Deuteronomic device to summarize the heart of the concerns expressed through the preaching of the law. The triennial confession in verses 13–15 assumes 14:22–29. The opening phrase of verse 13 is effectively a declaration that the laws have been faithfully observed – that all wickedness has been purged from the community, enabling intimacy with Yahweh to be enjoyed. The second half of the verse declares that the criterion of generosity to the landless has been fulfilled. The influence of Canaan has been resisted (verse 14a). In short, the law has been fulfilled (verse 14b), and the way is open to the unfolding fulfilment of the covenantal promises.

Verses 16–19 draw the law code to a close in a way that is strongly reminiscent of chapters 1 – 11. The repeated injunctions to obey, linked to the reassertion of the special status of Israel conferred by Yahweh's election, bring chapters 12 – 26 to a buoyant climax. These final verses, and chapter 26 as a whole, return to themes which have dominated the Mosaic preaching of the laws.

In many ways, 'law code' is a wholly inadequate designation for the

---

[64] There has been much discussion of the origins and significance of this unit (see Lohfink 1971b; 1971c).

phenomenon which we have observed in Deuteronomy 12 – 26. This is not a list of legal sentences. It is law pressed into the service of theological preaching. This is what makes this collection of laws so different from any other.

Conclusion: theology and ethics in the Deuteronomic laws

There can be no question that the Deuteronomic laws are profoundly theological. Chapters 12 – 26 are extremely complex, and in the course of our exegesis we came across many problems which we were not able to resolve satisfactorily. While we detected order in places, even order which corresponded very closely to that of the Decalogue, there were other parts of the collection where we could detect no rationale whatsoever behind the arrangement. (The Decalogue order suggested by Kaufman and others is ultimately not flexible enough to accommodate all the complications.) At some points, the hand of the Deuteronomist is very obvious, and the theological agenda extremely clear, in his carefully worked presentation. At others, there are only nuggets of theology in what appears to be a jumble of unlikely case law. But, having said all this, there is a huge weight of evidence to support the fact that these laws serve the message of the book as a whole, and share the same outlook as the framework.

I would suggest that chapters 12 – 26 are exactly what the framework suggests they are – a new application of the revelation at Horeb (the Decalogue and the Book of the Covenant) for the new situation which Israel is about to face in Canaan. The laws present Israel with the opportunity to keep moving forward in obedience with God, even after they have settled in the land.

In these laws, we see how Deuteronomic theology shapes the ethics of God's people. The ethical demands of these chapters result from the application of the Deuteronomic theology of worship, of the land and of human relationships to Israel's new existence.

The Deuteronomic theology of worship

The laws consistently declare that the primary responsibility of Israel in Canaan is to worship Yahweh, and to worship him at the place and in the way which he chooses. This worship is regulated by divine revelation; the choice of place and the manner of worship are both matters of God's sovereignty. Israel must constantly listen to the divine word, and allow that to define their worship. And then Israel must keep on the move, regularly going to the place chosen by God to enjoy his presence. Conversely, Israel must repudiate the ways of Canaan. As God's chosen people, her whole life must reflect the distinctiveness which God requires. This is the only way to live obediently in the land.

The Deuteronomic theology of the land

In Deuteronomy, one cannot speak about worship without speaking about land, for the land is pre-eminently the place where God is encountered. Yahweh brings Israel out of Egypt and gives her the land so that she may enjoy its bounty, but ultimately so that his people may enjoy his company. This is why the nation is called to the place of Yahweh's choice: so that there, at the heart of the land, they can enjoy the presence of the Lord. Enjoyment of the milk and honey of Canaan, won in the dark night of the Passover, is intimately linked to enjoyment of relationship with Yahweh himself. It is vital, then, that nothing is done to defile this land, because that must inevitably affect the relationship with its owner. This, in turn, leads to the third theological distinctive.

The Deuteronomic theology of human relationships

It is not only defilement of the land which interrupts Israel's relationship with God, but a breakdown of relationships among the people themselves. They stand as one people before one God in one land. They must do everything in their power to maintain justice and right relationships, and to guard equality and equity, so that the relationship for which they have been set apart can be enjoyed in all its fullness.

These three simple distinctives are all, in their own way, direct theological consequences of the exodus event itself. The nation has been redeemed, and now belongs to God. As his unique people, they must submit to him in worship. He has redeemed them from Egypt to enjoy a relationship with him, and to do so in his land. In the light of his redemption, they cannot treat one another in a way which is incompatible with the way he has treated them. Now that they have become an exodus people, a people of journey, they are destined to keep moving forward with Yahweh, their redeemer God.

In the exodus, Israel experiences God's redemption. At Horeb, God explains that experience and begins to unfold what it means to be his people. At Moab, Moses, God's spokesman, applies the theology of the exodus and the laws of Horeb to the new life facing Israel in Canaan. Now Israel must respond to the ethical demands which these laws place upon them.

Chapter Four

Ethics and the nations

We have seen that the laws of Deuteronomy are shaped by a theological agenda, which is clear both in the chapters either side of the collection, which provide its context, and in the presentation of the laws themselves. The ethics of the book are forged as this Deuteronomic theology is applied to life in the land.

For the most part, Deuteronomy is evidently a highly 'moral' book by our standards today. Its fundamental concern for right relationships among God's people, including a concern for the disadvantaged and protection of women's rights, even spills over into asylum laws more liberal than those of its neighbours. There is still one aspect of the teaching of the book, however, which causes enormous problems for many people today. How can a book claim to be ethical in the light of its teaching on the way Israel must deal with the Canaanites?

The question of what to do with the Canaanites, as we have already seen, is an important one in the whole theology of Deuteronomy, impinging as it does on the worship of Yahweh, the occupation of the land and even right relationships in Israel. We must not make the mistake, however, of isolating the teaching on the inhabitants of Canaan from the rest of the book's teaching on Israel's foreign policy.

It is true that Deuteronomy is usually caricatured as displaying a rather bloodthirsty nationalism, largely because of its teaching on warfare in chapters 7 and 20. But before we even begin to discuss the details of the Deuteronomic view of either the election of Israel or war, we must set this whole issue in the context of the book's preaching.

The nations in the preaching of Deuteronomy

There has been only one rounded study of the nations in Deuteronomy – Otto Bächli's *Israel und die Völker* – but even this only hints at the subtle role which they play in the whole Deuteronomic presentation (1962: 11, 30).

Basically the preaching of Moses refers to the nations only where they impinge on the experience and interests of Israel (Bächli 1962: 36–43).

147

Apart from the stereotyped list of the tribes to be expelled from Canaan (*e.g.* 7:1) and the use of encounters with specific nations in Transjordan as illustrations, there is no interest in what goes on outside the confines of God's people. The rest of the world is simply designated as *'ammîm* and *gôyîm* (peoples). Both the occupants of the land and Israel's neighbours are referred to in this vague way. Deuteronomy is not interested in the nations for their own sake; it is preoccupied with the story of Israel. This is summed up in Lemche's comment on the role of the Canaanites in the historical books of the Old Testament:

> The understanding of Canaan and Canaanites is stereotypical and inflexible, and makes it clear that the Canaanites and their land had no independent history of their own; they were only included in the historical narratives in order to further the intentions of the narrators. The biblical Canaanites thus had no historical role to play and the Old Testament cannot be used as information about the *historical* Canaanites, because the Canaanites of the Old Testament are not historical persons, but actors in a 'play' in which the Israelites have got the better, or the hero's part (1991: 152).

The Deuteronomist is equally unconcerned to give an accurate description of the lifestyle and behaviour of the nations inhabiting Canaan prior to the conquest. It is simply not the point of the Mosaic preaching. So the sweeping condemnation of the practices of these tribes in 12:31–32 is not so much a treatise on Canaanite religion (*i. e.* that every 'Canaanite' could be spotted by their readiness to sacrifice children), but a demand that Israel avoid being contaminated by the ways of Canaan, which are repugnant to God.

Moses, however, is concerned to define the distinctiveness of Israel not simply against a Canaanite background, but against that of all the nations; so he uses the terms *'ammîm* and *gôyîm* to reflect the basic dichotomy between Israel and 'the world'. Both terms are used indiscriminately to describe the nations to be expelled by Yahweh from Canaan.[1] Together, they are used to denote the whole world, and appear to be synonymous (*e.g.* 4:27; 28:64–65; 30:1–3; 32:8). But where *'ammîm* and *gôyîm* appear separately, a crucial distinction emerges.[2]

---

[1] *'ammîm*: 7:16, 19; 20:16; 33:17. *gôyîm*: 4:38; 7:1, 17, 22; 8:20; 9:1, 4, 5; 11:23; 12:2, 29; 19:1; 20:15.

[2] Labuschagne points out a tension between the 'peoples everywhere under heaven'(4:19) who are to be allowed space and those in the land who are to be denied it (1987: 242, 265). Also Deurloo 1994: 36.

When *gôyîm* is used to refer to nations in general outside Canaan, it always carries negative connotations. The *gôyîm* are presented as a threat and a potential danger, embodying the possibility of ensnarement of God's people.[3] Thus there are nations outside the land which will be the enemies of Israel, and which will pose essentially the same threat as those currently in it. When national supremacy is promised to Israel, it is over the *gôyîm* rather than the *'ammîm* (15:6; 26:19; 28:12).

In marked contrast, the predominant use of *'ammîm* is in a neutral, and even in places a positive, sense. The nations here are not a threat to the survival of God's people, but instead look on in amazement at Yahweh's love for Israel. They are the audience before whom the drama of election and redemption is played out, and as such, may even become the recipients of some derivative blessing themselves.

It is in the journey through Transjordan in 2:25 that we first become aware that the world is watching Israel on her journey with God. But when the fear of the *'ammîm* turns to envious amazement, and even confession, in 4:5–8, we too must begin to take notice.[4] I have argued that chapter 4 introduces the decision which Israel must make to obey the 'laws and statutes' (4:5, 8) as further defined by Moses in chapters 5 – 11 and then the laws of chapters 12 – 26. In these verses, even the voices of the nations are added to encourage Israel to live Yahweh's way in the world. These important verses show that like it or not, the life of God's people is 'an open book to the world' (C. J. H. Wright, 1996: 47). Israel's decisions all take place before the nations. Egypt, in particular, plays this role in 9:26–28, where she is depicted as looking on in anticipation that the 'exodus project' will eventually flounder because of the disobedience in Israel.

Deuteronomy repeatedly stresses that Israel is chosen from among all the *'ammîm* (see 7:6–7; 10:15; 14:2), who therefore provide the backdrop against which her privileges are expressed:

> All of the addresses and laws in Deuteronomy are issued to an Israel which is constantly conscious of its enemies; this steadfast gaze at the enemies, at 'the nations' over against which Israel must and will affirm its claims, is the most dominant characteristic of Deuteronomy (Martin-Achard 1960: 335–336).

In 7:6, two epithets in particular are attached to Israel as a result of the

---

[3] 29:15, 17; also 12:30; 17:14; 18:9, 14. In 29:23 they witness the resulting humiliation.

[4] The use of *gôyîm* by the nations themselves is to be expected, and is mirrored in the Israelite continuation of verses 7–8. It has little bearing on our discussion.

electing love of God – Israel is now the *sᵉḡullâ* of Yahweh, and is called to be an *'am qāḏôš*.

sᵉḡullâ (treasured possession) occurs three times in Deuteronomy (7:6; 14:2; 26:18) and once in Exodus (19:6). It was used in the world of ANE vassal treaties to denote 'most favoured nation' status.[5] Israel is invested with royal honour and significance, not in her own right, but through association with the great king, Yahweh himself. The *'ammîm* are the natural audience for Israel's preferment. Israel as the *sᵉḡullâ* may even be a kind of 'show-house' for the nations, as the place where God is present in the world.[6] If this is in mind, then Israel will be expected to behave in a way appropriate not only for a favoured vassal, but for the king himself. The phrase *'am qāḏôš* (holy people; used with *sᵉḡullâ* in both 7:6 and 14:2) emphasizes separation, rather than privilege or example, and so is less concerned with the nations looking on.[7]

As the book draws to a close, the idea of the nation as an audience to the course of Israel's relationship with God becomes more prominent. Three times in chapter 28 (verses 9–10, 25, 37) the *'ammîm* are depicted as interested onlookers.[8] Concern for the reputation of Yahweh and a sense of affronted national pride should motivate the people to obey. Overt concern for the nations themselves, however, is conspicuous only by its absence.

The idea of the nations acting as an audience for Israel is not unique. The same concept occurs in Exodus 34:10 (although here the audience is described as the *gôyîm*, and *'am* is reserved for the people of Israel; see also Dt. 32:43), which may have provided the inspiration for Deuteronomy. In Ezekiel, the concept of the nations as the audience of Israel's decision is developed further, using similar ideas but different vocabulary. The main development in Ezekiel is Yahweh's explicit concern that the nations may know that he is the Lord, which is, at most, incipient in Deuteronomy.[9]

---

[5] Weinfeld cites a cognate *sglt* in a letter from the Hittite emperor to the last king of Ugarit, Ammurapi to denote an especially favoured vassal (1991: 368). Also Lohfink 1969: 545; Greenberg 1951. In later biblical passages it is used of private treasure belonging to kings (1Ch. 29:3; Ec. 2:8).

[6] This has some contact with *e.g.* the Zion theology of some of the Royal Psalms. Durham argues: 'They are to be a people set apart, different from all other people by what they are and what they are becoming – a display people, a show-case to the world of how being in covenant with Yahweh changes a people' (1987: 263).

[7] The phrase occurs alone in 14:21 and 28:9. The latter has similar connotations of royal honour and respect paid by the surrounding nations.

[8] For parallels to 28:37 see Je. 18:16; 19:8; 24:9; 25:9, 18; 1 Ki. 9:7; 2 Ch. 7:20. Also Dt. 29:21–23.

[9] See Ezk. 5:5, 14; 16:14, 37; 20:9, 14, 22, 41–42; 22:4–5, 16; 28:25; 36:20–3, 34–38;

It would not be strictly true, however, to say that the nations in Deuteronomy are treated as an inanimate object, permanently 'beyond the pale', merely uninvolved observers of all that happens within Yahweh's land. We are given glimpses of the fact that while Yahweh's concern is primarily for Israel, it does not stop there.

The nations and the Deuteronomic theology of blessing

On two occasions, Deuteronomy refers to Yahweh's involvement with the nations in their own right. While the assignment (*hlq*) of the astral bodies to be worshipped (in error) by the *'ammîm* may not be a blessing in 4:19 (also 29:25), the apportionment (*hlq*) of land in 32:8–9 most certainly is.[10] This verb is normally used in Deuteronomy to refer to Yahweh's special dealings with the Levites (10:9; 12:12; 14:27, 29; 18:1, 8), and here it shows that, despite the deficiency in the 'portion' which they have received, Yahweh's interest in the nations cannot be denied. This becomes clearer when we see the positive effect the proximity of Israel appears to have upon specific nations in chapters 2 and 23.

The treatment of Edom, Moab and Ammon in the narrative of the conquest of Transjordan in chapter 2 is remarkable in two respects. The first is the explicit designation of the inhabitants of Seir, the descendants of Esau, as the brother(s) of Israel in 2:4, 8. In a book which makes such a play of the 'brotherhood' of Israel, this is striking enough, but the accompanying assertion that Yahweh has given *these* nations their lands (verses 5, 9, 19) in a way comparable to his gift of the land to Israel (verse 12) is nothing short of astonishing.[11] In each case, Yahweh insists that the land rights of these nations should be respected because of their genealogical relationship to Israel: the occupants of the hill country of Seir are the descendants of Esau; Moabites and Ammonites can claim descent from Lot. In the editorial parentheses (verse 10–12 and 20–23), the point is rammed home by

---

37:28; 38:23; 39:7, 13, 21–23, 27–29. See also Blauw: 'The nations are witnesses of Yahweh's deeds in Israel. This is their most prominent function' (1962: 26). He cites Pss. 22:28; 24:1; 33:8; 47:8; 48:10; 66:7; 67; 87; 93 – 100; 117.

[10] Zebulun's blessing (33:19) may also imply a mediation of blessing to the nations, as the prosperity of the seafaring merchants of Zebulun issues in the invitation of 'peoples' to share in some kind of sacrificial feast; but it is difficult to assert this with any confidence.

[11] *y*ᵉ*rušâ* (possession) is used in 2:5, 9, 12, 19 of land allocated to the nations. It is only once (3:20) used of Israelite land, and there of the Transjordan.

explicit assertions that Yahweh has actually intervened on behalf of these nations in the recent past (especially 2:21). While this is clearly intended to be a heavily ironic criticism of Israel's own timidity, that does not take away the startling implications. These nations have experienced blessing through their relationship to Israel. This is not political expediency, but the consequence of the place of these nations in the Deuteronomic theology of blessing.[12]

Further evidence of this emerges from an unexpected source: the regulations in chapter 23 regarding admission of foreigners (the products of mixed marriages with Edomites, Moabites, Ammonites and Egyptians, rather than 'converts') to the assembly. The ease (or lack of it) with which each group may enter the covenant community depends solely on how its nation has treated Israel in the past. The Ammonites, despite the absence of Israelite provocation (2:19–20), are said to have opposed Israel on the way, and are permanently excluded. Similarly, the Moabites' exclusion is the result of the 'Balaam affair' of Numbers 22 – 24 (see Gn. 19:36–37). That much is clear, as is the fact that the relationship of any nation with Yahweh is somehow dependent on that nation's relationship with Israel.

It is the rules for the Edomites and the Egyptians, however, which are most enlightening. The first problem is that according to the narrative of Numbers 20:14–21, alluded to in 2:6–8, the Edomites refused to aid the Israelites.[13] On these grounds, one would expect the Edomites to be excluded permanently from the assembly in the same way as the Moabites and Ammonites. But there is another factor at work here, which we have already seen in chapter 2. Edom is described as the 'brother' of Israel in 23:7 (2:4). This close 'family relationship' with Israel is enough to maintain a *relatively* privileged position, despite their behaviour prior to the conquest. The slightly more lenient treatment of Edom (although exclusion for three generations is hardly a liberal measure), in contrast to the effective exclusion of Ammon and Moab, the descendants of Lot, has the effect of demonstrating that lineal proximity to Israel is a blessing.

The situation is confused a little by the status accorded to the Egyptians in 23:7–8. Egypt, of course, has nothing to do with Israel, but incredibly, they are elevated above the descendants of Lot because they 'entertained' Israel in their country (presumably this is alluding to the

---

[12] It is hard to see how this could ever be reconciled with an attempt to develop (or reappropriate) a sacral view of Israel's wars.

[13] The emphasis on divine permission to buy food and water in 2:6 does not contradict Nu. 20:19. This may suggest a closer relationship with Edom in chapter 2 than with the other nations.

days of Jacob and Joseph, rather than more recent experience). Now that Israel has been freed, she should not forget what it means to be an alien (10:18–19), and should make a reciprocal gesture to the descendants of the Egyptians, albeit a small one. The benefit accruing to the Egyptians, however, because Israel now knows what it is to be an alien, does exceed that accruing to distant relatives who refused to entertain Israel on their way to the land.

The exodus experience controls the treatment of all foreigners who assimilate to the community of Israel. Christiana van Houten has dealt with the role of the alien in Deuteronomy at some length (1991: 68–108), and shows that, remarkably, the *gērîm* function in essentially the same way as the Levites, providing an index to the obedience of Israel (along with the widows and orphans). Both the framework and the laws demand justice for the alien (1:16; 24:14, 17, 19, 21; 27:19) and the right to enjoy the produce of God's land (14:29; 16:11, 14; 26:11, 12, 13). While 14:21 makes it clear that some differences are still maintained, the participation of the alien in the events of 29:11 and 31:12 make Deuteronomy's essentially positive view of the alien very clear. (See also the 'brother Hebrew' in chapter 15.)

It is clear, then, that whatever its teaching on warfare in Canaan, Deuteronomy's attitude to the nations is not quite so clear cut as is often assumed. It is fair to say that, to some small degree at least, blessing may fall upon those nations who cross Israel's path, if they respond wisely to Yahweh's people.

There is, however, one further question which we must mention. The whole of the book of Deuteronomy is conceived as unfolding the next stage in the ongoing fulfilment of the promises made to the Patriarchs. We have seen in our discussion of the covenant that the Genesis material envisaged an international dimension in the fulfilment of promise, which is also anticipated in Exodus 19:5–6. Is there any evidence that Deuteronomy expects any such worldwide blessing to unfold?

It is extremely interesting that Deuteronomy 7:7 and other verses share the designation *sᵉgullâ* with Exodus 19:5–6. Where Deuteronomy speaks of an *'am qāḏôš*, however, Exodus has *gôy qāḏôš*, and adds the phrase *mamleḵeṯ kōhᵃnîm* (kingdom of priests). On balance, it seems most likely that Deuteronomy draws on parts of the exodus tradition to serve its own theological agenda (see Song 1992: 38–41). A massive amount of work has been devoted to the ambiguous phrase *mamleḵeṯ kōhᵃnîm*, and scholars divide neatly into those who see this as implying an international role or status for Israel and those which restrict the nuance of the term to a description of Israel in relationship to Yahweh (whether in metaphorical or literal terms).[14] Either way, its absence in Deuteronomy is puzzling, especially as the idea of a corporate priesthood (whatever its role in the world) seems to fit well with the scheme of one people worshipping one God in one land. The best we can do is suggest that *mamleket kōhᵃnîm* is omitted to avoid allowing the book to be read as an attack on the priesthood, or to avoid undermining the crucial role of the Levites in the book's preaching. It is fairly clear, however, that the Deuteronomist has not applied Exodus 19:5–6 to international relations in any significant way.

The place where Deuteronomy comes closest to laying claim to the fulfilment of the promises on the international stage is 4:5–8. The language is not that of Exodus 19:6, but the thought is very close. Perhaps, however, it is closer still to the thrust of Genesis 12 itself. Now, at last, Israel is to be acknowledged as a great nation (*gôy gādôl*), which Braulik sees this a direct appeal to the promise to Abraham (1977: 76). This is hard to show conclusively, but may be supported by passages such as 9:26–28; 15:6 and 28:1–12, 37, where the nations are involved in some way in the fulfilment of patriarchal promise in Israel (although not in the sense of being recipients of derivative blessing).[15]

It may not be possible to show conclusively that the nuanced treatment of the nations in Deuteronomy rests in a belief that the nations are involved in the fulfilment of the patriarchal promise, but that does not take away from the fact that, at its fringes, the Deuteronomic theology of blessing extends even to them.

It is extremely important, then, to appreciate both the function which the nations perform in the preaching of Moses, and the way in which they are embraced to some small degree in this book's theology of blessing. It is even possible to argue that here, in 4:5–8 in particular, we have a seminal doctrine of the mission of Israel. But this is not the main role of the nations in Deuteronomy. For much of the time, Moses' preaching addresses only one international issue: that of the presence of the Canaanites in the land of promise. They are neither an audience, nor the recipients of blessing; they are a problem.

While the Canaanites occupy the land, none of the fundamental tenets of Deuteronomic theology can be lived out ethically there. The

---

[14] For the former (international) view see Bauer 1958; Martin-Achard 1959: 37–40; Wildberger 1960: 92–95; Hyatt 1971: 200; Childs 1974: 367; Cazelles 1977: 78; Durham 1987: 263. For the opposing view see Caspari 1929; Galling 1928; Scott 1950; Vriezen 1953: 61; Bächli 1962: 174; Moran 1962; Fohrer 1963; Mosis 1978.

[15] Skweres finds no reference to the nations amidst the proliferation of allusions to Genesis (1979: 87–191, 232–33).

Canaanites are an impediment to the worship of Yahweh. They are clearly an obstacle to enjoying life with Yahweh in his land, and until they are removed there is no hope of establishing a new, godly way of living there. That is why, above all else, the nations in Deuteronomy are presented as an ethical dilemma.

The nations as an ethical dilemma in Deuteronomy

Deuteronomy makes it clear that Israel is called to a life of decision in the land to which Yahweh has brought them. There is, however, one fundamental decision which must be made decisively at the very moment of their entry to Canaan; Israel must decide to deal with the nations according to Yahweh's command. This is the primary ethical dilemma of life in the land of promise.

Moses seems all too aware that, whether because of religious duplicity, humanitarian concern, fear, or even a pragmatic concern for an easy life, Israel may be reluctant to carry out God's commands. The presence of the nations will confront Israel with a real dilemma, but at this first point of decision the people of God must prove that they are determined to submit to his sovereignty, and willing to obey his laws and statutes in the land, come what may.

Deuteronomy is so insistent that the Canaanites must be removed from life in the land because the ways of the nations are inimical to the ways of Yahweh. Only once (in 9:4) does Moses refer to the inhabitants' wickedness bringing down divine judgment. For the most part, his preaching focuses on the danger which their continued presence would pose (*e.g.* 7:16). In part, this is a consequence of Moses' realistic view of those to whom he preaches, but largely it is because he is aware of the threat which the current inhabitants pose to the worship of God by his people in his way and in his land.

Nowhere is this justification for conquest clearer than in chapters 12 and 13. The abrupt demand for distinctiveness in 12:4 and the passionate appeal of 12:30–31, framing chapter 12, are quickly followed by a long discussion of how to root out the worship of other gods in chapter 13. The treatment meted out is severe, as such behaviour jeopardizes the covenant itself (13:18–19). Throughout the laws which follow, all things Canaanite are repudiated, and it is clear that Israel must act to purge its environment of pagan influence. There can be only one answer. Israel's first decision in the land of promise must be to go to war.[16]

---

[16] On Israel's wars, see von Rad 1991 (inc. Ollenburger's foreword); Craigie 1978b;

It is the Deuteronomic teaching on war, principally contained in chapters 7 and 20, which has caused ethical problems for modern readers, if not for ancient Israelites. These chapters have been dismissed as indefensible, vicious nationalism, which can have no relevance in the modern world. This is a pity, because such sentiments do justice neither to the wider Deuteronomic context nor to the passages themselves.

On any reading of the book, the divine command to destroy a nation is problematic. This, like the Deuteronomic doctrine of election, is a brute fact, there in the text for all to see.[17] The ethical dilemma presented by the practices of the nations living in the land is to be resolved in the most uncompromising way. There are, however, two important features of the text which must be taken into account if we are to be fair to this material. First, this is *theological preaching*, urging Israel on to wholehearted obedience. In this context, we should surely expect some hyperbole, at least. While that may not remove the ethical problems, it may soften them around the edges. Secondly, the text itself acknowledges that these are terribly harsh commands. Moses repeatedly accompanies his calls for obedience with reminders that this campaign is to be carefully circumscribed and controlled. This is no brutal free-for-all, but a unique command of the God who owns not only the land, but the whole earth. Both these features are an integral part of the three main passages which deal with the war of conquest.

It is in chapter 7 that the concept of *herem* (the ban) is first explained. Verses 1–2 announce that the nations occupying the land are to be destroyed (*ḥrm*). This root is the fulcrum of Deuteronomy's teaching on the war of conquest (see also Ex. 22:19).[18] It is usually assumed that the Deuteronomist has transformed the occupation of Canaan into a 'holy war', a divinely ordained slaughter of 'innocent' Canaanites,[19] but this connection has often been made without carefully examining how this word is used in the text. In the light of all that we have seen, we must at least admit the possibility of some theological subtlety in the Deuteronomist's presentation.

Lind 1980; Sa-Moon Kang 1989. On Deuteronomy in particular, see Weinfeld 1993; Rofé 1985b; Gottwald 1964.

[17] On the election of Israel, see Galling 1928; Rowley 1950; Vriezen 1953; Koch 1955; Martin-Achard 1960; Wildberger 1960; Shafer 1977; Rendtorff 1981; dictionary articles on *bḥr*: Wildberger in *THAT*.1, cols. 275–300; Bergman, Ringgren, and Seebass, in *TWAT*. 1, cols. 592–608.

[18] It may or may not have sacral associations. See the Mesha stele and Jos. 7:12–13 for a sacral nuance; and 2 Ki. 19:11; 2 Ch. 20:23 for a secular.

[19] Weinfeld traces development from Ex. 21–23, 34 (expel), to Nu. 33:50–56 ('P' moves towards extermination) to annihilation in D (1993: 142–152). He argues for an idealistic revision of 'history'. *Cf.* Rofé 1985b: 25.

The first thing to notice is that *ḥrm* appears to be used in one way at the beginning of chapter 7, and in another at the end. In verse 1–2, the command is given to 'destroy' (verbal form of *ḥrm*) the nations. The parallel shows that there is no specific religious dimension here. In verse 26, on the other hand, the nominal form, *ḥerem*, clearly does have sacral overtones. This verse brings together two important terms – *ḥerem* and *tôʿēḇâ* – in a unique way. The idols of the Canaanites not only are subject to *ḥerem* regulations themselves, but actually have the potential to bring the full force of the *ḥerem* down upon the Israelites.

Therefore, in this chapter, the idea of *ḥrm* is used to bring together the ideal prosecution of a military campaign and the avoidance of ritual contamination. This serves the Deuteronomist's purposes exactly, for he is concerned to see Israel established in a land purged of Canaanite idolatry as painlessly as possible. The aim of the destruction (*ḥrm*) is to remove what is subject to the *ḥrm* laws (the idols). In Deuteronomy, the root of the dilemma facing the Israelites is not the people themselves, but their idolatrous way of life. Failure to reject these practices would jeopardize the very existence of Israel by putting them in the position of the Canaanites and their idols (*viz. ḥrm*) before Yahweh. Precisely the same situation is envisaged in 13:16–18, the only other place where Israelites come under the ban, and where the nominal and verbal forms of *ḥrm* also occur together.

The intensification of the command to dispossess the nations (see *e.g.* Ex. 23:29–33; 34:11–17) to destruction is not primarily about warfare at all. It is a theological conviction, arising from the recognition that the Canaanites will be a snare in the land; their influence must be purged from the land if Israel is to survive. The rationale for the destruction, then, is the avoidance of contamination (7:5) – although it must be said that the result is still total destruction.

Further evidence that this is theological preaching rather than a detailed battle plan comes in verses 3–4. On the one hand, all enemies are apparently to be exterminated, and on the other, the survivors are to be kept at arm's length! If verse 1 is the Deuteronomic view in its entirety, then prohibiting marriage into the wrong kind of family seems to labour the point![20] This is preaching about a war that has not yet started, galvanizing troops to throw themselves wholeheartedly into the fray, to do what God asks of them. We cannot read this chapter as if it were anything else.

The messy business of war, even this war, would inevitably throw up

---

[20]Craigie shows a similar difference in modern theories of war and execution (1978a: 58; 1978b: 45–54).

many eventualities not covered here; but Moses is not worried about such detail. Even when, in verse 22, he draws on Exodus 23:29–33, affirming that some Canaanites will no doubt survive, he simply calls the Israelites to persist in their thoroughgoing cleansing of the land, rather than stopping to answer awkward questions about how these survivors got there.[21]

Throughout this chapter, it is clear that the Mosaic preaching is concerned to bring the Israelites to the conviction that shattering the structures of Canaanite society is a theological necessity (see also 7:16, 22–23). This is expressed not in terms of driving out or dispossessing the Canaanites, but of destroying them. If Israel is to exist as the obedient people of God, then they need a sterile environment. No compromise is acceptable, or Israel's relationship with Yahweh will be endangered, and they themselves will experience the fate decreed for the Canaanites. How this *preaching* was to be enacted, however, is another matter entirely.

The more practical discussion of war is left to chapter 20, as we saw in the previous chapter. But here too we see that these rules are theologically shaped and theologically motivated. They are placed in a section which aims carefully to restrict killing (judicial or otherwise) within Israel. The four sections, 20:1–9 (preparations and orations); 20:10–15 (normal conduct of war); 20:16–18 (special case of conquest); 20:19–20 (environmental concerns), are all quite restrained in their approach. I have already discussed this section at some length, so all that we need do is look again at verses 10–20, to see how the conquest is treated in the context of wars in general.

Placed as they are between the essentially humanitarian rules of verses 10–14 and the environmentally friendly model for siege warfare, the demand for the obliteration of the Canaanites strikes a jarring note. I would argue that this is a deliberate attempt to underline that the war of conquest is exceptional in the experience of Israel.

In contrast to verses 10–15, the issue in verses 16–18 is not simply military victory, but annihilation of a way of life. While victory is guaranteed from the outset by the patronage of Yahweh, obliteration of the Canaanite cult is the theological necessity (verse 18). This is the justification for the unequivocal (and startlingly literal) command in verses 16–17 to leave no survivors. Once more *ḥrm* is used, in what is essentially a blunt reminder of the teaching of chapter 7. Even this,

---

[21] There are interesting parallels with chapter 15 and the provision for the 'Hebrew', which seems to suggest that the Israelite community would not always be 'ethnically pure'.

however, does not remove the sense that this theologically necessary act is somewhat at odds with everything else in the laws. Nor does it supply us with any more detail on the specific way in which the prescriptions are to be carried out.[22]

There is one other passage of the text to which we must give some attention, for it is only in chapters 1 – 3 that we actually read of Israel at war in Deuteronomy. It is here that we see a little more of the model theological war of the Deuteronomist.

I argued earlier that the wars in the Transjordan are presented as a paradigm for the incipient conquest by the Deuteronomist (see 3:21). This is even clearer when we read the details of the campaigns in the light of chapters 7 and 20, for it is here that we see *ḥrm* in action.

In 2:31–35 and 3:1–7, the Deuteronomist has adapted the narratives of Numbers 21:21–23, 33–35 to serve the theological interests of his own book. The stereotyped (and brutal) description of the annihilation of both Transjordan tribes is the same in Numbers 21:35 and Deuteronomy 3:3, and almost identical in Deuteronomy 2:34, but the Deuteronomist has expanded the details to suit his theological purpose. In particular, he emphasizes that the obliteration of the dynasties of Sihon and Og meant that this tribal group would not trouble Israel again.[23] It is clear that in the war to follow, the crucial matter is the permanent dismantling of the Canaanite nation. That is the prime concern of the Deuteronomic preaching, rather than the execution of individuals.

Neither the national focus of the preaching nor the rhetorical nature of all Deuteronomy's teaching on this war can take away the horror of the fact that a nation (albeit an evil nation, according to 9:4) is to be destroyed. We must expect to recoil a little from this. The Deuteronomic teaching, however, is not bloodthirsty, or brutal, or indiscriminate. It is the preaching of a theological necessity. The dangerous religion of the Canaanites is an obstacle to all that Yahweh has for his people, and it must be destroyed, along with those who would keep it alive.

Conclusion

As Israel approaches the land, the nation is all too aware that it will not

---

[22] Mitchell (1993: 184–190) comes to a broadly similar conclusion in his detailed reading of the book of Joshua, arguing that the juxtaposition of existing foreigners in the land and narratives detailing the ideal prosecution of a campaign of annihilation is deliberate, producing an important and flexible ambiguity.

[23] It is possible that it the royal families and armies were the object of the destruction; *e.g.* the use of *mtm* implies 'warrior'; *cf.* the Akkadian *mutu*.

be easy to choose the way of Yahweh and to maintain the momentum of obedience in Canaan. The most crucial element of the imminent decision they face is the repudiation of all things Canaanite, for, in the view of Deuteronomy, on this hangs the entire future of the people of God.

Despite the acknowledgment that Israel in some way represents Yahweh to the nations round about, and a surprising benevolence towards the nations 'related' to Israel, the theology of the Deuteronomist inexorably demands that Canaanite culture be wiped from the face of the earth. The careful delimitation of how war must be waged does not remove the enormity of the command. But God has decreed that this is necessary. Now the issue for Deuteronomy is not primarily one of morality; it is a matter of obedience.

Chapter Five

Ethics and human nature

By this stage, we have become quite familiar with the ways in which the preaching of Moses uses history, law, ritual and straightforward exhortation to urge Israel onward in her journey with Yahweh. The language, structure and theology of the book together make a powerful plea for obedience. We have seen how Deuteronomy applies exodus theology to the new situation in Canaan to develop ethics appropriate for enjoying life with Yahweh, and even for dealing with the present inhabitants. But there is one strand of the book's theology which we have not yet examined, and which actually calls all of the preaching of the book into question. It is the Deuteronomic theology of human nature, which poses the question: 'Will Israel be able to obey?'

It is not easy to decide whether Deuteronomy is basically optimistic or pessimistic about the prospects of Israel, and opinions are divided.[1] We are now in a position to come to some conclusions of our own, as we review the four major parts of the text (the historical introduction, 1 – 3; the preaching, 4 – 11; the laws, 12 – 26; and the conclusion, 27 – 34), with this question, 'Can Israel obey the laws?' in mind.

Human nature in chapters 1 – 3

The primary function of the historical introduction is to prepare Israel for decision. Yet, in doing this, it sows seeds of doubt regarding the eventual response to the commands of Yahweh and his servant Moses. This invests the whole book with an air of uncertainty.

The opening four verses encapsulate this tension. On the one hand, the recent conquest of Sihon and Og is ample proof of the Israelites' ability to succeed when they do things God's way; yet, on the other, the forty years taken to travel the short distance from Horeb to Kadesh Barnea illustrates Israel's *penchant* for disobedience.

The rest of chapter 1, however, tempers any optimism inspired by the

[1] McBride 1987 and Mayes 1993 have argued that it is optimistic, and Stulman 1990 and 1992 that it is pessimistic. A good case can be presented for both.

victories in Transjordan. Israel has started well before (verses 6–8) yet stalled quickly (verse 46). The exciting possibilities of the divine command to advance amounted to nothing. The intervening verses are a sad commentary on Israel's propensity to disobey Yahweh.

The devolution of authority from Moses to the representatives of the people (verse 9–18) has disastrous effects. Before reaching Horeb, the leadership of Israel rested firmly in the hands of Yahweh and his chosen representative, Moses. Only when Moses was absent or ignored had disaster struck. But at this crucial point, as Israel begins the journey to the land itself, the principle of democracy is introduced. The results of this devolution of power are plain in verses 19–45. The anxiety provoked by the spies' report leads to outright rebellion. The people refuse to go a step further, even accusing God of hating them (verse 27). The excuses which follow in verse 28 are pathetic, providing the fuel for much of the irony in chapter 2. Even Moses' pleading in verses 29–30 cannot change the fact that the people refused to trust the God who was leading them with fire and cloud (1:32–33).

Yahweh's verdict on all this is swift and uncompromising (verses 34–40). The obliteration of the rebellious generation (verse 35) brings both a new beginning and a warning that the capability of one generation to fail so abysmally raises the possibility of subsequent generations doing exactly the same (as at Beth Peor in 3:29 and 4:3). The attempts in verses 41–45 to reverse the verdict of Yahweh by instigating war against the Amorites show little more than the Israelites' ignorance, and the need for this generation to be removed before Israel can hope to start again.[2]

The gloom lifts a little in 2:2, as the nation begins to move in the right direction once more, but verses 2–23 still reflect a basic suspicion of Israel's ability to act faithfully. Despite all that God has done for them (verse 7), all they can do is 'fear the giants', which they allege inhabit the land. The scathing parentheses point out that the Moabites and the Ammonites managed to occupy 'their land', despite the presence of 'giants'. The irony betrays how little can be expected from God's people.

One would expect the account of the campaigns against Og and Sihon in 2:24 – 3:11 to provide some grounds for optimism, but in fact the narrative emphasizes all that Yahweh does, rather than any remarkable

---

[2] 'Chapter 1 sets up what Deuteronomy is about. It will echo and anticipate disobedience and unwillingness to live by promise and instruction. Further, the chapter gives us clues about the purpose and context of Deuteronomy. It is a word of instruction about how to live in the land, addressed to a people whose history reflects persistent faithlessness and disobedience' (Miller 1990: 36).

acts on the part of Israel; 2:30–34 is written as if the real battle is over before the fighting begins, and all that is left for Israel to do is carry out the mopping up for God. In chapter 1, we see human initiative (1:22–23) resulting in disobedience, fear and ultimately a complete fiasco as Israel is routed. Chapter 2 provides the complete antithesis. When Yahweh is in control Israel succeeds almost without effort. Success and failure are set side by side as the inevitable result of divine and human initiative respectively. It seems, then, that Israel is incapable of progressing alone.

Chapter 3 concludes with the rejection of Moses' appeal to be allowed to enter Canaan. This awful climax casts a shadow over what follows.[3] Yet the assurance that the promise would be fulfilled under Joshua's leadership ensures that the scenario is not entirely gloomy. Israel may just be a step away from apostasy (3:29), but they are also a step away from finally making it into the land.

Human nature in chapters 4 – 11

If a thoroughly positive expectation that the Israelites will fulfil their obligation of covenantal obedience is to be seen anywhere in Deuteronomy, these chapters would seem the most likely. And that is what we find in the resounding call to obedience in 4:1–2 (Driver 1901: 63). The immediate return to Baal Peor in verses 3–4, however, demonstrates that there is no more evidence of a naïve hope of constant obedience here than in chapters 1 – 3.

There is a similar juxtaposition in verses 5–9, where the towering optimism of verses 5–8 is abruptly brought down to earth by the plaintive appeal of verse 9 to remember the covenant. The vigorous call to 'take heed to yourself' and 'watch yourself' is unique in Deuteronomy and suggests that obedience will never be easy, for Israel is prone to forget – and this forgetfulness is not mere absentmindedness, but a reluctance to absorb the crucial lessons of salvation history. The nation must make a conscious effort to learn and hand on the lessons of the past (verse 10), for only then is there hope of the situation of 4:6–8 becoming reality.

It is in the context of forgetting God that Horeb is adduced to strengthen the injunction to listen to the 'latter-day' revelation of the Mosaic preaching at Moab (verse 14). Horeb may have been the

---

[3] Moses shares the consequences of the sin of the nation, rather than suffering vicariously for the people, as suggested by Miller (1987; 1990: 42–44) and Lohfink (1960b). Olson goes too far when he makes the death of Moses the key to reading the whole book (1994).

definitive theophany, but it is not the final word from God. Ultimately the infant nation of Israel requires more than an *aide-mémoire;* a new revelation is needed to enable them to live in the land.

Specific appeal is made to the Horeb theophany both to dissuade the Israelites from idolatry (verses 15–31) to which they are particularly prone, and to remind them that Yahweh is involved in the life of the nation (verses 32–40). The reminder of Moses' exclusion from the land in 4:21–22 does little to lighten the atmosphere, and as the scope of potential apostasy widens to forgetting the covenant in verse 23 (*cf.* verses 9, 15), the vivid description of Yahweh's reaction to such unfaithfulness in verse 24 almost completes a dark picture.

In verses 25–26, it is clear that appealing to Israel's 'better nature' will never be enough to guarantee a life of perpetual bliss in the land. The uncertainty of Israel's future is unhappily resolved as the events discussed in more detail in chapter 30 are anticipated. Israel will disobey. God's people will be expelled from God's land. The *kî* clause introducing 4:25 is temporal, underlining that this is inevitable (as in 30:10); in fact, in verse 26 heaven and earth have *already been* called as witnesses against Israel. The nation is already on the road to judgment.[4]

If I am reading these verses correctly, then chapter 4, especially in its anticipation of chapter 30, seems to undermine all subsequent calls to obey. This tension is not easily resolved, even by those who argue that the chapter is late and/or composite; it is one we are forced to live with. This chapter *does* call Israel to obey while asserting that one day, in the distant future, the nation will fail spectacularly. The full extent of the Deuteronomic mistrust of human nature is beginning to be revealed.

It is significant that in the Deuteronomic scheme of things, the possibility of repentance emerges only in 4:29–31, *after* the land has been lost. Although many have used this to try to show an exilic date for these chapters, they have overlooked the way in which the theology of Deuteronomy has influenced these verses. The book depicts a journey which begins in Egypt, moves into Canaan, and then has to leave Canaan and return to a new 'Egpyt' before finally coming back to the land for good. This journey is schematic and theological, and *does not presuppose the Babylonian exile*. To try to impose historical details on these theological ideas is to do the text an injustice. Within this theological journey, it is only after expulsion from the land that Israel

---

[4] Performative verbs, however, tend to occur in the perfect (Waltke & O'Connor 1990: 486–487). See also Delcor 1966 on the role of heaven and earth.

can repent and enter into a new relationship with God, as we shall see in chapter 30.

Therefore, despite the constant insistence on the need for the Israelites to obey and an awareness of the likelihood of failure, there is no explicit call for repentance *in* the land.[5] The omission is even more surprising when chapters 1 – 3 show that the journey into the land hinges upon repentance. I think, then, that there is a strong possibility that the Deuteronomist has deliberately avoided any reference to (or call for) repentance in the land because it would only delay the next bout of disobedience. He believes that the standards he preaches are ultimately beyond the reach of Israel, and his suppression of repentance (and forgiveness) in the land shows that he is not interested in such interim solutions. Rather like Jeremiah, he will preach and wait for God's final remedy.

So Deuteronomy appears to move in an environment that has largely been purged of repentance and forgiveness. Repentance occurs before Israel reaches Moab and after expulsion from the land. Forgiveness, accordingly, is seen in the wake of the failures in the wilderness, but plays little part in the Deuteronomic presentation of life in the land. Even in the laws, the concern is to avoid defiling the land and ruining Israel's relationship with Yahweh, and forgiveness does not feature prominently (but see perhaps 21:8). This is evident in the startling absence of any mention of the day of atonement or sin-offerings. The most attractive explanation of the Deuteronomist's exclusion of references to forgiveness it is his view that Israel is doomed from the start. Doomed, that is, until Yahweh intervenes to forgive, and his covenant faithfulness underwrites all the failures which the journey ahead will bring (verse 31).

Incredibly, the chapter finishes on a fairly upbeat note. There is a strident affirmation of the privileged position of Israel, who has experienced both the transcendence and immanence of Yahweh at Horeb (verses 32–40), a reminder that God is giving Israel the land in the institution of the cities of refuge (verses 41–43) and a brief summary of the recent successes of Israel in verses 44–49. But even here, the reference to Beth-Peor (verse 46) is a painful reminder of Israel's weakness for idols. The whole chapter is framed between two references to Beth-Peor (Deurloo 1994: 34–37).

Chapter 4, then, is fundamentally ambivalent about the future of Israel. On one hand, it calls repeatedly for total obedience from Israel,

---

[5] This is in contrast to the pre-exilic prophets in Samuel–Kings, *e.g.* 1 Sa. 7:3; 2 Ki 17:13. See *e.g.* Wolff 1964; Holladay 1958: 117.

yet, on the other, it raises the possibility that Israel is doomed to fail until Yahweh intervenes eschatologically. I have already suggested that this chapter functions as an overture to the whole book. It will be interesting if this view is sustained, as, having acknowledged what lies ahead, Moses does all that he can to urge Israel to ensure that the day of disaster never comes.

The dark portents of chapter 4 are all but forgotten as Moses reminds Israel of the Decalogue, and calls her on to greater obedience to the laws and statutes which will embody the spirit of Horeb in a new land. There is much of relevance to our study in chapters 5 – 11, but I will simply pick out the five most prominent features, and discuss how they relate to the question of human nature.

Calls to obey

Not surprisingly, calls to obedience proliferate in these chapters.[6] These repeated appeals seem to imply that Israel has the ability to comply. On the surface, this is the case. There may be a sub-text, however. The forceful repetition of the demand of obedience may in fact reveal a certain amount of desperation, presupposing the waywardness of Israel. Within the rhetoric of Deuteronomy, even calls to obedience become ambiguous.

Calls to remember

The explicit calls to remember Yahweh and his acts (or not to forget them) and the extended treatment of the golden calf episode reveal that Israel is constantly at risk of forgetting Yahweh.[7] In an ideal world, the acts of Yahweh would have so transformed the national consciousness that no such appeal to remembrance would be required. But Israel is a people which is prone to forget, and thus to disobey. The memory motif inevitably tends to promote a pessimistic view of the people of God (Brueggeman 1978: 53–58; 1985: 21).

Lack of confidence in God's people

The pessimism inherent in continual reminders not to forget is echoed by some more general examples of the lack of confidence in the people of God. One such example (which is easily missed) comes in the wake of the Shema in 6:7–9 and again in 11:18–21. In both places, the wider context is the likelihood of Israel's failing to obey Yahweh and forgetting the allegiance they owe him. God's people, then, must

---

[6] *E.g.* 5:1, 31–33; 6:1–9, 13–15, 17–19, 20–25; 7:12–15; 8:1, 6; 10:17–20; 11:1, 8–15, 22–25.

[7] *E.g.* 6:10–14; 8:11, 17–19; 9:7; 11:16.

immerse themselves totally in the atmosphere of the divine word, because they need to counter their innate tendency to forget. All kinds of visual and memory aids are necessitated by their weakness.

Moses also shows no confidence in the nation's ability to resist the lure of idolatry. This is clearest in chapters 12 and 13, but is also present in chapter 7 (especially verses 25–26), and again in chapter 8. The temptations of Canaan are very real for Israel. The people of God are weak, and liable to be influenced by the idolatry rife in the land. The only solution with any hope of success is to eradicate the source of temptation. Self-discipline, it seems, is a complete non-starter.

Probably the most striking expression of a lack of confidence in Israel comes from the lips of Yahweh himself in 5:29 (compare Je. 32:40). This is consistent with Exodus 20:20 and the rest of chapters 5 – 11. God himself and his servant Moses long that Israel would walk in his ways, yet as the book goes on this seems to amount to little more than wishful thinking.

Lessons from history

We have already dealt with the lessons that Israel should glean from their experiences at Horeb, but it is not simply chapters 4 and 5 which emphasize the importance of learning from the past. In chapter 6, verse 16 alludes to previous sinful rebellion against Yahweh and sets the tone for the use of history in chapters 6 – 11 (Weinfeld 1991: 346).

The passage 8:2–5 is crucial for our discussion. It makes clear that the wilderness experience was necessary, not as an intrinsic part of the plan of God for the advancement of Israel, but as a contingency to deal with her recalcitrance. It is clear from the opening verse that Yahweh viewed Israel as a proud nation, of whom he could not be sure. This is a key point. Moses is unsure of the nation because God himself is unsure. So during the wilderness years he put Israel to the test. No outcome is reported, however, with the implication that Yahweh is still unsure of his people, and leaving open the likelihood that further testing is needed:

> The sermon of Moses indicates that the experiment in the wilderness was a test by which *God* also would learn something – whether Israel would keep the commandments (verse 2). The results of the experiment at that point are ambiguous. We are never told whether God received an answer or what that answer might be. That ambiguity or unanswered question is not unimportant for comprehending the purpose of Deuteronomy (Miller 1990: 116).

If the results of the test in chapter 8 seem inconclusive, then 9:22–24, drawing on the events of Numbers 11 – 14, are clearly negative. The events of Taberah, Kibroth Hataavah and Kadesh Barnea hold out little hope.

Things get little better in chapter 9. The reference to Anakites in 9:2 recalls the irony of chapter 2, and rekindles the worry that Israel will not have sufficient trust in God to carry out the instructions which he has given. But the significance of this allusion is nothing beside the extended account of the giving of the law at Sinai and its aftermath, which contains some of the strongest assertions of the intrinsic 'sinfulness' of the nation in the whole book (*e.g.* 9:7–8). The sweeping assessment of Israel's history to date leaves no room for doubt: the entire course of their journey has been an unmitigated disaster, for they are habitually disobedient (Driver 1901: 113).

It is important to see that these damning words are spoken at Moab, not at Horeb; in other words, they are addressed to a people who have had the Decalogue for forty years. But this revelation has done nothing to address the heart of their problem, which is their very nature (Craigie 1978a: 194). One wonders if the new revelation in progress will fare any better.

Even while the theophany was still in progress, Israel angered God (verse 8). The declarations of Yahweh's anger intensify as the chapter progresses, but care is taken in verse 22 to underline that God had plenty of examples of Israel's bad behaviour to choose from. They were not acting out of character at Horeb. In verses 23–24, the example *par excellence* of Israel's failure to live up to their calling is cited: the refusal to enter the land at Kadesh Barnea. This is the climax of the Deuteronomist's argument: Israel even refused the gift of land itself, as a result of their perennial refusal to trust or obey Yahweh (as in 9:7).

God's response to all this is simply to give Israel *another* chance. He again presents Israel with the law of Horeb, and commissions the Levites to disseminate this law (10:1–9). The relief is tempered by the fact that nothing has actually changed; there is no new solution, only a reaffirmation of the old way of doing things. The same law is given to the same people (Weinfeld 1991: 418). The undertaking given by Yahweh in 10:10 almost has the appearance of a stay of execution. This becomes painfully apparent when, after the new tablets are given, the people are called back to obedience in urgent and strident tones (verses 12–22). The appeal to 'circumcise your hearts' (verse 16) and to reject the stubbornness of the past, in the face of both the grace and holiness of Yahweh, is crucial, if perhaps beyond Israel's reach.

This, then, is a subtly pessimistic message. There is room for hope,

and forgiveness of some sort, as the nation is given another chance –
but another chance for what? A diagnosis of terminal stubbornness (9:7,
23–24) still hangs over the people. What hope can there be for the
future, beyond a brief period of respite before an apparently inevitable
slide into disobedience?

The past is not always referred to in a wholly negative sense.[8] The
more hopeful allusions, however, are of an entirely different order from
those displaying a pessimistic view of Israel's potential. In the case of
the former, it is always Yahweh's faithfulness and power in action
which constitute the ground for optimism, never Israel's part in carrying
through the operations. As such, they say nothing about Israel herself.
Israel's only ground for optimism is the grace and power of Yahweh,
not her record or her prospects.

Election and grace

Paradoxically, the passages highlighting God's choice of Israel also
contain frank condemnations of her. For example, 7:6–9 insists that the
choice of Israel was not the result of divine perception of inherent
goodness (or even potential). Election is expected to be seen as a
powerful moral corrective (*e.g.* 7:9–11; 9:4–6).

The assertion in 9:6 (in the middle of a passage on election) that Israel
is a stiff-necked people emphasizes that a full appreciation of election
involves both the grace of God and the total unworthiness of Israel.[9]
Later in the same chapter (9:24–29), Moses despairs of the people
whom God has chosen, invoking instead the promises to the patriarchs.
This fascinating passage describes Moses' own struggle to come to
terms with the apparent contradiction between the purposes of God for
Israel and their sinful nature.[10]

Even the doctrine of election in Deuteronomy is highly ambiguous.
Israel is the people of God, and therefore one expects a certain degree
of optimism about their future in line with the plans of Yahweh. Yet, at
the same time, Yahweh has chosen a sinful people, a terminally stubborn nation who are not qualitatively different from the Canaanites, and
whose record to date does not hold out much ground for hope. Israel
may be the people of God, but this says nothing about their moral fibre.

---

[8] *E.g.* 6:22; 7:15, 18–23; 10:22; 11:2–7.

[9] See also 9:13, 26 and Ex. 32:9; 33:3, 5; 34:9; Couroyer 1981: 216–215.

[10] 'Had it not been for Moses' intercession and God's forbearance Israel would have
perished at Horeb. She was spared only to rebel again and again. The incident of Horeb
should have revealed her stubborn character, and the prevailing prayer of Moses and the
mercy of Yahweh should have encouraged her to show proper loyalty to her sovereign
Lord. Alas, her character was refractory' (Thompson 1974: 142).

On the mountain of God itself, Israel is shown as a nation whose attempts to obey the law lasted only as long as it took for Moses to go up to Horeb with Yahweh. After the golden calf there is no declaration that Yahweh is slow to anger and abounding in love, forgiving wickedness, rebellion and sin (in contrast to Ex. 34:6–7), no act of atonement for this crass act of apostasy (in contrast to Ex. 32). There is nothing but the prayer of Moses, the silence of Yahweh and the replacement of the tablets.

Throughout chapters 4 – 11, Deuteronomy displays an ambivalent attitude to the possibility of Israel's being willing or able to fulfil her covenantal obligations. Resounding calls to obedience sit alongside dismissive scepticism which denies that such revolutionary obedience will ever become reality. A delicate balance is maintained between passionate exhortation and subversive questioning, as in much of the prophetic literature. As a result, the choice facing Israel is always a real one. This is underlined by the closing verses of chapter 11 (11:26–28). The possibilities of blessing and curse at the climax of the preaching not only ensure that the decision facing Israel is presented in the most striking way, but adds to the atmosphere of uncertainty regarding the ability of the nation to obey. The question of obedience, then, is left hanging in the balance.

Human nature in chapters 12 – 26

Deriving theological principles in chapters 12 – 26 is not quite as straightforward. For a start, it is part of the nature of law that it is intensely difficult to read behind law-forms to the view of human nature from which the legislator is working.[11] The proscription of practices may or may not arise from the belief that such practices are *likely*. Repeated calls to enact laws may or may not imply reluctance on the part of the hearers to obey. We are touching on the philosophy of law itself, which is much too large a subject to be tackled here.

In addition, in any collection of laws, idealism and pragmatism mix freely (see Daube 1959). Both are quite obvious in the discussion of poverty in chapter 15 and the king-law of chapter 17, but are much harder to separate elsewhere, for throughout the Deuteronomic laws the ideal of God's people in God's land is preached realistically. This

---

[11] Law may well 'serve as a system for encoding values, ethos and worldview' (Stulman 1992: 47), but that does not mean it is easy to make the reverse step. See his bibliography and brief methodological discussion. Further work is needed on this question.

makes it extremely difficult to draw any conclusions on human nature from the laws themselves.

Overall, Deuteronomy 12 – 26 is at pains to define what God's model society will look like in the land. We see this, for example, in the demands to worship Yahweh in the way he prescribes, the provision for celebration of festivals and establishment of a national polity. The laws admit no reason why these stipulations should not be followed rigorously (see *e.g.* the declaration of 26:13). Yet there is no shortage of material which apparently assumes the worst. Major areas of concern in the Deuteronomic laws include compromise in the cultic realm, economic exploitation, ritualism, injustice, laxity in religious obligation, lack of respect for authority and improper behaviour in personal relationships. Ultimately, however, no answer is given to the question of the likely outcome of these decisions. In Deuteronomy, this must be resolved by reading the laws in the context of the framework of chapters 1 – 11 and 27 – 34.

Human nature in chapters 27 – 34

For the purposes of this discussion, the concluding phase of the book can be divided into four sections: blessings and curses (chapters 27 – 28), the covenant at Moab (chapter 29), the new covenant (chapter 30) and the postscript (chapters 31 – 34). As we approach the end of the book, the subversive, pessimistic strand of Deuteronomic theology becomes more dominant.

Blessings and curses (chapters 27 – 28)

The question facing us now is whether the instructions for the vivid enactment at Shechem, or Moses' own oration of blessing and curse at Moab, gives any hint of which is the more likely outcome in the future of Israel.

Of the curses to be pronounced at Shechem (27:15–26), the last one is the most interesting. In the context of this short list, the sweeping obedience demanded in this summarizing verse (verse 26) may have been within Israel's reach. But if this applies not just to the preceding verses, but to the whole of the Deuteronomic law (which seems likely), including the obligation to love Yahweh with heart, soul and strength, to cleave to him and serve him, Israel seems bound to fail (Craigie 1978a: 276). As Moses seems to reiterate this in 28:1, harking back to chapters 5 – 6, 27:26 should be interpreted in this broad sense.

The blessings in verses 2–14 are almost too good to be true. For a moment, the failures and recalcitrance of Israel are forgotten in this glowing appraisal of the future possibilities of God's people. But can such blessings actually be realized? The weight of the curses which disobedience would usher in (verses 15–68) quickly seems to sweep away such possibilities. The length and scope of this second list of curses are unparalleled in the Old Testament; Moses wields the stick more vigorously than he brandishes the carrot (McCarthy 1978: 68).[12]

In the midst of the catalogue of failure, punishment and pain, three themes stand out. The first is the return to Egypt, which we have already seen. The second is threat of destruction (28:45, 48, 49–51, 61). The final image is that of scattering among the nations. Just as return to Egypt and/or destruction of the nation are, in effect, the reversal of the acts of Yahweh, so the expulsion of Israel is understood as the counterpart of the imminent experience of the Canaanites at the hand of the people of God (see verses 36–37, 64–65). Whereas the blessing was expounded in terms of an idealistic future, the consequences of the curse are spelled out as the complete reversal of what God has done – the overturning of his purposes in Israel. It is now Israel herself who takes the place of Canaan in the divine economy – driven out of the land back to 'Egypt' and reduced to a few scattered survivors. This is clearly a carefully crafted rhetorical unit which puts a question mark over any hope of a prosperous future as the book draws to a close.

The Moab covenant (28:69 – 29:29)

The next two chapters are the most important in the whole book for grasping the Deuteronomic theology of human nature.[13] We begin by looking at the covenant at Moab, which is the Deuteronomist's unique contribution to Israel's covenant theology.

In chapters 5 – 11, we saw that Moses preaches that the covenant at Horeb is not enough for life in the land. Even the new set of tablets are basically ineffective, for the Horeb covenant is not enough to transform the behaviour of Israel. Now, in the covenant at Moab, Yahweh does a new thing. This is not simply a reiteration or renewal of the Horeb covenant (as in Ex. 34).

Obviously, the Moab covenant differs from its predecessor in the laws which are attached to it. But there is a much more fundamental difference. The Horeb covenant carries no statement of its limitations,

---

[12] Hillers argues that it is a characteristic of ANE treaty curses to outstrip the blessings lists (1964: 33). Craigie acknowledges its rhetorical force: 'When the substance of Deut 28:15–68 is read with a knowledge of the subsequent history of Israel as a nation, the curses seem to assume an awful inevitability.' (1978a: 341).

[13] Lenchak shows that chapters 29 – 30 form a rhetorical whole (1993: 1–37). The crucial categories are obedience, blessing and choice.

or of its temporary nature. There is no recognition within the covenant itself that it will ultimately break down, and must be replaced by a 'better covenant'. This is exactly what sets the Moab covenant apart – the recognition that it is temporary, and, like Horeb, ultimately unable to deliver (Cholewinski 1985: 106). Its regulations may be an advance on those of Horeb, more demanding and certainly far more applicable to life in Canaan; but, just as Horeb promised no remedy to Israel's existential problems, neither does Moab in itself. Crucially, however, it does introduce the expectation that a subsequent covenant may make for a real change of heart in Israel.

The first three verses of chapter 29 support this interpretation. This 'heading' couples its short reminder of salvation history with a piercing analysis of Israel's moral, intellectual and spiritual incapacity (Miller 1990: 202–206). The problem of Israel is highlighted and yet no solution is offered. In fact, it is made plain that laws in and of themselves can offer no solution – for laws cannot open minds or eyes or ears. A simple restatement of covenantal ideals will lead them nowhere. Yahweh must intervene if Israel is to hear.[14] The reminder of the power of Yahweh in 29:4–7 shows that he is a God who can intervene to provide a covenant which can deal with the deepest of Israel's problems – her own flawed nature.

Verses 1–7 can now be read together. Their message is that God has the power to change Israel, but has not done so yet (verse 3). Israel is still the same stubborn nation which rebelled at Horeb, Kadesh Barnea and elsewhere. The one change is that Moab has replaced Horeb, and, while the nation's quest for obedience may end in the same way, the Moab covenant has shown Israel that there is good reason to hope. Israel may not be able to respond as she ought 'today' (29:3, 27), but a time is coming when she will.

Verses 9–14 deal with the ratification of this covenant itself. There is no doubt over Yahweh's commitment to his people (e.g. verses 12–14), but their current ability to respond is less clear. Their previous exposure to idolatry in Egypt and during the journey through the desert is used to warn them against rejecting Yahweh (verses 15–16), and this leads naturally into verses 17–28, which form yet another denunciation of idolatry. The most severe rejection of covenant-breakers in the entire book (29:18–20) describes a situation where Yahweh's faithfulness produces only complacency. The divine response in verses 19–20 is a refusal to forgive this hypothetical individual, which resonates with the absence of forgiveness in the earlier part of the book.

[14] Lohfink 1963: 128 n.5; Miller 1990: 206; Keil 1864: 447.

This individual drama is then replayed on the national stage in verses 21–27, as verse 17 proves to be a description of the whole nation.[15] National catastrophe results from national breach of covenant. The likelihood of each individual falling into apostasy translates into the nation as a whole spurning the grace of Yahweh (Driver 1901: 326)

The comparison with Sodom and Gomorrah emphasizes the seriousness of the plight of Israel. They are morally and spiritually inured against all overtures of Yahweh. All the curses of this book are declared to have fallen on Israel as the nations look on. The warnings of chapter 28 are now depicted as future reality, as Israel is expelled from the land of Canaan, and stripped of the very context for her relationship with Yahweh (29:28).

The chapter closes with a cryptic allusion to the secret things and the revealed things in verse 28. This refers most naturally to the content of chapter 29, and, although it is difficult to tie this down with any precision, I would suggest that 'the revealed things' refer to the insights of this 'Moab covenant' – in other words, the understanding that this revelation is contingent, and will one day be superseded. The 'secret things', then, look to a new covenant, which will not simply call Israel to obey, but will enable them to do it, by dealing with the enduring problem of human nature.[16] In the meantime – which is clearly expected to be a substantial period – Israel must do all that she can to obey, knowing that ultimately she is doomed to fail, at least until this eschatological intervention.

This covenant at Moab, then, is about theology more than about ritual. The advances on Horeb are in the content of the laws, now applied to the incipient occupation, and in the admission that laws do not change people. Both the Horeb and Moab covenants are fatally flawed, because they can do nothing about the problem of human nature.

The new covenant (chapter 30)

If the covenant at Moab reveals the need for something to be done about human nature, then the new covenant promised in chapter 30 meets that need. One day, the 'secret things' will be revealed, and God will act to change his people.

In 30:1, we move forward in time to the day when both curse *and* *blessing* have been experienced in the life of the nation (in contrast to 29:21). As in chapter 4, a long period of occupation leads inexorably to

---

[15] A similar idea occurs in the Annals of Asshurbanipal (*ANET* 300) but the role of the nations is unique.

[16] Driver 1901: 328; Thompson 1974: 234; Craigie 1978a: 360. Mayes takes it with what follows (1981: 368).

expulsion from the land, but now a greater hope begins to dominate Israel's horizons, as the Deuteronomist looks to a deep-rooted repentance in exile (verse 1). At the beginning of the previous chapter, Moses makes it plain that stubborn Israel is destined to fail – for she is inherently disobedient and Yahweh has not given them minds to understand, eyes to see or ears to hear. In chapter 30, the divine intervention which Israel needs so desperately is seen to be on the way.

National repentance (30:2–3), rather than apostasy, is now inevitable. The journey of Israel resumes once more, this time accompanied by conformity to the command of 6:3–4 for wholehearted obedience. Now the blessing of God is experienced in all its fulness (verse 5). In 30:6 all this is traced to the telling intervention by Yahweh.

That verse picks up the command of 10:16 given to Israel, and states that, in the wake of their persistent refusal and inability to conform to Yahweh's laws on their own, he will act and perform the necessary surgery.[17] Israel is effectively helpless in the present. Only after this future act will obedience be a realistic possibility in the life of God's people (verse 8), and the full potential of life with God in the land open up for Israel (verse 10).

Verses 1–10 have a basic symmetry. The section begins and ends with the need for obedience. Verses 3–5 and 7–9 deal with the restoration of the divine order and renewed fulfilment of promise. At the centre stands verse 6, with its emphasis on the change brought about by God (Vanoni 1981). The Deuteronomist makes it clear that Israel will not truly obey the command (and indeed cannot) until after they have experienced the blessing, all the horror of the curse, and the new thing of Yahweh's 'circumcision of the heart'. This relativizes not simply Horeb, as Cholewinski would argue, but Moab as well. Both are only transitional moments in Israel's journey to transformation.

This is basically a prototype of the new covenant thought which we see in Jeremiah and Ezekiel.[18] One day Yahweh will solve the problem of the human heart. Until Yahweh's climactic (eschatological) action, the only satisfactory option open to Israel is to strive to obey the law which they have been given in the preceding chapters.

Verses 11–20 stand in many ways as a conclusion to the Deuteronomic preaching. After the explicit statement of Israel's need to be transformed comes one of the most powerful calls to decision in the

---

[17] See Craigie 1978a: 363; Buis & Leclerq 1963: 187 (also Je. 4:4).

[18] Buis 1968: 11–13; Cholewinski 1985: 109–110. Cholewinski admits that Deuteronomy is more primitive than Jeremiah and Ezekiel, but ascribes this to an attempt to provide a precursor to that material in retrospect!

whole of the Bible (Miller 1990: 213–214). Israel must set herself to choose life.

I have already discussed the problems of these verses at some length, and tentatively suggested that verses 11–14 should be read as the decision to be made *after* the instigation of the new covenant, while verses 15–20 bring Moses' listeners at Moab back to the present, calling them to obey today in the light of the hope of future transformation laid before them. Even though Israel needs Yahweh's intervention, the call to obey 'today' remains. Even though Israel will finally learn her lesson only through the trauma of expulsion, a life of decision still stands before her. Even though these verses deal with ultimate solutions, they return to the necessity of covenant faithfulness in the present.

Verses 15–20 are probably the most eloquent exposition of the Deuteronomic theology of daily life in the entire book. Today at Moab, and every day in the land, the Israelites are confronted with a decision in the light not only of their failures in the past, but also the hope which chapter 30 holds out for the future. This proud people must learn to live in hope, devoting themselves humbly to following Yahweh and his law, resolved to repent when they fail, and looking forward to the day when Yahweh fulfils his promise to end their frustration at their failure by transforming their moral and spiritual laxity into the power to obey. This is what the Deuteronomist calls them to when he urges them to 'choose life'.

The postscript (chapters 31 – 34)

The final narrative and poetic sections return in several places to the key question of Israel's 'nature'. After the initially upbeat exhortation to the nation and Joshua in 31:1–13, Moses turns in verses 14–29 to the subject which has occupied much of chapters 29 – 30. Moses' anticipation of Israel's future apostasy is now reiterated by Yahweh himself in 31:16–18. This verdict on human nature is bleak in the extreme.[19]

The context of the Song of Moses is therefore one of strong negative expectation. If anything, the atmosphere darkens as chapter 31 leads into chapter 32 (see especially verses 19–21). Verse 21 is the most deterministic statement from the mouth of Yahweh in the book.[20] He states

[19] 'The words of God are not primarily prophetic; they portray rather divine insight into the basic character of the people and their constant tendency to unfaithfulness' (Craigie 1978a: 372).

[20] 'In verses 24–29 the propensity for disobedience is assumed by Moses because of a history of such behaviour. In verse 21, however, the text goes further and echoes a word

that he knows the *yēṣer* of Israel. This is, in effect, the sinful nature of Israel.[21] The law is no ultimate solution to this, but can only hope to restrain Israel's sin and make them more aware of it, and increasingly conscious of their need for Yahweh to deal with this twistedness.

Yahweh's declaration of Israel's natural bias to evil is immediately echoed by the words of Moses, who reiterates the inability of law to solve Israel's predicament (see chapters 10, 29). Here it cannot even restrain, but simply reveals the sinfulness of the people (31:26–27).[22] The Levites (who experience Israel's obedience or disobedience in concrete terms) have a prominent role in confronting the people. Heaven and earth are once again called as witnesses (4:26; 30:19), and testify to the stubborn disobedience of Israel (31:28, 32:1). Israel's culpability is clear. The picture is completed by the ominous declaration of Moses just before his song begins in verse 29. The knowledge revealed by Yahweh in verse 21 is repeated by his servant. Israel's future does not look bright, because she is, by nature, sinful.

The song itself opens with a call to heaven and earth to listen to the words of Moses (32:1–2), and then turns to the response demanded of Israel and the likelihood of her showing such a response. As Moses praises God (verses 3–4), it is clear that the words and life of Israel should echo his proclamation. But instead of affirmation of the divine faithfulness, there is silence, followed by a pointed castigation (verses 5–6). Israel is denounced as morally disfigured (*mûm*, 15:21; 17:1), perverse ('*iqqēš*, 2 Sa. 22:27) and foolish (*nābāl*), in need not of moral instruction but of surgery. A lyrical rehearsal of the history of the nation follows, which picks up many key Deuteronomic ideas.

The song returns to the theme of the essential waywardness of the people in verse 15. The riches lavished on Israel lead only to rebellious obesity:

> The general statement of the first line of verse 15 is then made intensely personal by the shift in number to the second person singular – you *grew fat ...!* The condemnation falls not only on the impersonal 'Jeshurun' or 'Israel' but on each individual within that larger community (Craigie 1978a: 382).

---

first heard in the story of beginnings in Genesis 6:5 and 8:21–22: to wit, that there is within the human heart and will a tendency to disobey God' (Miller 1990: 224).

[21] See von Rad 1966a: 190; Mayes 1973: 262–63; 1981: 378. Mayes argues that the law is given as the means to overcome this tendency. I would argue that the law can do nothing about it.

[22] 'The ominous note of the law as witness has nothing to do with anything within the *law*; Moses knows what is in the *heart* of the people' (Miller 1990: 233).

This verse and those following are a poetic representation of the past, present and future of Israel, rather than alluding to specific events. While I remain sceptical of any attempt to fit the song into a rigid 'covenant-lawsuit' form, the suggestion that we have Israel accused before the bar of God is very helpful. It is as if Moses is standing outside space and time, characterizing the life of God's people in the most painful terms. The impersonal reflection of verses 16–17 gives way to the direct address of verse 18: Israel has abandoned her God.

The divine verdict on the nation in verse 20 is similar to that of Moses in verses 5–6: they are a 'subversive generation' (REB). As this poetic generation experiences Yahweh's loving-kindness, rebels, suffers chastisement and sees rescue, it calls the nation in every generation to covenant faithfulness.

The litany of Israel's moral weakness continues in verses 23–27, where the punitive action of Yahweh is halted only by the typically Deuteronomic remembrance that the international reputation of God is inextricably bound up with the fate of Israel. This abatement of the wrath of God, however, presages yet another statement of the moral torpor of Israel (verses 28–29).

Israel is almost beyond help. The nation languishes in darkness, and yet it is at this darkest point that the possibility of rescue begins to emerge. The rest of the song is devoted to the retribution Yahweh exacts on those he has used as his tools (verse 21). The focus shifts from addressing Israel to addressing the nations who oppress her in the poetic scheme. The final cry of triumph proclaims the tentative restoration of relationship with Israel (verse 43). The atoning action of Yahweh restores the land as the locus of relationship and creates new possibilities for Israel.[23]

Initially there is a closing down of hope in the song. Israel is a nation without a future, capable only of disobeying, locked in un-wisdom by her very nature. She is perverse and twisted. Yet as the song continues, a note of optimism begins to emerge. Moses realizes that Yahweh will not abandon Israel to disobedience. There is hope for Israel in even Yahweh's punitive and purgative intervention. This is not developed, but it is presented as the beginnings of an answer. It is striking that here, in the last words of Moses the lawgiver, we see the realization that the law is not the way of salvation for Israel. Thus the closing words of Moses in 32:46–47 take on a new depth of meaning. The key to

---

[23] 'The poem will end appropriately with the thought of Israel, freed not only from the calamities which it has so long endured, but also from its sin and so restored completely to Jehovah's favour' (Driver 1901: 381).

enjoying life in the land in the short term is indeed to follow the words of Yahweh as spelled out in Deuteronomy. But this is tempered with a pessimism springing from the realization that Israel is by nature a rebellious nation. Obedience cannot last for long. The ultimate function of the law is not, then, to enable obedience, but to expose disobedience, paving the way for the divine intervention which will eventually enable real obedience, and a new intimacy with God himself.

As the book ends, this basic Deuteronomic tension persists. The tribes are blessed by Moses, but only in the context of his exclusion from the land because of his sin (32:52). The report of Moses' blessing the tribes is placed between a double reminder of his significant resting-place at Nebo outside the land (see 34:4). The repeated assertion that Moses could see the land but not enter it seems to bode only ill for Israel. The closing verses deliberately emphasize Moab (and Baal-Peor), powerfully reminding them of the decision to be faced.

Despite the evident significance and holiness of Moses, the most prominent fact is that he died outside the land as a result of disobedience. The inference can only be that there is little hope of Israel as a whole surpassing him. His death outside the land eloquently illustrates the theology which he preached. Sailhamer has forcefully argued that the narrative strategy of the Pentateuch as a whole contrasts Abraham, who lived by faith before the law, and Moses, who failed to keep the law once it had been given. He argues that *the Pentateuch itself* presents the way of Abraham as better than the way of Moses (1995: 270). My reading of Deuteronomy supports his case.

Ultimately, there is hope only in the intervention of God for Israel. The law cannot be kept, even by the greatest of us. As Israel stands at Moab, faced with a lifetime of decision in the land, Moses' message is simply that lasting obedience can be maintained and lasting prosperity achieved only by trusting in the grace of Yahweh.

Conclusion

The preaching of Deuteronomy powerfully calls Israel to obedience in the light of the revelation of Yahweh at Moab. I have shown, however, that a subversive strand of the book gradually overturns any confidence that God's covenant people are capable of consistently living up to his ideal. Deuteronomic theology ultimately rests on the conviction that human nature is deeply flawed, and can be transformed only by God. This basic conviction underwrites all the ethical teaching of the book.

Throughout Moses' preaching, there is a complex interplay of optimism and pessimism. The excitement of the new opportunities at Canaan mingles with a deep awareness of Israel's consistent preference for apostasy in the past, even at times of great religious importance. This tension is resolved only in the closing chapters of the book, where it becomes clear that the theology of Deuteronomy is a theology based on grace. In the covenant at Moab, Moses the lawgiver declares that law, whether given at Horeb or at Moab, is no solution to the problem of Israel's sinful nature. They are, like many who listened to Jesus' parables, people to whom God has not given minds to understand, or eyes to see, or ears to hear. Only God can remedy that situation – which is exactly what he promises to do.

Chapter 30 ensures that Deuteronomy is ultimately an optimistic book. Its doctrine of the sinfulness of human nature may mean that Israel is bound to fail, but the promise of God's radical intervention, setting up a new covenant which does change the hearts of his people, means that the book is transformed by a theology of hope. God is going to intervene. That is why Moses can preach on (30:15–20), calling Israel to persevere in obedience, walking with Yahweh, facing a lifetime of decisions. God's people may be bound to fail today, but they are not trapped in failure for ever, for God's solution is coming.

Conclusion

Theology and ethics in Deuteronomy

I set out to study Deuteronomy in the hope of gaining some insight into how one might apply the ethical teaching of the Old Testament to the modern world in which we live. I believe that the text of this remarkable book has provided us with exactly that.

On reading the book as a whole, it quickly became apparent that Deuteronomy from beginning to end has a distinctive understanding of Israel's relationship with God. This 'Deuteronomic theology' is characterized by an emphasis on the exodus as the formative event in the life of the nation, and the belief that Yahweh is now Israel's absolute ruler who must be obeyed in every detail of life, and that he has given Israel a land in which to enjoy relationship with him together. Every part of the text reflects this same theological perspective.

Just as we can speak of the theology of Deuteronomy, so we can speak of its ethics. The ethics of the book are nothing more that its theology applied to the details of life. The theology of the exodus translates into a concern for equality among those whom God has rescued. The theology of God's sovereignty translates into a willingness to allow him to define worship, and to remain different from other nations. The theology of the land translates into a determination to ensure that everyone can enjoy the produce of Canaan, and to maintain justice in every sphere of life, so that Israel's relationship with God may not be interrupted. These are the key features of the book's ethics, although there are many other facets to its applied theology.

It is important, however, to understand that Deuteronomy does not see itself as the last word on ethics for Israel. Israel is a nation constantly on the move, constantly facing new challenges and different ethical dilemmas. This book is theology applied to one specific situation, as Israel prepares for life in the land of promise. But Deuteronomy insists that the journey of Israel will go on. The life of God's people will always be a constant succession of decisions. As Moses takes the theology of the exodus and the revelation at Horeb and applies them to the new opportunities and dangers in Canaan, so it will be necessary to repeat the process of applying theology to life again and again, if Israel is to live faithfully for Yahweh throughout her future.

Deuteronomy suggests it will always be difficult to speak of the ethics of the Old Testament, because the ethics of the people of God result from applying theology to an ever-changing situation. If that theology is also changing, as God reveals more of himself to his people, then the situation becomes even more complex.

But that is not to say that there is no point in attempting to construct 'the ethics of the Old Testament'; simply that to do so faithfully means taking into account the dynamic nature both of Old Testament theology and the way in which it is applied to Israelite national life. It is probably here that the Christian church has most to learn from the Old Testament. In Christ, we may have experienced a new exodus; we may have seen God's sovereignty redefined in terms which transcend national boundaries, and watched the locus of God's relationship with humanity shift from a place to a global community; but it is here, in the Old Testament, that we see theology applied to the details of life in the most thoroughgoing and painstaking way. It is here that we see how to make godly decisions – how to choose life over death. The challenge, of course, is to repeat the process which we see in action in Deuteronomy, but with a theology transformed by Christ, and to a world which is quite unlike that of Moses.

There is a final point which is crucial to understanding both the theology and ethics of Deuteronomy. We have seen that this book teaches that ultimately all merely human efforts to obey the law, to make godly decisions and to live out Deuteronomic theology in practice are bound to fail. They are bound to fail because human beings are intrinsically flawed, as the example of Moses himself shows. All the ethical teaching of the book is conditioned by this basic theological conviction. In the last analysis, ethics can do nothing to solve Israel's problems. Solutions must wait until the day when God intervenes to establish a new covenant, which deals not just with the changing situations in which Israel finds herself, but with the moral perversity which is inherent in her character.

We have seen the inauguration of this new covenant. In Christ, God has intervened to solve the problem of sinful human nature. But even now, we have not seen the full outworkings of that solution. We still continue to struggle to obey, to make godly decisions. The complete fulfilment of Deuteronomy 30 remains elusive, and will do so until the day of God's final intervention in human history, when finally we shall be able to live in the way which God requires, to love him with heart and soul and strength. This ancient book reminds us, perhaps more than anything else, that the goal of all theology, and the goal of all ethics, is to show us the grace of God, and to encourage us to throw ourselves on him, or, to use the words of Moses, to 'choose life' as we embrace the God who has chosen us in Christ.

Bibliography

Abba, R. (1977), 'Priests and Levites in Deuteronomy', *VT* 27: 257–267.

Alexander, T. D. (1982), 'A Literary Analysis of the Abraham Narrative in Genesis' (unpubl. PhD diss.: Queen's University, Belfast).

——(1993), 'Genealogies, Seed, and the Compositional Unity of Genesis', *TynB* 44: 255–270.

Amsler, S. (1977), 'La motivation de l'éthique dans la parénèse du Deutéronome', in Donner, H., Hanhart, R., & Smend, R. (eds), *Beiträge zur alttestamentlichen Theologie: Festschrift für Walther Zimmerli* (Göttingen: Vandenhoeck & Ruprecht), 11–22.

Anbar, M. (1985), 'The Story of the Building of an Altar on Mount Ebal', in Lohfink, N. (ed.), *Das Deuteronomium: Entstehung, Gestalt und Botschaft* (BEThL 68: Leuven: Leuven University Press), 304–310.

Andersen, F. I., & Forbes, A. D. (1989), *The Vocabulary of the Old Testament* (Rome: Pontifical Institute).

Bächli, O. (1962), *Israel und die Völker: Eine Studie zum Deuteronomium* (AZTANT 41: Stuttgart: Zwingli Verlag).

Bailey, K. E. (1976), *Poet and Peasant* (Grand Rapids: Eerdmans).

Baltzer, K. (1970), *Das Bundesformular* (Neukirchen: Neukirchener Verlag); ET *The Covenant Formulary* (Oxford: Oxford University Press, 1971).

Barr, J. (1961), *The Semantics of Biblical Language* (Oxford: Oxford University Press).

Barton, J. (1974), 'The Relation of God to Ethics in the Eighth Century Prophets' (unpubl. DPhil. diss.: Oxford).

——(1978), 'Understanding Old Testament Ethics', *JSOT* 9: 44–64.

——(1979), 'Natural Law and Poetic Justice in the Old Testament', *JTS* NS 30: 1–14.

——(1981), 'Ethics in Isaiah of Jerusalem', *JTS* NS 32: 1–18.

——(1983), 'Approaches to Ethics in the Old Testament', in Rogerson, J. (ed.), *Beginning Old Testament Study* (London: SPCK).

——(1996), 'The Basis of Ethics in the Hebrew Bible', *Semeia* 11–22.

Bauckham, R. J. (1989), *The Bible in Politics: How to Read the Bible Politically* (London: SPCK).

Bauer, J. B. (1958), 'Könige und Priester, ein heiliges Volk (Ex. 19, 6)', *BZ* NF 2: 283–286.

Baumann, E. (1956), 'Das Lied Moses auf seine gedankliche Geschlossenheit untersucht', *VT* 6: 414–424.

Begg, C. T. (1994), '1994: A Significant Anniversary in the History of Deuteronomy Research', in García Martínez *et al.* (1994), 1–12.

Bellefontaine, E. (1975), 'The Curses of Deuteronomy 27: Their Relationship to the Prohibitives', in Flanagan, J. W., & Robinson, A. W. (eds), *No Famine in the Land: Festschrift for J. L. McKenzie* (Missoula: Scholars), 49–61.

——(1979), 'Reviewing the Case of the Rebellious Son', *JSOT* 13: 13–39.

Bickerman, E. (1950–51), 'Couper une alliance', *Archives d'Histoire du Droit Orientale* 5: 133–156.

Birch, B. C. (1988), 'Old Testament Narrative and Moral Address', in Tucker, G. M., Petersen, D. L., & Wilson, R. R. (eds), *Canon, Theology and Old Testament: Essays in Honor of B. S. Childs* (Philadelphia: Fortress), 75–91.

——(1991), *Let Justice Roll Down: The Old Testament, Ethics and the Christian Life* (Louisville: Westminster/John Knox).

Birch, B. C., & Rasmussen, L. L. (1976), *Bible and Ethics in the Christian Life* (Minneapolis: Augsburg).

Blair, E. P. (1961), 'An Appeal to Remembrance: The Memory Motif in Deuteronomy', *Int* 15: 41–47.

Blank, S. H. (1950–51), 'The Curse, Blasphemy, the Spell and the Oath', *HUCA* 23/1: 73–94.

Blauw, J. (1962), *The Missionary Nature of the Church* (New York: McGraw-Hill).

Boston, J. R. (1968), 'The Wisdom Influences Upon the Song of Moses', *JBL* 87: 166–178.

Braulik, G. (1970), 'Die Ausdrücke für Gesetz im Buch Deuteronomium', *Biblica* 51: 39–66.

——(1971), 'Spuren einer Neuarbeitung des deuteronomistischen Geschichtswerkes in 1 Kön 8, 52–53, 59–60', *Biblica* 52: 20–33.

——(1977), 'Weisheit, Gottesnähe und Gesetz – zum Kerygma von Deuteronomium 4, 5–8', in Braulik, G. (ed.), *Studien zum Pentateuch: Festschrift für W. Kornfeld* (Vienna: Herder), 165–195, repr. in Braulik (1988a), 53–93.

——(1978a), *Die Mittel deuteronomischer Rhetorik erhoben aus*

Deuteronomium 4:1–40 (AnBib 68: Rome: Pontifical Institute).

——(1978b), Review of Mittmann (1975), *Biblica* 59: 351–383.

——(1984), 'Law as Gospel: Justification and Pardon according to the Deuteronomic Torah', *Int* 38: 5–14.

——(1985), 'Die Abfolge der Gesetze in Deuteronomium 12 – 26 und der Dekalog', in Lohfink, N. (ed.), *Das Deuteronomium: Entstehung, Gestalt und Botschaft* (BEThL 68, Leuven: Leuven University Press), 252–272.

——(1986a), 'Das Deuteronomium und die Menschenrechte', *ThQ* 166: 8–24.

——(1986b), *Deuteronomium 1, 1 – 16, 17* (NEchB: Würzburg: Echter Verlag).

——(1988a), *Studien zur Theologie des Deuteronomiums* (SBAB 2: Stuttgart: Katholisches Bibelwerk).

——(1988b), 'Zur Abfolge der Gesetze in Deuteronomium 16, 18 – 21, 23. Weitere Beobachtungen', *Biblica* 69: 63–92.

——(1991), *Die deuteronomischen Gesetze und der Dekalog* (SBS 145: Stuttgart: Katholisches Bibelwerk).

——(1992), *Deuteronomium II: 16, 18 – 34, 12* (NEchB: Würzburg: Echter Verlag).

Breit, H. (1933), *Die Predigt des Deuteronomisten* (Munich: Kaiser).

Brekelmans, C. (1985), 'Deuteronomy 5', in Lohfink, N. (ed.), *Das Deuteronomium. Entstehung, Gestalt und Botschaft* (BEThL 68, Leuven: Leuven University Press), 164–173.

Brichto, H. C. (1973), 'Kin, Cult, Land and Afterlife', *HUCA* 44: 1–54.

Brown, R. (1993), *The Message of Deuteronomy* (Leicester: IVP).

Bruce, W. S. (1909), *The Ethics of the Old Testament* (2nd edn, Edinburgh: T. & T. Clark).

Brueggemann, W. (1978), *The Land* (OBT: Philadelphia: Fortress).

——(1985), 'Imagination as a Mode of Fidelity', in Butler, J. T., Conrad, E. W., & Ollenburger, B. C. (eds), *Understanding the Word: Essays in Honour of B. W. Anderson* (JSOTS 37: Sheffield: Sheffield Academic Press), 1–27.

Buis, P. (1968), 'La Nouvelle Alliance', *VT* 18: 1–15.

Buis, P., & Leclerq, J. (1963), *Le Deutéronome* (Sources bibliques: Paris: Gabalda).

Carmichael, C. M. (1967), 'Deuteronomic Laws, Wisdom and Historical Traditions', *JSS* 12: 198–206.

——(1974), *The Laws of Deuteronomy* (Ithaca: Cornell University Press).

——(1976), 'On Separating Life from Death: An Explanation of Some Biblical Laws', *HTR* 69: 1–7.

——(1977), 'A Ceremonial Crux: Removing a Man's Sandal as a Female Gesture of Contempt', *JBL* 96: 321–336.

——(1979), 'A Common Element in Five Supposedly Disparate Laws', *VT* 29: 129–142.

——(1982), 'Forbidden Mixtures', *VT* 32: 394–415.

——(1985), *Law and Narrative in the Bible* (Ithaca: Cornell University Press).

Caspari, A. (1929), 'Das Priestliche Königreich', *ThBl* 8: 105–110.

Cazelles, H. (1967), 'Passages in the Singular within Discourses in the Plural of Dt. 1–4', *CBQ* 29: 207–219.

——(1977), 'Alliance du Sinai, alliance de l'Horeb et renouvellement de l'alliance', in Donner, H., Hanhart, H., & Smend, R. (eds), *Beiträge zur alttestamentlichen Theologie: Festschrift für Walther Zimmerli* (Göttingen: Vandenhoeck & Ruprecht), 69–79.

Childs, B. S. (1970), *Biblical Theology in Crisis* (Philadelphia: Fortress).

——(1974), *Exodus* (OTL: London: SCM).

——(1985), *Old Testament Theology in a Canonical Context* (London: SCM).

——(1992), *Biblical Theology of the Old and New Testaments* (London: SCM).

Cholewinski, A. (1976), *Heiligkeitsgesetz und Deuteronomium* (AnBib 66: Rome: Pontifical Institute).

——(1985), 'Zur theologischen Deutung des Moabbundes', *Biblica* 66: 96–111.

Christensen, D. L. (1991), *Deuteronomy 1 – 11* (WBC: Waco: Word).

Clark, G. R. (1992), *Hesed in the Hebrew Bible* (JSOTS 157: Sheffield: Sheffield Academic Press).

Clements, R. E. (1965a), 'Deuteronomy and the Jerusalem Cult Tradition', *VT* 15: 300–312.

——(1965b), *God and Temple* (Oxford: Blackwell).

——(1976), *A Century of Old Testament Study* (Guildford: Lutterworth).

——(1984), 'Christian Ethics and the Old Testament', *Modern Churchman* 26: 13–26.

——(1992), 'Loving One's Neighbour: Old Testament Ethics in Context' (The Ethel M. Wood Lecture, University of London).

Clines, D. J. A. (1978), *The Theme of the Pentateuch* (JSOTS 10: Sheffield: Sheffield Academic Press).

Couroyer, B. (1981), 'Avoir de nuque raide': ne pas incliner l'oreille', *RB* 88: 216–225.

Craigie, P. C. (1978a), *The Book of Deuteronomy* (NICOT: Grand Rapids: Eerdmans).

——(1978b), *The Problem of War in the Old Testament* (Grand Rapids: Eerdmans).

Crenshaw, J. L., & Willis, J. T. (eds) (1974), *Essays in Old Testament Ethics* (New York: Ktav).

Crüsemann, F. (1981), 'Die Eigenständigkeit der Urgeschichte', in Jeremias, J., & Perlitt, L. (eds), *Die Botschaft und die Boten: Festschrift für H. W. Wolff* (Neukirchen: Neukirchener Verlag), 11–29.

Dahood, M. (1966), *Psalms* I (AB: New York: Doubleday).

Daube, D. (1959), 'Concessions to Sinfulness in Jewish Law', *JJS* 10: 1–13.

——(1961), 'Direct and Indirect Causation in Biblical Law', *VT* 11: 246–269.

——(1969a), 'The Culture of Deuteronomy', *Orita* 3: 27–52.

——(1969b), 'Repudium in Deuteronomy', in Ellis, E. E., & Wilcox, M. (eds), *Neotestamentica et Semitica: Studies in Honour of Matthew Black* (Edinburgh: T. & T. Clark), 236–239.

Davidson, R. (1959), 'Some Aspects of the Old Testament Contribution to the Shape of Christian Ethics' *SJT* 12: 373–387.

Davies, E. W. (1981), 'Inheritance Rights and the Hebrew Levirate Marriage', *VT* 31: 138–144, 257–268.

Davies, G. I. (1979), 'The Significance of Deuteronomy 1:2 for the Location of Mount Horeb', *PEQ* 111: 87–101.

Delcor, M. (1966), 'Les attaches littéraires: l'origine et la signification de l'expression biblique "prendre à témoin le ciel et la terre" ', *VT* 16: 8–25.

Deurloo, K. A. (1994), 'The One God and All Israel', in García Martínez *et al.* (1994), 32–46.

DeVries, S. J. (1975a), *Yesterday, Today and Tomorrow. Time and History in the Old Testament* (Grand Rapids: Eerdmans).

——(1975b), 'Deuteronomy: Exemplar of a Non-Sacerdotal Appropriation of Sacred History', in Cook, J. I. (ed.), *Grace Upon Grace: Essays in Honor of Lester J. Kuyper* (Grand Rapids: Eerdmans), 95–105.

Diepold, P. (1972), *Israels Land* (BWANT 15: Stuttgart: Kohlhammer).

Dion, P. E. (1991), 'Deuteronomy 13: the Suppression of Alien Religious Propaganda During the Late Monarchical Era', in Halpern, B., & Hobson, D. W. (eds), *Law and Ideology in Monarchic Israel* (JSOTS 124: Sheffield: Sheffield Academic Press), 147–216.

Driver, G. R., & Miles, J. C. (1952–55), *The Babylonian Laws* (2 vols., Oxford: Oxford University Press).

Driver, S. R. (1901), *A Critical and Exegetical Commentary on Deuteronomy* (ICC: 3rd edn, Edinburgh: T. & T. Clark).

Dumermuth, F. (1958), 'Zur deuteronomischen Kulttheologie und ihren Voraussetzungen', *ZAW* 70: 59–98.

Durham, J. I. (1987), *Exodus* (WBC: Waco: Word).

Eichrodt, W. (1967), *Theology of the OT* II (London: SCM), ET of *Theologie des Alten Testaments* II/III (5th edn, Göttingen: Vandenhoeck & Ruprecht, 1964).

Eissfeldt, O. (1917), *Erstlinge und Zehnte im Alten Testament* (Leipzig: Hinrichs).

——(1956), 'Silo und Jerusalem' (SVT 4: Leiden: Brill), 138–148.

——(1958), *Das Lied Moses* (Berichte über die Verhandlung der Sächsischen Akademie der Wissenschaften zu Leipzig 104/5).

Emerton, J. A. (1962), 'Priests and Levites in Deuteronomy', *VT* 12: 129–138.

——(1982), 'The Origin of the Promises to the Patriarchs in the Older Sources in the Book of Genesis', *VT* 32: 14–32.

——(1990) (ed.), *Studies in the Pentateuch* (SVT 41: Leiden: Brill).

Epsztein, L. (1986), *Social Justice in the Ancient Near East and the People of the Bible* (London: SCM).

Eslinger, L. M. (1981), 'The Case of an Immodest Lady Wrestler, Deuteronomy xxv: 11–12', *VT* 31: 269–281.

Finkelstein, J. J. (1981), *The Ox That Gored* (Transactions of the American Philosophical Society 1/2: Philadelphia: American Philosophical Society).

Firmage, E. (1990), 'The Biblical Dietary Laws and the Concept of Holiness', in Emerton, J. A. (ed.), *Studies in the Pentateuch* (SVT 41: Leiden: Brill), 177–208.

Fishbane, M. (1985), *Biblical Interpretation in Ancient Israel* (Oxford: Clarendon).

Fitzmyer, J. A. (1967), *The Aramaic Inscriptions of Sefire* (Rome: Pontifical Institute).

Fletcher, V. E. (1971), 'The Shape of Old Testament Ethics', *SJT* 24: 47–73.

Fohrer, G. (1963), '"Priesterliches Königtum", Ex. 19, 6', *T-Z* 19: 359–362.

Fowler, M. D. (1987), 'The Meaning of lipnê YHWH in the Old Testament', *ZAW* 99 (1987), 384–390.

Frankena, R. S. (1965), 'The Vassal Treaties of Esarhaddon and the Dating of Deuteronomy', *OTS* 14 (1965), 122–154.

Galling, K. (1928), *Die Erwählungstraditionen Israels* (BZAW 48: Giessen: Töpelmann).

García López, F. (1977–78), 'Analyse littéraire de Deutéronome 5–11', *RB* 84 (1977), 481–522, and 85 (1978), 1–49.

García Martínez, F. Hilhorst, A. van Ruiten, J. T., & van der Woude, A. S. (eds) (1994), *Studies in Deuteronomy in Honour of C. J. Labuschagne on the Occasion of his 65th Birthday* (SVT 53: Leiden: Brill).

Goldberg, M. L. (1984), 'Gifts or Bribes in Deuteronomy', *Int* 38: 15–25.

Goldingay, J. (1981), *Approaches to Old Testament Interpretation* (Leicester: IVP).

——(1985), 'Divine Ideals, Human Stubbornness and Scriptural Inerrancy', *Transformation* 2 (4): 1–4.

——(1984), 'Diversity and Unity in Old Testament Theology', *VT* 34: 153–168.

——(1987), *Theological Diversity and the Authority of the Old Testament* (Grand Rapids: Eerdmans).

Gordon, C. H. (1965), *Ugaritic Textbook* (Analecta Orientalia 38: Rome: Pontifical Institute).

Gottwald, N. K. (1964), 'Holy War in Deuteronomy: Analysis and Critique', *Review and Expositor* 61: 296–310.

Greenberg, M. (1951), 'Hebrew sglh, Akkadian sikiltu', *JAOS* 71: 172–174.

Grossfeld, B. (1988), *Targum Onqelos to Deuteronomy* (Edinburgh: T. & T. Clark).

Guilding, A. E. (1948), 'Notes on the Hebrew Lawcodes', *JTS* 49: 43–52.

Gunneweg, A. H. J. (1965), *Leviten und Priester* (Göttingen: Vandenhoeck & Ruprecht).

Halbe, J. (1975a), 'Passa-Massot im deuteronomischen Festkalendar: Komposition, Entstehung und Programm von Deuteronomium 16, 1–8', *ZAW* 87: 147–168.

——(1975b), 'Erwägungen zum Ursprung und Wesen des Massotfestes', *ZAW* 87: 324–345.

——(1985), 'Gemeinschaft, die Welt unterbricht', in Lohfink, N. (ed.), *Das Deuteronomium: Entstehung, Gestalt und Botschaft* (BEThL 68: Leuven: Leuven University Press), 55–75.

Halpern, B. (1981), 'The Centralisation Formula in Deuteronomy', *VT* 31: 20–38.

——(1991), 'Jerusalem and the Lineages in the seventh century BCE: Kinship and the Rise of Individual Moral Liability', in Halpern & Hobson (1991), 1–107.

Halpern, B., & Hobson, D. W. (eds) (1991), *Law and Ideology in Monarchic Israel* (JSOTS 124: Sheffield: Sheffield Academic Press).

Hamilton, J. M. (1992), *Social Justice and Deuteronomy: The Case of Deuteronomy 15* (SBLDS 136: Atlanta: Scholars).

Haran, M. (1979), 'Seething a Kid in its Mother's Milk', *JJS* 30: 24–35.

Hasel, G. F. (1982), *Old Testament Theology: Basic Issues in the Current Debate* (3rd edn, Grand Rapids: Eerdmans).

Hempel, J. (1914), *Die Schichten des Deuteronomium* (Leipzig: Voigtländer).

——(1954), 'Die Würzeln des Missionswillens im Glauben des Alten Testaments', *ZAW* 66: 244–272.

——(1962), 'Ethics in the Old Testament', *IDB*, vol. E–J, 153–157.

——(1964), *Das Ethos des Alten Testaments* (BZAW 67: Berlin: Töpelmann).

Hillers, D. R. (1964), *Treaty Curses and the OT Prophets* (Biblica et Orientalia 16: Rome: Pontifical Institute).

Hoffner, H. A. (1969), 'Some Contributions of Hittitology to Old Testament Study', *TynB* 20: 48–51.

Holladay, W. L. (1958), *The Root SUBH in the Old Testament* (Leiden: Brill).

Houston, W. (1993), *Purity and Monotheism. Clean and Unclean Animals in Biblical Laws* (JSOTS 140: Sheffield: Sheffield Academic Press).

van Houten, C. (1991), *The Alien in Israelite Law* (JSOTS 107: Sheffield: Sheffield Academic Press).

Houtman, C. (1984), 'Another Look at Forbidden Mixtures', *VT* 34: 226–228.

Huffmon, H. B. (1966), 'The Treaty Background of Hebrew yada'', *BASOR* 181: 31–38.

Huffmon, H. B., & Parker, S. B. (1966), 'A Further Note on the Treaty Background of Hebrew yada'', *BASOR* 184: 36–38.

Humbert, P. (1960), 'Le substantif to'ebah et le verbe t'b dans l'Ancien Testament', *ZAW* 72: 17–37.

Hyatt, J. P. (1970), 'Were there an Ancient Historical Credo in Israel and an Independent Sinai Tradition?', in Frank, H. T., & Reed, W. L. (eds), *Translating and Understanding the Old Testament* (Nashville: Abingdon), 152–170.

——(1971), *Exodus* (NBC: London: Marshall, Morgan & Scott).

Janzen, W. (1994), *Old Testament Ethics: A Paradigmatic Approach* (Louisville: Westminster/John Knox).

Jenson, P. P. (1992), *Graded Holiness* (JSOTS 106: Sheffield: Sheffield Academic Press).

Jeremias, J. (1958), *Jesus' Promise to the Nations* (London: SCM), ET of *Jesu Verheissung für die Völker* (Stuttgart: Kohlhammer, 1956).

Joyce, P. M. (1987), *Divine Initiative and Human Response in Ezekiel* (JSOTS 51: Sheffield: Sheffield Academic Press).

Kaiser, W., Jr (1983), *Toward Old Testament Ethics* (Grand Rapids: Zondervan).

——(1992), 'New Approaches to Old Testament Ethics', *JETS* 35: 289–299.

Kalluveettil, P. (1982), *Declaration and Covenant: A Comprehensive Review of Covenant Formulae from the Old Testament and Ancient Near East* (AnBib 88: Rome: Pontifical Institute).

Kaufman, S. A. (1978–79), 'The Structure of the Deuteronomic Law', *Maarav* 1/2: 105–158.

Keel, O. (1980), *Das Böcklein in der Milch seiner Mutter und Verwandtes im Lichte eines altorientalischen Bildmotivs* (OBO 33: Freiburg: Schweiz Universitatsverlag).

Keil, C. F. (1864), *The Fifth Book of Moses*, in Keil, C. F., & Delitzsch, F., *Commentary on the Old Testament* 1 (*The Pentateuch*), (repr. Grand Rapids: Eerdmans, 1988). (From *Biblischer Commentar über die Bücher Moses* 2: *Leviticus, Numeri und Deuteronomium* (Leipzig: Dörffling & Franke, 1862.)

Kilian, R. (1966), *Die vorpriesterlichen Abrahamsüberlieferungen, literarkritisch und traditionsgeschichtlich untersucht* (BBB 24: Bonn: Peter Hanstein).

Kitchen, K. A. (1965), *Ancient Orient and Old Testament* (London: Tyndale).

Kleinert, P. (1872), *Untersuchungen zur alttestamentlichen Rechts- und Literaturgeschichte* I: *Das Deuteronomium und der Deuteronomiker* (Leipzig: Velhagen & Klasing).

Kline, M. G. (1963), *The Treaty of the Great King* (Grand Rapids: Eerdmans).

Knapp, D. (1987), *Deuteronomium 4: Literarische Analyse und theologische Interpretation* (Göttingen: Vandenhoeck & Ruprecht).

Koch, K. (1955), 'Zur Geschichte der Erwählungsvorstellung in Israel', *ZAW* 67: 205–266.

Kuyper, L. J. (1952), 'The Book of Deuteronomy', *Int* 6: 321–340.

Labuschagne, C. J. (1987), *Deuteronomium I a* (De Predeking van het Oude Testament: Nijkerk: Callenbach).

Lemche, N. P. (1976), 'The Manumission of Slaves – The Fallow Year – The Sabbatical Year – The Jobel Year', *VT* 26: 38–59.

———(1991), *The Canaanites and their Land: The Tradition of the Canaanites* (JSOTS 110: Sheffield: Sheffield Academic Press).

Lenchak, T. A. (1993), *'Choose Life', A Rhetorical-Critical Investigation of Deuteronomy 28, 69 – 30, 20* (AnBib 129: Rome: Pontifical Institute).

Levenson, J. D. (1975), 'Who Inserted the Book of the Torah?', *HTR* 68: 203–233.

———(1980), 'The Theologies of Commandment in Biblical Israel', *HTR* 73: 13–33.

———(1981), 'From Temple to Synagogue: 1 Kgs 8', in Halpern, B., & Levenson, J. D. (eds), *Traditions in Transformation: Turning Points in Biblical Faith: Festschrift for F. M. Cross* (Winona Lake: Eisenbrauns), 143–146.

Lewy, I. (1962), 'The Puzzle of Deuteronomy xxvii', *VT* 12: 207–211.

L'Hour, J. (1963), 'Une Code criminelle dans le Deutéronome', *Biblica* 44: 1–28.

———(1964), 'Les interdits to'ebah dans le Deutéronome', *RB* 71: 481–503.

Lilley, J. P. U. (1993), 'Understanding the Herem', *TynB* 44: 170–177.

Lind, M. C. (1980), *Yahweh is a Warrior: The Theology of Warfare in Ancient Israel* (Scottdale: Herald).

Locher, C. (1986), *Die Ehre einer Frau in Israel: Exegetische und rechtsvergleichende Studien zu Deuteronomium 22, 12–21* (OBO 70: Freiburg: Schweiz Universitatsverlag).

Lohfink, N. (1960a), 'Darstellungskunst und Theologie in Dtn. 1:6 – 3:29', *Biblica* 41: 105–134.

———(1960b), 'Wie stellt sich das Problem Individuum-Gemeinschaft in Deuteronomium 1, 6 – 3, 29?', *Scholastik* 35: 403–407.

———(1962a), 'Der Bundesschluß im Land Moab: Redaktiongeschichtliches zu Dt 28, 69 – 32, 47', *BZ* NF 6: 32–56.

———(1962b), 'Die deuteronomische Darstellung des Übergangs der Führung Israels von Mose auf Josue', *Scholastik* 37: 32–44, repr. in Lohfink (1990a), 83–97.

———(1963), *Das Hauptgebot: eine Untersuchung literarischer Einleitungsfragen zu Dt. 5 – 11* (AnBib 20: Rome: Pontifical Institute).

———(1964), 'Verkündigung des Hauptgebots in der jüngsten Schicht des Deuteronomiums', *Bibel und Leben* 5; appeared in a modified form as 'Höre, Israel! Auslegung von Texten aus dem Buch Deuteronomium' (Die Welt der Bibel 18, 1965), repr. in Lohfink (1990a), 167–192.

———(1965), 'Zur Dekalogfassung von Dt 5', *BZ* NF 9: 17–32.

——(1969), 'Dt 26:17–19 und die Bundesformel', *ZkTh* 91: 517–553 repr. in Lohfink (1990a), 211–262.

——(1971a), 'Die Sicherung der Wirksamkeit des Gotteswortes durch das Prinzip der Schriftlichkeit der Tora und durch das Prinzip der Gewaltenteilung nach den Ämtergesetzen des Buches Deuteronomium 16, 18 – 18, 22', in Wolter, H. (ed.), *Testimonium Veritati: Festschrift für W. Kempf* (Frankfurt: Knecht), 143–155.

——(1971b), 'Zum "kleinen geschichtlichen Credo", Dtn 26, 5–9' *Theologie und Philosophie* 46: 19–39, repr. in Lohfink (1990a), 263–290.

——(1971c), 'Un exemple de théologie de l'histoire dans l'ancien Israël. Deut 26, 6–9', *Archivio fie filosofia* 39: 189–199, repr. in Lohfink (1990a), 291–303.

——(1984), 'Zur deuteronomischer Zentralisationsformel', *Biblica* 65: 297–328, repr. in Lohfink (1991b), 147–177.

——(1985) (ed.), *Das Deuteronomium: Entstehung, Gestalt und Botschaft* (BEThL 68: Leuven: Leuven University Press).

——(1989a), 'Die 'huqqim umispatim', im Buch Deuteronomium und ihre Neubegrenzung durch Dtn. 12:1', *Biblica* 70: 1–27.

——(1989b), 'Dtn 12: 1 und Gen 15:18: Das dem Samen Abrahams geschenkte Land als der Geltungsbereich der deuteronomischen Gesetze', in Gorg, M. (ed.), *Die Väter Israels: Beiträge zur Theologie der Patriarchenübelieferungen im Alten Testament: Festschrift für J. Scharbert* (Stuttgart: Katholisches Bibelwerk), 183–210, repr. Lohfink (1991b), 257–287.

——(1990a), *Studien zum Deuteronomium und zur Deuteronomischen Literatur* I (SBAB 8: Stuttgart: Katholisches Biblewerk).

——(1990b), 'Gibt es eine deuteronomische Bearbeitung im Bundesbuch?', in Brekelmans, C., & Lust, J. (eds), *Pentateuchal and Deuteronomistic Studies* (BEThL 94: Leuven: Leuven University Press), 91–113.

——(1990c), 'Das deuteronomische Gesetz in der Endgestalt – Entwurf einer Gesellschaft ohne marginale Gruppen', *BN* 51: 25–40.

——(1991a), *Die Väter Israels im Deuteronomium. Mit einer Stellungnahme von Thomas Römer* (OBO 111: Freiburg und Göttingen: Schweig Universitatsverlag).

——(1991b), *Studien zum Deuteronomium und zur Deuteronomischen Literatur* II (SBAB 12: Stuttgart: Katholisches Bibelwerk).

——(1994), 'Moab oder Sichem – wo wurde Dtn 28 nach der Fabel des Deuteronomiums proklamiert?', in García Martínez *et al.* (1994), 139–153.

Maag, V. (1960), 'Malkut Jhwh', in *Congress Volume* (SVT 7: Leiden: Brill 1960), 137–142.

Maarsingh, B. (1961), *Onderzoek naar de Ethiek van de Wetten in Deuteronomium* (Winterswijk: Van Amstel).

McBride, S. D. (1987), 'The Polity of the Covenant People. The Book of Deuteronomy', *Int* 41: 229–244.

McCarthy, D. J. (1965), 'Notes on the Love of God in Deuteronomy and the Father–Son Relationship between Yahweh and Israel', *CBQ* 27: 145–146.

——(1978), *Treaty and Covenant* (AnBib 21a: Rome: Pontifical Institute).

McConville, J. G. (1984), *Law and Theology in Deuteronomy* (JSOTS 33: Sheffield: Sheffield Academic Press).

——(1987), 'Using Scripture for Theology: Unity and Diversity in Old Testament Theology', in Cameron, N. M. de S. (ed.), *The Challenge of Evangelical Theology: Essays in Application and Method* (Edinburgh: Rutherford House), 39–57.

——(1992), '1 Kings viii 46–53 and the Deuteronomic Hope', *VT* 42: 67–79.

——(1993), *Grace in the End: A Study in Deuteronomic Theology* (Carlisle: Paternoster).

McConville, J. G., & Millar J. G. (1994), *Time and Place in Deuteronomy* (JSOTS 179: Sheffield: Sheffield Academic Press).

McKeating, H. (1979), 'Sanctions against Adultery in Ancient Israelite Society, with Some Reflections on the Methodology in the Study of Old Testament Ethics', *JSOT* 11: 57–72.

Maimonides (1967), *Sefer ha–Mitswot*, in *The Commandments: Sefer ha-Mitswot of Maimonides*, trans. Chavel, C. B., & Kafah, Y. (London: Soncino).

Maloney, R. P. (1974), 'Usury and Restrictions on Interest-Taking in the Ancient Near East', *CBQ* 36: 1–20.

Martin-Achard, R. (1959), *Israël et les Nations* (Cahiers Théologiques 42: Neuchâtel: Delachaux).

——(1960), 'La signification théologique de l'élection d'Israël', *ThZ* 16: 331–341.

Mayes, A. D. H. (1973), 'The Nature of Sin and its Origin in the Old Testament', *Irish Theological Quarterly* 40: 250–263.

——(1980), 'Exposition of Deuteronomy 4:25–31', *Irish Biblical Studies* 2: 67–85.

——(1981), *Deuteronomy* (NCB: London: Marshall, Morgan & Scott).

——(1987), 'Deuteronomy 4 and the Literary Criticism of Deuteronomy', *JBL* 100: 23–51.

——(1993), 'On Describing the Purpose of Deuteronomy', *JSOT* 58: 13–33.

——(1994), 'Deuteronomy 14 and the Deuteronomic Worldview', in García Martínez *et al.* (1994), 165–181.

Mendenhall, G. E. (1954), 'Covenant Forms in Israelite Tradition', *The Biblical Archaeologist* 17/2: 26–46, 17/3: 49–76.

——(1974), 'Samuel's Broken *Rîb*: Deut. 32', in Flanagan, J. W., & Robinson, A. W. (eds), *No Famine in the Land: Festschrift for J. L. McKenzie* (Missoula: Scholars), 63–74.

Merendino, R. P. (1969), *Das deuteronomische Gesetz. Eine literarkritische, gattungs- und überlieferungsgeschichtliche Untersuchung zu Dt 12 – 26* (BBB 31: Bonn: Peter Hanstein).

Mettinger, T. N. D. (1982), *The Dethronement of Sabaoth: Studies in the Shem and Kabod Theologies* (Coniectana Biblica, OT, 18: Lund: CWK Gleerup).

Milgrom, J. (1963), 'The Biblical Diet Laws as an Ethical System: Food and Faith', *Int* 17: 288–301.

——(1973), 'The Alleged Demythologisation and Secularisation in Deuteronomy', *IEJ* 23 (1973), 156–161.

——(1976), 'Profane Slaughter and a Formulaic Key to the Composition of Deuteronomy', *HUCA* 47: 1–17.

——(1991), *Leviticus 1 – 16* (AB: New York: Doubleday).

Miller, P. D., Jr (1969), 'The Gift of God. The Deuteronomic Theology of the Land', *Int* 23: 454–465.

——(1970), 'Apotropaic Imagery in Prov 6:20–22', *JNES* 29: 129.

——(1987), 'Moses, My Servant: A Deuteronomic Portrait of Moses', *Int* 41: 245–255.

——(1990), *Deuteronomy* (Interpretation: Louisville: John Knox).

Minette de Tillesse, G. (1962), 'Sections "tu", et sections "vous", dans le Deutéronome', *VT* 12: 29–87.

Mitchell, G. (1993), *Together in the Land: A Reading of the Book of Joshua* (JSOTS 134: Sheffield: Sheffield Academic Press).

Mittmann, S. (1975), *Deuteronomium 1:1 – 6:3 literarkritisch und traditionsgeschichtlich untersucht* (BZAW 139: Berlin: Töpelmann).

Moran, W. L. (1962), 'A Kingdom of Priests', in McKenzie, J. L. (ed.), *The Bible in Current Catholic Thought* (New York: Herder & Herder), 7–20.

——(1963a), 'The Ancient Near Eastern Background of the Love of God in Deuteronomy', *CBQ* 25: 77–87.

——(1963b), 'The End of the Unholy War and the Anti-Exodus', *Biblica* 44: 333–342.

——(1966), 'The Literary Connection between Lev 11:13–19 and Deut 14:12–28', *CBQ* 28: 271–277.

Mosis, R. (1978), 'Ex 19:5b–6a: Syntaktischer Aufbau und lexicalische Semantik', *BZ* NF 22: 1–25.

Muilenburg, J. (1969), 'Form Criticism and Beyond', *JBL* 88: 1–18.

Neufeldt, E. (1955), 'Prohibitions against Loans at Interest in Ancient Hebrew Laws', *HUCA* 26: 355–412.

Neusner, J. (1987), *Sifre to Deuteronomy* I, II (Brown Judaic Studies 98 and 101: Atlanta: Scholars).

Nicholson, E. W. (1967), *Deuteronomy and Tradition* (Oxford: Blackwell).

——(1973), *Exodus and Sinai in History and Tradition* (Oxford: Blackwell).

——(1977), 'The Decalogue as the Direct Address of God', *VT* 27: 422–433.

——(1986), *God and His People* (Oxford: Clarendon).

Noth, M. (1952), 'Die Vergegenwärtigung des AT in der Verkündigung', *EvTh* 11.

——(1972), *A History of Pentateuchal Traditions* (Englewood Cliffs, NJ: Prentice Hall); ET of *Überlieferungsgeschichte des Pentateuch* (Stuttgart: Kohlhammer, 1948).

——(1981), *The Deuteronomistic History* (JSOTS 15: Sheffield: Sheffield Academic Press); ET of *Überlieferungsgeschichtliche Studien* (2nd edn, Tübingen: Max Niemayer, 1957), 1–110.

O'Donovan, O. M. T. (1973), 'The Possibility of a Biblical Ethic', *TSFB* 67: 15–23.

Ogletree, T. W. (1983), *The Use of the Bible in Christian Ethics* (Philadelphia: Fortress).

Olson, D. T. (1994), *Deuteronomy and the Death of Moses* (OBT: Minneapolis: Fortress).

Otto, E. (1991), 'Forschungsgeschichte der Entwürfe einer Ethik im Alten Testament', in *Verkündigung und Forschung* 36/1: 3–37.

——(1993a), 'Town and Rural Countryside in Ancient Israelite Law', *JSOT* 57: 3–22.

——(1993b), 'Vom Bundesbuch zum Deuteronomium: Die deuteronomische Redaktion in Dtn 12 – 26', in Braulik, G., Gross, W., & McEvenue, S. (eds), *Biblische Theologie und gesellschaftlicher Wandel: Festschrift für N. Lohfink SJ* (Vienna: Herder, 1993), 261–278.

van Oyen, H. (1967), *Ethik des Alten Testament* (Geschichte der Ethik, Band 2: Gütersloh: Gütersloher Verlagshaus).

Patrick, D. (1985), *Old Testament Law* (Atlanta: Scholars).

Paul, S. M. (1970), *Studies in the Book of the Covenant in the Light of Cuneiform and Biblical Law* (SVT 18: Leiden: Brill).

Perlitt, L. (1969), *Bundestheologie im Alten Testament* (Neukirchen: Neukirchener Verlag).

——(1980), 'Ein einzig Volk von Brüdern', in Lührman, D., & Strecker, G. (eds), *Kirche: Festschrift für G. Bornkamm zum 75 Geburtstag* (Tübingen: Mohr), 27–52.

——(1991), *Deuteronomium 1, 1 - 18* (BK V/1: Neukirchen: Neukirchener Verlag).

——(1994), 'Der Staatsgedanke im Deuteronomium', in Balentine, S. E., & Barton, J. (eds), *Language, Theology and The Bible: Essays in Honour of James Barr* (Oxford: Clarendon), 182–198.

Petschow, H. (1965), 'Zur Systematik und Gesetzestechnik im Codex Hammurabi', *Zeitschrift für Assyriologie* 57: 146–172.

Phillips, A. (1970), *Ancient Israel's Criminal Law* (Oxford: Blackwell).

——(1981), 'Another Look at Adultery', *JSOT* 20: 3–25.

Plöger, J. G. (1967), *Literarkritische, formgeschichtliche und stilkritische Untersuchungen zum Deuteronomium* (BBB 26: Bonn: Peter Hanstein).

Polzin, R. (1980), *Moses and the Deuteronomist* (New York: Seabury).

Poulter, A. J. (1989), 'Rhetoric and Redaction in Deuteronomy 8; Linguistic Criticism of a Biblical Text' (unpubl. PhD diss., Cambridge University).

Preuss, H. D. (1982), *Deuteronomium* (Erträge der Forschung 164: Darmstadt: Wissenschaftliche Buchgesellschaft).

von Rad, G. (1953), *Studies in Deuteronomy* (London: SCM); ET of *Deuteronomium-Studien* (FRLANT 58: 2nd edn, Göttingen: Vandenhoeck & Ruprecht, 1948).

——(1966a) *Deuteronomy* (OTL: London: SCM); ET of *Das fünfte Buch Mose: Deuteronomium* (Göttingen: Vandenhoeck & Ruprecht 1964).

——(1966b), *The Problem of the Hexateuch and Other Essays* (London: Oliver & Boyd); ET of *Das formgeschichtliche Problem des Hexateuchs* (BWANT 78: Stuttgart: Kohlhammer, 1938); 'The Problem of the Hexateuch', 1–78; 'The Promised Land and Yahweh's Land in the Hexateuch', 79–93; 'A Rest for the People of God', 94–102.

——(1991), *Holy War in Ancient Israel* (Grand Rapids: Eerdmans); ET of 3rd edn of *Der heilige Krieg im Alten Israel* (AZTANT 20: Göttingen: Vandenhoeck & Ruprecht, 1951).

Rendtorff, R. (1981), 'Die Erwählung Israels als Thema der deuteronomischen Theologie', in Jeremias, J., & Perlitt, L. (eds), *Die*

Botschaft und die Boten: Festschrift für H. W. Wolff (Neukirchen: Neukirchener Verlag), 76–86.

Reventlow, H. G. (1979), 'Basic Problems in Old Testament Theology', *JSOT* 11: 2–22.

Rodd, C. S. (1994), 'New Occasions Teach New Duties. 1. The Old Testament in Christian Ethics', *ExpT* 105 (1994–5), 100–106.

Rofé, A. (1985a), 'The Covenant in the Land of Moab: Dt 28:69 – 30:20', in Lohfink, N. (ed.), *Das Deuteronomium: Entstehung, Gestalt und Botschaft* (BEThL 68: Leuven: Leuven University Press), 310–320.

——(1985b), 'The Laws of Warfare in the Book of Deuteronomy: Their Origins, Intent and Positivity', *JSOT* 32: 32–44.

——(1987), 'Family and Sex Laws in Deuteronomy', *Henoch* 9: 131–159.

——(1988), 'The Arrangement of the Laws in Deuteronomy', *EThL* 64: 265–287.

Rogerson, J. W. (1982), 'The Old Testament and Social and Moral Questions', *Modern Churchman* 25: 28–35.

Römer, Th. (1990), *Untersuchung zur Väterthematik im Deuteronomium und in der deuteronomistischen Tradition* (OBO 99: Freiburg und Göttingen: Schweiz Universitatsverlag).

Römer, W. H. Ph. (1974), 'Randbemerkungen zur Travestie von Deut 22, 5', in Heerma van Voss, M. S. H. G., Houwink ten Caate, Ph. H. J., & van Ochelen, N. A. (eds), *Travels in the World of the OT: Studies presented to M. A. Beek* (Assen: Van Gorcum), 217–222.

Rose, M. (1975), *Der Ausschliesslichkeitsanspruch Jahwes* (BWANT 106: Stuttgart: Kohlhammer).

Rowley, H. H. (1939), *Israel's Mission to the World* (London: SCM).

——(1945), *The Missionary Message of the Old Testament* (London: Carey, Kingsgate).

——(1950), *The Biblical Doctrine of Election* (London: Lutterworth).

——(1967), *The Worship of Israel* (London: SPCK).

Ruprecht, E. (1979a), 'Vorgegebene Tradition und theologische Gestaltung in Gen xii 1–3', *VT* 29: 171–188.

——(1979b), 'Der traditionsgeschichtliche Hintergrund der einzelnen Elemente von Gen xii 2–3', *VT* 29: 444–464.

Sailhamer, J. (1995), *Introduction to Old Testament Theology: A Canonical Approach* (Grand Rapids: Zondervan).

Sa-Moon Kang (1989), *Divine War in the OT and ANE* (BZAW 177: Berlin: Töpelmann).

Schluter, M. (1984), 'Can Israel's Law and Historical Experiences be applied to Britain Today?', *Jubilee Centre Research Paper* 3 (Cambridge: Jubilee Centre).

Schluter, M., & Clements, R. (1989), 'Reactivating the Extended Family: From Biblical Norms to Public Policy in Britain', *Jubilee Centre Research Paper* 2 (Cambridge: Jubilee Centre).

——(1990), 'Jubilee Institutional Norms: A Middle Way between Creation Ethics and Kingdom Ethics as the Basis for Christian Political Action', *EQ* 62: 37–62.

Schmid, H. H. (1963), *Gerechtigkeit als Weltordnung* (Tübingen: Mohr).

Schottroff, W. (1969), *Der altisraelitische Fluchspruch* (WMANT 30: Neukirchen: Neukirchener Verlag).

Schulz, H. (1969), *Das Todesrecht im Alten Testament* (BZAW 114: Berlin: Töpelmann).

Scott, R. B. Y. (1950), 'A Kingdom of Priests, Ex. xix 6', *OTS* 8: 213–219.

Seebass, H. (1983), 'Gehörten Verheissungen zum ältesten Bestand der Väter-Erzählungen?', *Biblica* 64: 189–209.

Segal, J. B. (1963), *The Hebrew Passover: From the Earliest Times to A.D. 70* (London: Oxford University Press).

Segal, M. H. (1967), *The Pentateuch: Its Composition and Authorship and Other Biblical Studies* (Jerusalem: Magnes).

Seitz, G. (1971), *Redaktionsgeschichtliche Studien zum Deuteronomium* (BWANT V, 13: Stuttgart: Kohlhammer).

van Seters, J. (1972), 'The Conquest of Sihon's Kingdom: A Literary Examination', *JBL* 91: 182–197.

——(1975), *Abraham in History and Tradition* (New Haven: Yale University Press).

Shafer, B. E. (1977), 'The Root bhr and Pre–Exilic Concepts of Chosenness in the Hebrew Bible', *ZAW* 89: 20–42.

Skweres, D. (1979), *Die Rückverweise im Buch Deuteronomium* (AnBib 79: Rome: Pontifical Institute).

Smend, R. (1982), 'Ethik III. Altes Testaments', *Theologische Realenzyklopädie* 10 (Berlin: Töpelmann), 423–435.

Smith, G. A. (1931), *The Historical Geography of the Holy Land* (25th edn, London: Hodder & Stoughton).

Song, T. G. (1992), 'Sinai Covenant and Moab Covenant: An Exegetical Study of the Covenants in Exodus 19:1 – 24:11 and Deuteronomy 4:45 – 28:69' (unpubl. PhD diss.: CNAA; Cheltenham).

Spriggs, D. C. (1974), *Two Old Testament Theologies: A Comparative Evaluation of the Contributions of Eichrodt and von Rad to our*

Understanding of the Nature of Old Testament Theology (SBT 2/30: London: SCM).

Staerk, W. (1894), *Das Deuteronomium, sein Inhalt und literarische Form* (Leipzig: J. C. Hinrichs).

Steuernagel, C. (1894), *Der Rahmen des Deuteronomiums* (Halle: J. Krause).

——(1900), *Deuteronomium und Josua* (HKAT: Göttingen: Vandenhoeck & Ruprecht).

Stulman, L. (1990), 'Encroachment in Deuteronomy. An Analysis of the Social World of the Deuteronomic Code', *JBL* 109: 613–632.

——(1992), 'Sex and Familial Crimes in the D Code', *JSOT* 53: 47–63.

Thompson, J. A. (1964), *The Ancient Near Eastern Treaties and the Old Testament* (London: Tyndale).

——(1974), *Deuteronomy* (TOTC: Leicester: IVP).

Toombs, L. E. (1965), 'Love and Justice in Deuteronomy: A Third Approach to the Law', *Int* 19: 399–411.

Vanoni, G. (1981), 'Der Geist und der Buchstabe. Überlegungen zum Verhältnisse der Testamente und Beobachtungen zu Dtn 30: 1–10', *BN* 14: 65–98.

de Vaux, R. (1961), *Ancient Israel* (London: Darton, Longman & Todd).

Veijola, T. (1991), 'Höre Israel! Der Sinn und Hintergrund von Deuteronomium vi 4–9', *VT* 42: 528–541.

Vriezen, Th. C. (1953), *Die Erwählung Israels nach dem Alten Testament* (AZTANT 24: Zurich: Zwingli Verlag).

von Waldow, H. E. (1974), 'Israel and her Land: Some Theological Considerations', in Bream, H. N., Heim, R. D., & Moore, C. A. (eds), *A Light Unto My Path: Old Testament Studies in Honour of J. M. Myers* (Philadelphia: Temple University Press), 493–508.

Waltke, B. K., & O'Connor, M. (1990), *Biblical Hebrew Syntax* (Winona Lake: Eisenbrauns).

Waterhouse, S. W. (1963), 'A Land Flowing With Milk and Honey', *AUSS* I: 152–166.

Weinfeld, M. (1961), 'The Origin of Humanism in Deuteronomy', *JBL* 80: 241–247.

——(1970), 'The Covenant of Grant in the Old Testament and in the Ancient Near East', *JAOS* 90: 184–203.

——(1972), *Deuteronomy and the Deuteronomic School* (Oxford: Oxford University Press).

——(1973), 'On Demythologisation and Secularisation in Deuteronomy', *IEJ* 23: 230–237.

——(1991), *Deuteronomy 1 – 11* (AB: New York: Doubleday).

——(1993), 'The Ban on the Canaanites in the Biblical Codes and its Historical Development', in Lemaire, A., & Otzen, B. (eds), *History and Traditions of Early Israel: Studies Presented to Eduard Nielsen* (SVT 50: Leiden: Brill), 142–160.

Welch, A. C. (1924), *The Code of Deuteronomy* (London: James Clark).

Wellhausen, J. (1889), *Die Composition des Hexateuchs und der historischen Bücher des ATs* (Berlin: Georg Reimer).

Wenham, G. J. (1970), 'The Structure and Date of Deuteronomy' (unpubl. PhD diss.: London University).

——(1971), 'Deuteronomy and the Central Sanctuary', *TynB* 22: 103–118.

——(1972), 'Betulah, a Girl of Marriageable Age', *VT* 22: 326–348.

——(1979), 'The Restoration of Marriage Reconsidered', *JJS* 30: 36–40.

——(1981), *Numbers* (TOTC: Leicester: IVP).

——(1985), 'Law and Legal System in the Old Testament', in Wenham, G. J., & Kaye, B. N, *Law, Morality and the Bible* (Leicester: IVP), 24–52.

——(1987), *Genesis 1 – 15* (WBC: Waco: Word).

Wenham, G. J., & McConville, J. G. (1980), 'Drafting Techniques in some Deuteronomic laws', *VT* 30: 248–252.

Westermann, C. (1974), *Genesis 1 – 11* (BK: Neukirchen: Neukirchener Verlag).

Wiener, H. M. (1926), 'The Arrangement of Deuteronomy 12 – 26', *JPOS* 6: 185–195.

Wildberger, H. (1960), *Jahwes Eigentumsvolk* (AZTANT 37: Zurich: Zwingli Verlag).

Wilson, I. (1992), 'Divine Presence in Deuteronomy' (unpubl. PhD diss.: Cambridge University).

——(1995), *Out of the Midst of the Fire* (SBLDS 151: Atlanta: Scholars).

Wilson, R. R. (1988), 'Approaches to Old Testament Ethics', in Tucker, G. M., Petersen, D. L., & Wilson, R. R. (eds), *Canon, Theology and Old Testament: Essays in Honor of B. S. Childs* (Philadelphia: Fortress), 62–74.

Wolff, H. W. (1964), 'Das Kerygma des deuteronomistischen Geschichtswerks', in *Gesammelte Studien zum Alten Testament* (Theologische Bücherei 22: Munich: Kaiser), 308–324.

——(1966), 'The Kerygma of the Yahwist', *Int* 20: 131–158; ET of 'Das Kerygma des Jahwisten', *EvTh* 24 (1964), 73–98.

Wright, C. J. H. (1983), *Living as the People of God* (Leicester: IVP).

——(1990), *God's People in God's Land* (Exeter: Paternoster).

——(1992a), 'The Ethical Authority of the Old Testament: A Survey of Approaches', *TynB* 43: 101–120, 203–232.

——(1992b), 'Ethical Decisions in the Old Testament', *EJT* 1: 125–140.

——(1993), 'Bibliography on Biblical Ethics', *Transformation* 10/3: 27–33.

——(1995), *Walking in the Ways of the Lord: The Ethical Authority of the Old Testament* (Leicester: IVP).

——(1996), *Deuteronomy* (NIBC: Carlisle: Paternoster).

Wright, G. E. (1954), 'The Levites in Deuteronomy', *VT* 4: 325–330.

——(1961), 'The Old Testament Basis for Christian Mission', in Anderson, G. H. (ed.), *Christian Mission* (New York: McGraw-Hill), 17–33.

——(1962), 'The Lawsuit of God', in Anderson, B. W., & Harrelson W. (eds), *Israel's Prophetic Heritage: Festschrift for J. Muilenburg* (New York: Harper & Row), 26–67.

Yaron, R. (1966), 'Restoration of Marriage', *JJS* 17: 1–12.

Zevit, Z. (1976), 'The 'Egla Ritual of Deuteronomy 21: 1–9', *JBL* 95: 377–339.

Index of authors

Index of Scripture references